CHINA'S DILEMMA
The Taiwan Issue

CHINA'S DILEMMA

The Taiwan Issue

SHENG LIJUN

I.B.Tauris *Publishers*
LONDON · NEW YORK

First published in Singapore in 2001 by
Institute of Southeast Asian Studies
30 Heng Mui Keng Terrace
Pasir Panjang
Singapore 119614

Internet e-mail: publish@iseas.edu.sg
World Wide Web: http://www.iseas.edu.sg/pub.html

First published in Europe and the United States of America in 2001 by
I.B.Tauris & Co Ltd
6 Salem Road, London W2 4BU
175 Fifth Avenue, New York NY 10010
www.ibtauris.com

The responsibility for facts and opinions in this publication rests exclusively with the author and his interpretations do not necessarily reflect the views or the policy of the publishers.

ISEAS Library Cataloguing-in-Publication Data

Sheng, Lijun.
China's dilemma : the Taiwan issue.
  1.   Chinese reunification question, 1949–
  2.   China—Foreign relations—Taiwan.
  3.   Taiwan—Foreign relations—China.
  4.   United States—Foreign relations—China.
  5.   China—Foreign relations—United States.
  6.   United States—Foreign relations—Taiwan.
  7.   Taiwan—Foreign relations—United States.
  8.   China—Politics and government—1976–
  9.   Taiwan—Politics and government—1988–
  I.   Title.
DS777.55 S54   2001   sls2000063073

ISBN 1-86064-732-4 paperback
ISBN 1-86064-731-6 hardback

Typeset by International Typesetters Pte. Ltd.
Printed in Singapore by Stamford Press Pte. Ltd.

CONTENTS

PART IV
CONCLUSION

Introduction

The rise of China is an important phenomenon in post-Cold War international relations and one which has brought about to many contending views. Not since China–United States rapprochement in the early seventies and China's reform policy which opened the country up to the outside world in the late seventies, has China created such academic interest.

China's foreign policy has long been influenced by its relations with the Soviet Union and the United States. And in China–United States relations, the Taiwan issue has always been a crucial factor. China's Taiwan policy is very sensitive to the U.S. stance on this key issue. Its importance to China–United States relations as well as to stability in East Asia was demonstrated by the events that followed Lee Teng-hui's "private" visit to Cornell University in the United States in June 1995 and his announcement of "special state-to-state relations" with China in July 1999.

The Taiwan issue has never been confined to the Chinese on both sides of the Taiwan Strait as the United States has always had a role to play. And its influence is likely to continue. A considerable part of this book is therefore devoted to an examination of how China–United States relations have affected the Taiwan issue.

China has never treated the Taiwan issue in isolation: it is integral to its overall strategy. Its displeasure with Taiwan since 1995 has not merely been because of Taiwan's persistent drift away from reunification, but also because of China's view that Taiwan is helping the United States to contain it and undermine its overall strategy for the next century. This strategy is to keep a low profile in international affairs and concentrate on domestic modernization for the time being. The "one country two systems" formula which China intends for Taiwan is more to prevent Taiwan's further drift towards independence than to bring about immediate reunification. Reunification before conditions are ripe would create more problems for China.

The Taiwan issue has not developed as the result of the intentions of only one party. Between China, the United States and Taiwan different interests and strategies, fluid and tricky domestic politics, mutual suspicion and misperception of each other have come into play, leading to one crisis after another.

The United States first revived the issue, after it had lain dormant for ten years, with its sale of 150 F-16 fighters to Taiwan in 1992. Then, it formally upgraded its relations with Taiwan in 1994. But it was its issuing of a visa to Taiwan's president Lee Teng-hui on 22 May 1995 to allow him to visit his alma mater Cornell University in the United States, that really inflamed relations between China and Taiwan.

Taiwan has also played an active part in the triangle. In July 1999, Lee Teng-hui made waves by raising the controversial "two states" theory. He explained that the controversy would benefit Taipei in the end: "The more controversy, the better. Only this way will everyone pay attention to the key of the Republic of China's existence. When the whole world knows the Republic of China's difficult situation, afterwards it will be easier to do things."[1]

Lee's outspokenness and controversial statements since 1994 have been part of a calculated strategy to keep Taiwan at the forefront of international attention. Winning over diplomatic allies would not in itself tilt the balance in Taiwan's favour (Taiwan has fewer than 30 diplomatic allies), so Taiwan has to ensure it continues to receive international media coverage to remind the world of its existence and plight. By the same token Taiwanese leaders and high officials travel abroad in an attempt to gain more international sympathy, necessary for Taiwan's survival as a sovereign state. And Taiwan puts a lot of effort and money into the countries that support it diplomatically and into its "pragmatic diplomacy". Moreover, the Taiwan issue is likely to be revived on the international front by Taiwan every time things quieten down.

Taiwan has been the most proactive of the three in the China–United States–Taiwan triangle in challenging the status quo. It changed its "one China only" position to that of "one China, two governments", then "one China, two entities", followed by "one China, two equal entities", "one China, two equal political entities", "one China, two legal entities in the international arena", then "two equal political entities" without mentioning "one China", and most recently "two special states". In the foreseeable future Taiwan will likely continue to lead the initiative. This is significant for regional stability. How China will react when Taiwan moves from a de facto independence to a de jure one is another uncertainty.

Chinese strategic thinking has been deeply influenced by Mao's belief that the "main contradiction" should be solved first and that "minor contradictions" are easier to resolve once the "main contradiction" has been tackled. China has embraced this philosophy when dealing with the territories of greater China. In the 1970s, China did not want to take over Macao when the Portuguese government first approached Beijing about the territory's hand-over. Hong Kong's hand-over did not occupy much of the Chinese authorities' attention until the early 1980s when the issue was formally brought to the Chinese leaders by the British government. Reunification with Taiwan has been treated in a similar manner: Beijing was enthusiastic about reunification in the late 1970s and the early 1980s following the normalization of relations between China and the United States. Later, when it was realized this was out of the question for the time being, the issue was dropped from its top agenda, although it was still listed as one the three main tasks for the 1980s. China then concentrated on what it considered to be the most fundamental element of its overall strategy, i.e. reform and modernization. However, after 1995, the Taiwan issue was forced back onto China's top agenda by Lee Teng-hui's intensified push of his "pragmatic diplomacy".

Here China is faced with a dilemma. While it wants to concentrate its energy and resources on modernization, it is having to divert resources to curtail Taiwan's creeping independence. China's agenda, which is to concentrate on modernization now and deal with the Taiwan issue at a later stage, when conditions are ripe, is being pushed aside by Taiwan's assertiveness. A further dilemma for China is that a mild response is ineffective while a display of strength, such as missile "testing" and military exercises like those carried out in the Taiwan Strait in 1995–96, is also undesirable.

China is also suspicious of Washington and has long been resisting its involvement in the Taiwan issue. However, in order to constrain Taiwan's moves towards independence, it has had to get Washington involved. For example, Washington was asked to exert pressure on Taipei to return to talks in 1997–98 and to return to the "one China" framework after Lee put forward his "two states" theory in 1999. The United States' involvement may bring short-term stability to the situation but in the long run it may complicate China's reunification efforts. However, China, has no better choice at the moment.

Taiwan's refusal to reunify with China hinges on three main issues: 1) a disparity in living standards; 2) different economic levels; and 3) democracy. The first two do not hold water since there is a difference in living standards and economic levels not only between Hong Kong and China but also within China itself.

The democracy question is something that needs careful exploration. This book examines in depth the evolution of China's perception of the Taiwan issue. Taiwan's insistence that "China must respect Taiwan's democratic system" has now been replaced by the demand for "democracy and freedom" in China as another precondition for any reunification talks, i.e. "democratic reunification", calling on China to emulate its democracy. This invites two questions. The first is, which model is better suited to reunification — an ideology-free or an ideology-laden one?

China's "one country two systems" formula is ideology-free, emphasizing that neither side should impose its political and social systems onto the other. Taiwan's formula, on the other hand, ideologicalizes cross-strait relations and thus increases tension since China feels that Taiwan is threatening to replace its political and social system.

Taiwan's democratic system should be given due credit, but should not be overestimated. It still has many flaws: heavy money politics, serious triad involvement, wide-spread vote-buying and the use of government institutions and resources for election purposes, disregard for electoral laws, campaign violence, gangsterism and political mud-slinging. Taiwanese society is also plagued by serious social evils such as corruption and crime. There may indeed be more press freedom and freedom of political choice than ever before, but this alone does not constitute liberal democracy. People in Taiwan generally still do not actively and widely use their individual rights to protect and enhance their daily lives. It is often the case that after elections in which people used their individual rights, they revert to old practices. A sense of democracy does not pervade everyday life.

The second question is, is it better for Taiwan to stay inside or outside China in order to promote democratization in China?

Historically, democratization has been used to improve governance, and not to split or challenge sovereignty. Many Chinese are convinced that Taiwan's linking of reunification with China's democratization to its "pragmatic diplomacy", is a ploy to gain Western support of its independence. These tactics have in fact greatly jeopardized democratization prospects in China.

The liberal democracy may be stable but the democratization process itself is likely to be unpredictable and even violent, and the state may then be more militant. Taiwan will be an easy target for this militancy. Like many Taiwanese who have strong *bei qing* [a complex that they are being victimised by mainlanders], people in the mainland will then likely have such *bei qing*, but in a reverse way. Chinese mainlanders are likely to take the view that the people in Taiwan have joined the West to weaken and contain China when it was in difficulty, instead of helping it. Parties will readily exploit national sentiment for power. Reunification will be a catchy call and convenient political capital. There is no guarantee that a democratizing state and even a mature democracy will not use force when national survival and territorial integrity are at risk.

This book also demonstrates that the Taiwan problem is now one of the most difficult issues that the Communist Party of China (C.C.P.) has ever encountered in its 80 years of history, for it has little of what traditional Chinese strategists called *tianshi*, *dili* and *renhe* [situational, geographical and human and social advantages]. In terms of *renhe* [human and social advantages], during the Chinese Civil War for example, the C.C.P. had massive support from the grass-roots, intellectuals and even other elite social groups for its "united front policy". In the case of Tibet, it eventually managed to obtain wide support from "liberated Tibetan serfs", at least between the 1950s and 1960s, for its rule and reform there. In Hong Kong, it is enjoying considerable support from the business community and many other social sectors. In terms of *dili* [geographical advantage and hence enhanced military deterrence], the C.C.P. had credible military strength in Tibet after it totally wiped out the Tibetan force at Changdu in 1950. Its deterrence over Hong Kong is very apparent. And where *tianshi* [situational advantage] is concerned, before the end of the Cold War, China had the Soviet card to play. China does not have such advantages over Taiwan, especially in terms of *renhe* [human and social advantages]. People in Taiwan have, over time, become increasingly cohesive in rejecting China's formula for reunification. This situation is unlikely to change soon.

This book is an analysis of China's Taiwan policy, not of the China–United States–Taiwan triangle. Therefore, Taiwan's China policy and the U.S. China policy, which are not the focus of the book, are discussed only when they give a better understanding of China's Taiwan policy. This book focuses on the period from the early 1990s, especially after Lee Teng-hui's United States trip in June 1995 to September 1999.

In this book, the term "China", after 1949, refers to the People's Republic of China (P.R.C.), whereas the term "Taiwan" refers to the Republic of China (R.O.C.), comprising the islands which make up Taiwan and other islands it occupies. The term "Taiwanese", when used to describe people, refers to all the people in Taiwan including mainland Taiwanese. The *pinyin* system of transliteration is used for Chinese names and words, whereas Wades-Giles transliteration is used for those in Taiwan. Newspapers cited in the book, if they are website editions, do not carry page numbers.

I must express my gratitude to the Singapore Institute of Southeast Asian Studies, where I am a fellow, for funding this research project and providing research facilities and assistance.

My gratitude also goes to specialists, scholars and officials in the following Chinese and Taiwanese institutes and organizations for having discussions with me: (from China) the Central Committee of the C.C.P., the Central Leading Group of the Taiwan Affairs, the Association for Relations Across the Taiwan Strait, the P.L.A. Academy of Military Sciences, the Centre for Peace & Development Studies, the Centre of International Studies of the State Council, the Asia-Africa Development Research Institute of the Development Research Centre of the State Council, the China Institute of Contemporary International Relations, the Institute of World Economic and Politics, the Institute of Taiwan Studies of China Academy of Social Sciences, the Institute of American Studies, the Taiwan Studies Society, the Institute of International Relations of Beijing University, the Shanghai Institute for International Studies, the Institute of Asia Pacific Studies of Shanghai Academy of Social Sciences, the Centre for American

Studies of Fudan University, the Institute of Taiwan Studies of Xiamen University; and (from Taiwan) the Mainland Affairs Council, the Strait Exchange Foundation, the Council for Economic Planning & Development of Executive Ruan, the Chinese Council of Advance Policy Studies, the Democratic Progressive Party, the Taiwan Independence Party, the Chinese Association for Eurasian Studies, the Institute of International Relations, the Institute of European and American Studies of Academia Sinica, the National Sun Yat-Sen University, the Department of Political Science of National Taiwan University, and the Cross-Strait Interflow Prospect Foundation.

Notes

1. Jason Blatt, "Taipei 'to Face Beijing Force'", *South China Morning Post* (hereafter cited as *SCMP*), Hong Kong, 11 August 1999.

Part I

Background

1

A Historical Review

Mainland China and the island of Taiwan were linked by a land bridge in ancient times, but are now separated by the Taiwan Strait, which is about 72 nautical miles at the narrowest point and 140 nautical miles at the widest.

Mainland Chinese people began commercial activities on Taiwan island much earlier than the establishment of the first Chinese local government there, which was during the Yuan Dynasty (1271–1368).[1] In 1662 the Ming General Zheng Chenggong (Cheng Cheng-kung: his Japanese name was Koxinga) expelled the colonial Dutch occupiers from the island, claiming that "Taiwan is China's territory". The general refused to withdraw his troops in exchange for goods offered by the defeated Dutch army. It was after this that China began to pay more attention to Taiwan.

Taiwan at first resisted the establishment of the Qing Dynasty which replaced the Ming Dynasty out of its proclaimed loyalty to the latter. Then, before being defeated by the Qing troops, Taiwan asked for vassal status as Korea and Vietnam once had. The Qing Emperor, Kang Xi, turned down this request, insisting that Taiwan was Qing China's territory, not a vassal state. Taiwan remained a territory (Qing court upgraded it to a province in 1885) until the Qing court, and after being defeated, signed it over to Japan with a treaty in 1895.[2] Before then, China's claim of sovereignty over Taiwan had never been challenged (the Dutch had only wanted to use or rent Taiwan as a trading port).

The Role of the United States in Taiwan before the 1990s

Taiwan attracted the attention of a few Americans as early as the mid-nineteenth century when the United States began to expand into the Asia-Pacific region. Inconclusive proposals were made for the occupation, purchase or colonization of the island as a coaling station and trading port. M.C. Perry, who led a U.S.

fleet to visit the island in 1854, even proposed that Taiwan be procured as a front post for the United States to ensure stability in the Western Pacific. Perry also wrote that if the United States controlled Taiwan, it would be able to control China.[3]

An American consul in Taiwan and other officials, as well as private shipping companies, assisted the Japanese invasion of the island in 1874, which led to Japan's annexation of the Ryukyu Islands five years later.[4] The cession of Taiwan from China to Japan in 1895 ended further American involvement in Taiwan for nearly half a century.

The Cairo Declaration of 1 December 1943 committed the United States and other Allied powers to restoring to China "all the territories Japan has stolen from the Chinese", including Taiwan and Penghu (the Pescadores).[5] This commitment was reaffirmed in the Potsdam Proclamation of 26 July 1945,[6] and was honoured by the United States through the provision of military assistance to the Kuomintang (K.M.T.) government for the repossession of these islands when the Japanese surrendered a month later.[7] When, in February 1947, there was a revolt against the K.M.T. government on Taiwan, the United States refused to become involved on the grounds that this was an internal affair of China.[8] Although no Japanese representatives were present when the Cairo Declaration was signed, the Japanese government later expressed its acceptance officially in writing.

It was at one time largely accepted that the origin of the conflict between China and United States over Taiwan was the Communist take-over of mainland China in 1949. This interpretation emphasizes the ideological aspect of China–United States conflict over Taiwan. However, there is also evidence that during World War II, the United States secretly set up a special group, headed by a U.S. intelligence officer, George Keer, to study and implement a programme, code-named "X Island Program". The aim of this was to occupy Taiwan and train personnel for the purpose of setting up a provisional military government on the island. From 1942, together with other U.S. military intelligent units, this group studied the feasibility of making Taiwan independent, neutralized, or placed under the trusteeship of either the United States or the United Nations. The plan was also supported by some U.S. officials such as Dean Acheson, George Kennan, Dean Rusk and John Foster Dulles. For various reasons, these proposals were not adopted.

It is notable that all these activities were conducted in the early 1940s when China was an ally of the United States in its war against Japan, and the Chinese Communist Party (C.C.P.) had not yet broken away from the K.M.T.-led resistance coalition and was far from showing any sign of replacing the K.M.T. This points to geo-political rather than ideological interest in Taiwan on the part of the United States.[9] In recently de-classified C.I.A. documents that Taiwan has just bought, some scholars in Taiwan claim to have found clear evidence that the United States intended to support the establishment of an indigenous government on the island against the mainland K.M.T., even before the Communist take-over of the mainland in 1949.

Nevertheless, the conflict became open after the Chinese Communist take-over of the mainland. By May 1949 the Chinese Communists had amassed about 300,000 assault troops across the strait from Taiwan.[10] No one expected the K.M.T. troops to hold out for long. In December 1949, the U.S. State Department circulated a confidential policy memorandum to its information officers forecasting the imminent fall of Taiwan.[11] For a brief period, the United States decided to pursue a policy of non-intervention and sought to disengage itself from Taiwan, preferring to determine its China policy after the "the dust had settled".[12]

This situation was dramatically reversed by the outbreak of the Korean War in 1950. U.S. President Harry Truman immediately reversed the policy of non-intervention by dispatching the U.S. Seventh Fleet to the Taiwan Strait. Beijing interpreted this as a hostile action intended to block reunification and overthrow the new Republic. On the other hand, Washington perceived the Korean War as deliberately engineered by the Soviet Union and China as part of Communist expansion in Asia.

In this context, the United States retained Taiwan as an ally and an outpost in the frontline of U.S. defence in the Western Pacific. The United States changed its previous position on China's sovereignty over Taiwan. From 1950 to 1972, the United States held that the status of Taiwan was "undetermined".[13] In May 1951, the United States dispatched a Military Assistance Advisory Group (M.A.A.G.) to Taiwan. Economic aid was to follow. In 1954 it signed a Mutual Security Treaty with Taiwan. For almost three decades, the United States supported Taiwan's challenge to Beijing's claim that the P.R.C. was the sole legal government of China. This antipathy between the P.R.C. and the United States continued throughout the 1950s and 1960s.

In the early 1970s, Washington decided on rapprochement with the P.R.C. U.S. President Richard Nixon visited China in early 1972, and the two countries issued the Shanghai Communiqué. In this communiqué, Beijing reaffirmed its position:

> [T]he Government of the People's Republic of China is the sole legal government of China; Taiwan is a province of China which has long been returned to the motherland; the liberation of Taiwan is China's internal affair in which no other country has the right to interfere; and all U.S. forces and military installations must be withdrawn from Taiwan.

On the other hand, the United States only "acknowledged" that "all Chinese on either side of the Taiwan Strait maintain that there is but one China and that Taiwan is a part of China". Although "[t]he United States Government does not challenge that position", it did not explicitly recognize Chinese sovereignty over

Taiwan. Despite U.S. affirmation that the objective was ultimately "the withdrawal of all U.S. forces and military installations from Taiwan", it nevertheless reaffirmed its "interest in a peaceful settlement of the Taiwan question".[14] Despite its historical value, the Shanghai Communiqué did not solve key issues in the China–United States relationship over the Taiwan issue. The United States continued to recognize the K.M.T. government on Taiwan and U.S. troops remained there.

The Watergate scandal in 1972–74 scotched any intention Nixon might have had of normalizing relations with Beijing. Any moves his successor Gerald Ford might have contemplated were sacrificed to higher priorities, notably the effort to restore a credible American position in East Asia following the collapse of South Vietnam in 1975. Between 1972 and 1979, before the establishment of diplomatic relations between the P.R.C. and the United States, Beijing expressed disapproval of the slow pace with which the United States dealt with the Taiwan issue. Beijing claimed that there was a Ford-Kissinger promise to sever diplomatic relations with the K.M.T. government on Taiwan.[15]

During his first few years in office President Jimmy Carter seemed to back away from any commitment on the Taiwan issue. This was evident during Secretary of State Cyrus Vance's visit to Beijing in 1977. Although this was a setback for China–United States relations, during this period China was preoccupied with a succession crisis. Under the new leadership of Deng Xiaoping in Beijing and fresh efforts on the part of President Carter, the two countries restarted moves towards normalizing relations in 1978.[16]

In the Joint Communiqué on the Establishment of Diplomatic Relations between the United States of America and the People's Republic of China, dated 1 January 1979, the United States recognized the P.R.C. as the sole legal government of China. It agreed to terminate formal diplomatic relations and the mutual defence treaty with the K.M.T. government in Taiwan and to withdraw all remaining U.S. forces from the island. However, the United States continued to "acknowledge", but did not explicitly recognize, "the Chinese position that there is but one China and Taiwan is part of China". The United States stated that it would "maintain commercial, cultural and other unofficial relations with the people of Taiwan".[17] In the normalization negotiations, the Carter Administration insisted that it would continue to sell weapons to Taiwan. Beijing expressed strong opposition to this.[18] Nevertheless, both sides agreed to normalize their relations. Thus, the Taiwan issue was touched upon, but not resolved in the normalization process, leaving behind many potential conflict points.

The issue of Taiwan's legal status is one such point of conflict. The United States, in both the Shanghai Communiqué of 1972 and the Normalization Communiqué of 1979, chose only to acknowledge, but not openly *recognize*, the Chinese position that Taiwan is part of China. The difference between *acknowledge* and *recognize* is particularly important. The former only points to a fact and does not imply that the United States supports it and is willing to accept the consequent obligations, whereas the latter implies support of Beijing's claim that Taiwan is a province of the P.R.C. and a willingness to accept all the legal consequences arising therefrom.[19]

Related to the issue of Taiwan's legal status, the United States also refuses to recognize that China and Taiwan are in a state of civil war. By doing so, the United States avoids the application of article 2(7) of the United Nations (U.N.) Charter which prohibits U.N. intervention in the domestic affairs of a member state, as well as the enforcement of rules of war under international law, including the principle of neutrality and the prohibition of arms sales to an insurgent group in a foreign civil war.[20] When asked whether an armed attack from the mainland against Taiwan would be considered a civil war situation in which the United States or the U.N. could not be legally involved, Washington replied: "[I]t would not be regarded as a civil war."[21]

Thus, by not supporting Beijing's territorial claim over Taiwan and by refusing to recognize the confrontation between the P.R.C. and the R.O.C. as a civil war, the United States can legally continue to sell arms to Taiwan, leaving open the possibility of future military intervention.

Given the U.S. stance on Taiwan's legal status, Beijing suspects it intends to pursue a "two Chinas" or "one China, oneTaiwan" policy. This suspicion was reinforced by a White House statement that the United States would be "neutral on the question of whether there should be reunification".[22]

A second point of conflict is U.S. arms sales to Taiwan and the Taiwan Relations Act (T.R.A.). When the United States ended diplomatic relations with the R.O.C. in 1979, it declared its intention of maintaining unofficial relations with the people of Taiwan. On 26 January 1979, President Carter put forward a bill which provided the legal basis for these "unofficial relations". The proposed bill met with opposition in Congress because it was considered inadequate. So a revised version, called the Taiwan Relations Act, was adopted and signed into law by President Carter on 10 April 1979 (Public Law 96–8), and implemented by an executive order in June 1979.

The T.R.A. was a heavy blow to Beijing, especially in the wake of normalization of relations with the United States. It also hindered the development of China–United States relations. For a start, U.S. credibility was damaged. Through the T.R.A. the United States was considered to be "unilaterally taking back much of what they had agreed to give China on the Taiwan issue".[23] At the time of China–United States normalization, the United States had fully accepted three conditions with regard to Taiwan. Two of these were to withdraw U.S. troops and to abrogate the United States–Taiwan Mutual Defence Treaty. However, under the Act, although the U.S. government agreed to withdraw U.S. troops, it did not suspend the U.S. defence commitment. Moreover, it supported continued arms sales to Taiwan and intervention through various means against

Beijing's efforts to reunify with Taiwan. The third condition was severance of diplomatic relations with the K.M.T. government in Taiwan. On the surface, the United States accepted the demand by withdrawing formal diplomatic recognition, but the T.R.A. restored de facto diplomatic relations and treated Taiwan as a de facto independent political entity. Beijing claimed that the Act was "tantamount to a de facto revitalization" of the United States–Taiwan Mutual Defence Treaty.[24] Moreover, China–United States normalization did not produce a confidence crisis in Taiwan which was expected to facilitate an earlier reunification, because continued arms sales and the T.R.A. sent the message to Taiwan's K.M.T. government that the United States was rejecting Beijing's reunification efforts.

Before long, China–United States relations were once again plunged into crisis by the Taiwan issue. During his presidential campaign in 1980, Ronald Reagan attacked Carter's China policy and made various pro-Taiwan remarks on the issues of Taiwan's legal status, the T.R.A. and U.S. arms sales to Taiwan. After the Reagan Administration was installed in January 1981, Beijing responded by pressing its demands with respect to Taiwan. These demands were that:

1. the two communiqués (the Shanghai Communiqué of 1972 and the Normalization Communiqué) should have precedence over the T.R.A.;
2. Reagan should not reinstitute the six Taiwan consular offices closed down at the time of U.S. derecognition, as he had pledged to do during his 1980 presidential campaign;
3. arms sales to Taiwan should be terminated;
4. the Reagan Administration should explicitly recognize and in action respect China's sovereignty over Taiwan;
5. the T.R.A. should be abolished or at least revised.

After much bargaining, Beijing and Washington finally worked out a communiqué on 17 August 1982, which placed a ceiling on the quantity and quality of U.S. arms sales to Taiwan. It read:

> [T]he United States Government states that it does not seek to carry out a long-term policy of arms sales to Taiwan, that its arms sales to Taiwan will not exceed, either in qualitative or in quantitative terms, the level of those supplied in recent years since the establishment of diplomatic relations between the United States and China, and that it intends to gradually reduce its arms sales to Taiwan, leading, over a period of time, to a final resolution.[25]

However, Washington not only interpreted the "final resolution" to be one of peaceful reunification with Beijing but also raised the ceiling on U.S. arms sales to Taiwan by using the level of its arms sales in 1979, the highest watermark of the Carter Administration. It also recalculated the level by taking inflation into account.[26] What is more, U.S. officials revealed in private that "the qualitative restrictions on arms sales to Taiwan would also be interpreted in relative rather than absolute terms. That is, the United States would be willing to sell Taiwan more advanced weapons systems as older ones became obsolete or if American production of them ceased".[27] Finally, Washington interpreted the ceiling on the quality of arms sales to Taiwan as applying to actual weaponry, which excluded its provision of high defence production technology that could raise the quality of Taiwan's weapon systems. Later in the 1990s, highly advanced U.S. weapons, such as six *Knox*-class frigates, were *leased*, not *sold*, to Taiwan to avoid the application of the 17 August 1982 Communiqué.

Although China–United States relations became largely stable after the communiqué (up until the Tiananmen incident in 1989), Beijing has remained highly suspicious of U.S. actions with regard to Taiwan. This background provides a better understanding of how China perceived increased U.S. arms sales to Taiwan after the Cold War, as well as the U.S. decision to upgrade its relations with Taiwan in 1994 and to allow Taiwan's President Lee Teng-hui to enter the United States for a "private visit" in 1995.

China's Taiwan Policy before the 1990s

During the Mao Zedong era, China's policy towards Taiwan was largely based on Mao's determination to liberate Taiwan through force. However, in the mid-1950s, China began launching peaceful political initiatives by proposing negotiations with the K.M.T. government in Taiwan, although in essense it did not deviate from its liberation-through-force policy.

In the mid-1950s, Beijing first proposed such negotiations in conversations with the Americans in Geneva (which were later continued in Warsaw). In April 1955, Chinese Premier Zhou Enlai suggested negotiations with the "responsible local authorities" in Taiwan. He followed this up in June 1956, when he publicly expressed China's willingness to discuss concrete steps for a peaceful solution of the Taiwan problem with the K.M.T. in Taiwan. In April 1957, Mao also publicly expressed the willingness of the C.C.P. to co-operate with the K.M.T. In October 1958, in an announcement issued in the name of Defence Minister Peng Dehuai, but actually written by Mao himself, Beijing once again called on Taipei to enter into negotiations for a peaceful solution of the Taiwan problem.

Taiwan dismissed all these initiatives as propaganda. Nevertheless, the two sides did establish contact through secret channels, and worked out some tentative proposals and arrangements for reunification, which were similar to the "one country, two systems" formula which is now proposed by China (see Part III). However, the Cultural Revolution, which began in China in 1966, brought these secret talks to an end.

At the start of the Deng Xiaoping era in late 1978, Beijing abandoned its policy of liberating Taiwan through force and formed a new policy of "peaceful reunification".[28] Subsequently it launched a series of peaceful initiatives towards Taiwan. Deng, on many occasions, expressed his hope for a peaceful reunification. In January 1979, the Standing Committee of China's National People's Congress (N.P.C.) sent "A Message to Compatriots in Taiwan".[29] On 30 September 1981, Ye Jianying, chairman of the Standing Committee of the N.P.C., announced a nine-point proposal for solving the Taiwan issue:

1. unfettered movement, trade and communications between Taiwan and the P.R.C.;
2. autonomy for Taiwan and the retention of Taiwan's own armed forces;
3. a role for Taiwan officials in the P.R.C.'s national political system;
4. retention of Taiwan's capitalist economy;
5. financial aid for Taiwan from the central government when in need;
6. freedom for people from Taiwan to settle on the Chinese mainland;
7. a profitable role for Taiwanese capitalists in China's economic modernization;
8. talks between the K.M.T. and the C.C.P. for reunification; and
9. the welcoming of proposals from the masses on how reunification should be accomplished.[30]

These various statements were more conciliatory and offered more specific concessions to Taiwan than ever before. Apart from the proposal that "three direct links and four exchanges"[31] should be established before political negotiations took place, Beijing also guaranteed in these statements that after reunification the present economic and social system, the armed forces, economic and cultural relations with foreign countries and the way of life, would remain unchanged. It also appealed for an end to the military confrontation over the Taiwan Strait. On the same day that "A Message to Compatriots in Taiwan" was issued, China's Defence Ministry announced the end of the two-decade-long symbolic bombardment of the Jinmen (Quemoy) and other off-shore islands.[32] Beijing also began to reduce its troop concentrations in Fujian Province facing Taiwan. It called for reunification talks with Taipei and promised that after reunification Taiwan would enjoy a high level of autonomy.

Beijing's initiatives towards Taiwan received great publicity. The weeks following Ye's announcement saw dozens of gestures, ranging from suggestions that Taiwan jurists establish ties with the mainland, to offers for the repatriation of Chiang Kai-shek's remains to the family tombs in his native town, Fenghua. China also took specific unilateral action to encourage trade, such as ending customs duties on goods from Taiwan and encouraging Taiwanese businessmen to co-operate economically with China.[33] China also promised Taiwan that it would be able to retain its intelligence, administrative and legal systems. In the new Constitution of 1982, it added a special provision, i.e. Provision 31, which allowed for the setting up of a special administrative region which would operate under a special new law. This was targeted towards both Taiwan and Hong Kong.[34]

On 26 June 1983, Deng proposed talks on an equal footing and co-operation between the two parties (the C.C.P. and K.M.T.): "[We] will not raise it as talks between the central government and a local government". He noted that after reunification, two different systems could be practised on the mainland and in Taiwan.[35] On 22 February 1984, Deng officially announced the "one country two systems" formula for reunification. According to Xu Jiatun, a former member of the Central Committee of the C.C.P. and the former director of China Xinhua News Agency in Hong Kong (now self-exiled in the United States because of the 1989 Tiananmen incident), the "one country, two systems" formula was originally targeted at reunification with Taiwan but was later also proposed for Hong Kong.[36]

China designed the peaceful reunification policy in the late 1970s when the United States was ready to shift its diplomatic recognition from the R.O.C. to the P.R.C. China expected its new Taiwan policy to facilitate the normalization of relations between China and the United States and bring about a crisis of confidence in Taiwan, which would result in quicker and easier reunification. Once people in Taiwan concluded that they would get no support from the international community, particularly the United States, and realized that the Taiwan question would be resolved by the Chinese people themselves, then they would be much more likely to take the best terms they could get from Beijing.

However, Beijing was over-confident that China–United States relations would develop rapidly following the normalization. It had expectations of an early reunification, because it believed that Washington would accommodate its demands at the expense of Taiwan.[37] However, the U.S. attitude towards Taiwan thwarted any Chinese plans for an early reunification. Nevertheless, China did not reverse its basic Taiwan policy, which was to build up China's own strength through modernization while seeking the best opportunity to bring about earlier reunification at minimum cost. China saw its best chance at reunification would be with a successful, modernized and booming economy, with expanding trade and a market full of business opportunities and attractive to Western investments. Once it was economically successful China would likely have more leverage in international affairs. Washington would be more willing to accommodate its wishes for reunification if it stood to benefit from China's co-operation in other matters. By that time Taiwan would also be more likely to take the best terms it could get from Beijing. Even if it were to refuse, Beijing would be able to enforce reunification at much lower cost. The international repercussions would be greatly reduced if it did not impose socialist rule immediately on Taiwan, but instead tolerated a "one country, two systems" arrangement. There would be fewer repercussions if China was successful in developing the special economic zones and in ensuring the continued prosperity of Hong Kong under the "one country, two systems" formula. China believed that its future position would be strengthened so long as it could maintain internal stability and concentrate on building up its strength as quickly as possible.

With this strategy in mind, Beijing concentrated its efforts on keeping Taiwan more diplomatically isolated until such an opportunity arose. Through a series of peaceful proposals and more conciliatory moves, China hoped to win more international support and draw attention to Taiwan's persistent refusal of peaceful proposals. In this way, the blame for any consequent tensions and conflict in the Taiwan Strait could be shifted to Taiwan. China hoped these initiatives would discourage Taiwan's predilection for independence. If the best option (reunification through negotiation) could not be achieved, China hoped for at least the maintenance of the status quo and a slowdown of the drift towards independence until such time as it became strong enough to deal with the issue, at which point it would have more options, more confidence and there would be less cost. At the same time, Beijing tried hard to encourage bilateral trade and investment in the hope that increasing integration between the two economies would not only facilitate earlier reunification but also put the mainland in a stronger bargaining position.

This new Taiwan policy which espouses the "one country, two systems" formula for reunification has remained unchanged since the late 1970s.

Cross-Strait Relations before 1995

The K.M.T. government in Taiwan successfully withstood the shock of China–United States normalization in the late 1970s and China's subsequent diplomatic initiatives and pressure. This is partly due to international support from some major powers, in particular the United States through its Taiwan Relations Act and continued arms sales, and partly due to Taiwan's strong tenacity and determination to survive.

In the mid-1980s, as a result of efforts on both sides of the Taiwan Strait, there began a thaw in cross-strait relations. Between November 1987, when Taiwan under Chiang Ching-kuo lifted the ban on travelling to the mainland, and the end of 1995, these were 8.5 million visits to the mainland by Taiwanese people, of which 1.5 million were in 1995 alone.[38] Cross-strait telephone calls totalled 220 million during the same period.[39] In 1995, the volume of mail and telephone calls from China to Taiwan ranked second highest out of the total volume of foreign mail and calls, while that from Taiwan to China ranked first for the island's foreign mail and telecommunications. In 1989 cross-strait letters numbered about 19 million and by 1995 the number had increased to 30.4 million. In 1989, the number of telephone calls from China to Taiwan was 1.8 million. By 1995 the number had increased to 40.8 million.[40]

Most impressive of all was the development in cross-strait economic relations. By 1990, Taiwan businessmen were investing US$1 billion annually in China, and three years later their investments had grown to US$2.5 billion annually.[41] In 1995, according to China, over 27,000 Taiwanese companies were investing in the mainland with contracted investment exceeding US$24 billion (Taiwan's spin on it was that 25,000 Taiwanese companies had relocated to the mainland with investment totalling US$25 billion.[42]) Taiwan's investment in China in 1995 was equal to 1.25 per cent of its GDP, the highest rate among the countries in the world, with Japan coming in second (0.06 per cent) and the United States third (0.04 per cent) in terms of the GDP ratio.[43] Next to Hong Kong, Taiwan was the largest source of outside investment in the mainland.[44]

Indirect trade between the two sides has also increased rapidly since November 1987, reaching, according to Taiwan, US$100 billion by the end of 1994.[45] According to Taiwan's Board of Foreign Trade (B.O.F.T.), in 1994 bilateral trade jumped 20.1 per cent from a year before to hit a record high of US$16.51 billion. Exports to the mainland climbed 15.1 per cent from the previous year to US$14.65 billion, while imports soared 83.0 per cent to US$1.86 billion. This trade accounted for 9.3 per cent of Taiwan's overall trade in 1994.

In 1995, despite tensions across the Strait, Taiwan's total volume of exports to the mainland had risen from US$4.4 billion in 1990 to US$17.9 billion. In that year, the total volume of imports and exports reached US$3.0 billion and US$17.8 billion respectively, an increase of 66.3 per cent and 22.2 per cent respectively over the previous year. As a result, Taiwan enjoyed a trade surplus of US$14.8 billion with the mainland, 1.65 times that of the previous year. All the cross-strait trade figures in 1995 set record high levels.[46]

Together with the development in the economic relations, the two sides also took steps to increase their overall mutual contacts. Since the late 1970s, Beijing had been pushing vigorously for formal political contacts and earlier talks on reunification. By 1995, Taiwan had agreed to negotiate their differences and handle cross-strait affairs involving what Taiwan called "common power" (*gong quan li*), not officially but through a semi-official organization, i.e. the Strait Exchange Foundation (S.E.F.), established in February 1991. Beijing accepted this informal arrangement and set up a counterpart organization called the Association for Relations across the Taiwan Strait (A.R.A.T.S.). It was hoped that this semi-official organization would facilitate the process to talks on final reunification.

In September 1990, Taiwan set up the National Unification Council (N.U.C.) as an advisory body for the President. In January 1991, Taiwan's Executive Yuan set up the Mainland Affairs Council (M.A.C.) to make overall plans for handling mainland affairs. In February 1991 and March 1991 respectively, Taiwan's N.U.C. and Executive Yuan adopted the "Guidelines for National Unification". On 30 April 1991, Taiwan announced that "the period of mobilization for the suppression of Communist rebellion" would be terminated on 1 May and the "temporary provisions" of the constitution in force during the "mobilization" period would be annulled simultaneously. In other words, Taiwan would no longer treat the C.C.P. as a rebellious organization. In July 1992, the Executive Yuan passed the "Regulations on Relations between People in the Taiwan area and on the Mainland".

A.R.A.T.S. and S.E.F. had several informal meetings in 1992. On 12 October 1992, Chinese President Jiang Zemin, using his capacity as Secretary General of the C.C.P., noted: "Under the 'one China' prerequisite, [the two sides] can discuss everything, including the method for a formal negotiation, to find a way both sides deem appropriate".[47] In April 1993, a groundbreaking meeting took place in Singapore between Taiwan's Koo Chen-fu, chairman of the S.E.F., and his mainland counterpart Wang Daohan of A.R.A.T.S. At this, the first "Wang-Koo meeting", Koo and Wang signed the "Cross-Strait Agreement on the Use and Inspection of Affidavits", the "Cross-Strait Agreement on Matters Related to Inquiry by Registered Letters and Relevant Compensation", the "Agreement on the System for Connection and Talks between the Two Sides", and the "Joint Agreement of the Wang-Koo Meeting".

Subsequently, the two sides conducted 15 rounds of negotiations to discuss in depth problems arising from exchanges between the two sides. China pushed for another Wang-Koo meeting to upgrade the level of the talks on some important issues in the hopes that they would lead to earlier reunification negotiations. The second Wang-Koo meeting was scheduled for 20 July 1995. Preparatory talks between S.E.F. Vice Chairman Chiao Jen-ho and Tang Shubei, Vice Chairman and Secretary General of A.R.A.T.S. took place in early 1995.

However, the second Wang-Koo meeting never took place. Lee's United States visit and Beijing's subsequent angry response led to tensions across the Strait, and plunged cross-strait relations to their lowest point since the late 1970s.

Notes

1. Chen Kongli, ed., *Taiwan Lishi Gangyao* [A History of Taiwan] (Beijing: Jiuzhou Publishing House, 1996), p. 28.
2. See "The Treaty of Peace Between Japan and China (17 April 1895)", in *Treaties and Agreements With and Concerning China 1894–1919,* edited by John V.A. MacMurrary

(New York: Oxford University Press, 1921), vol. 1, pp. 18–19. The treaty is generally known as the Treaty of Shimonoseki in Japanese or the Treaty of Ma Guan in Chinese.

3. Peng Qian, Yang Mingjie and Shu Deren, *Zhongguo Weishenmu Shu Bu* [Why China Says No] (Beijing: New World Publishing House, 1996), p. 138.

4. Wan Wenlan, *Zhongguo Jindaishi* [A Contemporary History of China] (Beijing: People's Press, 1962), pp. 220–1; Huang Chia-mo, *Meiguo Yu Taiwan 1784–1895* [The United States and Taiwan 1784–1895] (Taiwan: Zhongyang Yanjiuyuan [Central Research Institute] Press), 1966, pp. 135–42, 259–74.

5. *Foreign Relations of the United States 1943* (Washington, D.C.: Government Printing Office [GPO], 1961), pp. 448–9.

6. See Proclamation Defining Terms for Japanese Surrender, 26 July 1945 in *Department of State Bulletin*, no. 318 (1945), p. 137.

7. Gene T. Hsiao, "The Legal Status of Taiwan in the Normalisation of China–American Relations", in *China–American Normalisation and Its Policy Implications,* edited by Gene T. Hsiao and Michael Witunski (New York: Praeger Publishers, 1983), p. 30.

8. John W. Garver, "Arms Sales, the Taiwan Question, and China–U.S. Relations", *Orbis* 26, no. 4 (Winter, 1983): 1001.

9. Peng et al., *Zhongguo Weishenmu Shu Bu*, op. cit., pp. 138–43.

10. Edwin K. Snyder, *The Taiwan Relations Act and the Defence of the Republic of China* (Berkeley: Institute of International Studies, University of California, 1980), p. 1.

11. Ralph N Clough, *Island China* (Cambridge, MA: Harvard University Press, 1978), p. 7.

12. A. Doak Barnett, *U.S. Arms Sales: The China–Taiwan Tangle* (Washington, D.C.: The Brookings Institution, 1982), p. 16. Also see William M. Bueler, *U.S. China Policy and the Problem of Taiwan* (Boulder: Colorado Associated University Press, 1971), Chapter 1.

13. Garver, op.cit., p. 1001; Hsiao and Witunski, op. cit., p. 43.

14. All citations are from *Beijing Review* 15, no. 9 (3 March 1972): 4–5.

15. *New York Times*, 7 September 1977, quoted in Steven I. Levine, "China Policy during Carter's Year One", *Asian Survey* 18, no. 5 (1978): 441. Ford immediately denied any such promise.

16. For China–United States relations between the Shanghai Communiqué of 1972 and the normalization of 1979, see Michel Oksenberg and Robert B. Oxnam, eds., *Dragon and Eagle: United States–China Relations, Past and Future* (New York: Basic Books, 1978).

17. See the "Joint Communiqué on the Establishment of Diplomatic Relations between the United States and the People's Republic of China, and United States", *Beijing Review* 21, no. 51 (22 December 1978). The Chinese text uses the word *"chengren"*, which, if translated into English, means "recognize" instead of "acknowledge" as in the English text, see *Renmin Ribao* [People's Daily] (Beijing), 17 December 1978, p. 1.

18. Jimmy Carter, *Keeping Faith* (New York: Bantam Books, 1982), pp. 186–202.

19. Hsiao and Witunski, op. cit., p. 62.

20. Ibid.

21. See U.S. House of Congress, *Taiwan Legislation: Hearings Before the Committee on Foreign Affairs*, 96th Cong., 1st Sess., 7 and 8 February 1979 (Washington D.C.: GPO, 1979), pp 46–47.

22. Ibid., p. 39.

23. Garver, op. cit., pp. 1018–9.

24. China Xinhua News Agency (Beijing) (hereafter cited as Xinhua). "A Key Link in Development of China–U.S. Relations", 18 June 1981, in *Foreign Broadcast Information Service* (hereafter cited as *FBIS*) 19 June 1981, pp. B1–2. See also Zhang Dezhen, *Heige De Yatai Zhixing* [Haig's Trip to the Asian and Pacific Region], *Renmin Ribao*, 23 June 1981.

25. See the Communiqué in *Beijing Review* 25, no. 34 (23 August 1982).

26. Harry Harding, *A Fragile Relationship: The United States and China since 1972* (Washington D.C.: The Brookings Institution, 1992), p. 117.

27. Ibid.

28. Zhai Zuojun et al., *Gongheguo Sishinian Dashi Shuping* [Comments on Major Events in the Forty Years of the P.R.C.] (Beijing: Dang'an Press, 1989), p. 287.

29. The Standing Committee of the National People's Congress of the P.R.C., "A Message to Compatriots in Taiwan", *Beijing Review* 22, no. 1 (5 January 1979): 17.

30. See *Beijing Review* 24, no. 40 (5 October 1981): 10–11.

31. The "three direct links" referred to direct trade, transportation and postal services between the mainland and Taiwan; the "four exchanges" referred to the establishment of exchanges between relatives and tourists, academic groups, cultural groups and sports representatives.

32. See Zhai et al., op. cit., p. 287.

33. See Kenneth S. Chern. "The Impact of the Taiwan Issue on Sino-American Relations, 1980–82", in *China in Readjustment,* edited by Leung Chi-keung and Steve S.K. Chin (Hong Kong: University of Hong Kong Press, 1983), p. 381. Also Barnett, op. cit., p. 24.

34. For the new constitution, see *Renmin Ribao*, 6 December 1982.

35. Deng Xiaoping, "*Zhongguo Dalu He Taiwan Heping Tongyi De Shexiang*" [An Idea for the Peaceful Reunification of the Chinese Mainland and Taiwan], in *Jianshe You Zhongguo Tese De Shehui Zhuyi* [Build Socialism with Chinese Characteristics] (Beijing: People's Press, 1987), pp. 17–19. "*Yige Zhongguo Shi Wuke Zhengbian De Shishi*" [One China is an Indisputable Fact], *Renmin Ribao*, 12 August 1999.

36. Xu Jiatun, *Xu Jiatun Xianggan Huiyilu* [Years in Hong Kong] (Taipei: Lien Ho Pao, 1994), p. 324.

37. This belief has been consistent since the early Mao era. Wang Binnan, China's chief negotiator with the Americans in the 1950s, recalled that Mao asked him to tell his American counterpart during the China–United States negotiations in 1958 that the United States was a big country and China was a big country too. The United States should not offend and confront China just for the sake of a small island like Taiwan. See *Renmin Ribao*, 17 December 1978, p. 8.

38. China Central TV (Beijing) (hereafter cited as CCTV) (overseas), News Program, 28 February 1996.

39. Central News Agency (Taipei), "Taiwan: Mainland Affairs Council Chairman Says Taiwan Ready For Talks with China", Reuters News Service, Reuters Business Briefing (hereafter cited as Reuters), 25 January 1996.

40. CCTV, "Taiwan: Flowers and Moon-cakes Fly Across The Strait", Reuters, 19 February 1996.

41. John R. Faust and F. Judith Kornberg, *China in World Politics* (Boulder: Lynne Rienner Publishers, 1995), p. 42.
42. Central News Agency, "Taiwan: Mainland Affairs Council Chairman Says Taiwan Ready for Talks with China", Reuters, 25 January 1996.
43. Central News Agency, "China: Taiwan Biggest Investor in Mainland China in Terms of Proportion of GDP", Reuters, 9 April 1997.
44. Faust and Kornberg, op. cit., p. 42.
45. Central News Agency, "Taiwan: Mainland Affairs Council Chairman Says Taiwan Ready for Talks with China", Reuters, 25 January 1996.
46. *China Daily*, 7 October 1996, p. 4.
47. *"Yige Zhongguo Shi Wuke Zhengbian De Shishi"* [One China is an Indisputable Fact], *Renmin Ribao*, 12 August 1999.

2

Lee's U.S. Visit
and China's Response

On 22 May 1995, the United States, in a reversal of a 16-year ban on United States visits by high ranking R.O.C. officials, granted a visa to President Lee Teng-hui for a 6-day "private" visit to his alma mater, Cornell University, in Ithaca, New York. This prompted a crisis in both China–United States relations and cross-strait relations.

Since the United Nations shifted its recognition from the R.O.C. to the P.R.C. in 1971 and the United States followed suit in 1979, Taiwan has been working hard to break its diplomatic isolation. In May 1994, the Clinton Administration refused Lee a visa to visit the United States, but allowed him a refuelling stop in Hawaii on his way to Central America, restricting him to the airport grounds in Honolulu while his plane was being refuelled. Lee landed at the airport in Honolulu but refused to disembark from the plane in protest. However, this did not deter his efforts to return to the United States.

In 1991, the Taiwan alumni of Cornell contributed US$1 million for an academic chair. This was followed by the establishment of the Lee Teng-hui Professorship of World Affairs at Cornell University in 1994 through a US$2.5 million endowment provided anonymously by Lee's friends in Taiwan. In early 1995, the university invited Lee to be the main speaker at its June alumni observance. During a rally in April 1995, described as the largest political gathering of Asian students ever at Cornell, the "Taiwan Speak-Up Committee" collected more than 2,000 signatures urging Clinton to grant Lee a visa to visit the university. In order to ensure that the visa was issued, a Taiwan think-tank, headed by Lee's right-hand man, Liu Tai-ying, hired the Washington lobbying firm of Cassidy & Associates in 1994 for US$4.5 million and a promise of a large bonus if Congress voted in favour of Lee's visa.[1]

Traditionally, Taiwan's allies in the United States have been conservative Republicans. However, Cassidy was headed by a former aide to Democratic Senator George McGovern and included among its senior lobbyists Jody

Powell, press secretary to former U.S. President Jimmy Carter, and Bob Beckel, a Carter Administration political operative. The firm's account executive for Taiwan was Gerald Warburg, who had been a principal aide to former Senator Alan Cranston, a Democrat from California.

In November 1994, the Republicans won a landslide victory in the U.S. Congress, and many key positions were taken up by conservative friends of Taiwan. Organized by Cassidy, the new Taiwan lobby also included Democrats and centrist Republicans, activated by a letter-writing and telephone campaign in favour of Lee's visa and pro-Taiwan resolutions from more than 30 state legislatures.[2]

By early April 1995, the House of International Relations Committee voted 33-to-0 to support the visa. Taiwan's friends in Congress such as Senator Frank Murkowski of Alaska, chairman of the Foreign Relations Sub-committee on East Asia, and Jesse Helms of North Carolina, who had long advocated closer ties with Taiwan, helped spear-head lopsided Congressional resolutions in favour of a Lee visit.

At a meeting on 18 May with President Clinton at the White House, Senator Charles Robb broached the visa issue. The President agreed,[3] and announced, on 22 May, that Lee would be granted a visa. Taiwan's allies in the United States also wanted Lee to be allowed to attend the annual meeting of the United States–Taiwan Economic Council in Anchorage, Alaska in September 1995.

Lee was overjoyed with the U.S. decision which led to the first visit, albeit a "private" one, to the United States by a R.O.C. president since the republic was founded in 1912 (Chiang Ching-kuo only visited the United States as Defence Minister). He was in the United States from 8 to 11 June 1995.

Three days after Lee returned from the landmark visit, Taiwan's Premier Lien Chan also made landmark visits to the Czech Republic, Austria and Hungary. These three European countries did not have diplomatic relations with Taiwan and formally recognized the P.R.C. as the sole legal government of China. Canada also allowed a "private" visit by Taiwan's Vice Premier Hsu Li-teh.

At the same time, Taiwan intensified its bid for U.N. membership. It announced, also in June, that it would donate US$1 billion to create a U.N. fund for developing nations if it was admitted into the world body. It urged the international society to support such a request. The Taiwanese Deputy Foreign Minister Fang Chin-yen said: "If we can join the United Nations, the Republic of China would like to donate 0.44 per cent of its Gross National Product. That is US$1 billion."[4] It denied that it was considering applying first for U.N. observer status and then U.N. membership, insisting that Taiwan was "seeking to enter the United Nations as full member."[5] At the same time, Taiwan commissioned its fifth *Perry*-class missile frigate (called *Ziyi* in Chinese *Pinyin*), and sent one navel fleet (called *Dun Mu* in Chinese *pinyin*) to visit Singapore. Germany announced that it would remove Taiwan from its list of "areas of tension". This gave Taiwan easier access to German arms sales (Taiwan has long had its eye on German submarines).

China's response to all this was angry.

Response to the United States

The U.S. policy reversal came as a tremendous shock to Beijing. Chinese President Jiang Zemin rushed back from a trip to Shanghai to discuss the incident. Only weeks before, the U.S. Secretary of State, Warren Christopher, had given Chinese Foreign Minister Qian Qichen his firm assurance that a visa would not be granted to Lee. For a while, Beijing seemed to be at a loss as to what to do and failed to respond immediately. However, when it came, China's response was stern. It accused Washington of deviating from the commitment it had made in the three China–United States joint communiqués, and of damaging the foundation of China–United States relations as well as the United States government's international reputation by permitting Lee's visit.[6] It said that the U.S. decision was a "belligerent act on a par with the Korean and Vietnam wars" and "a wanton wound inflicted upon China" while "China had done nothing harmful to the United States".[7] China also:

1. issued a stiff formal protest to the U.S. ambassador to China, Stapleton Roy;
2. recalled its ambassador to the United States, Li Daoyu;
3. postponed indefinitely a trip to the United States by its Defence Minister Chi Haotian;
4. cut short Air Force Chief of Staff General Yu Zhenwu's trip to the United States half-way through his tour of U.S. airbases and consultations with U.S. officials;
5. cancelled a visit to Washington by its State Councillor Li Guixian;
6. postponed talks between Chinese and U.S. experts on nuclear energy co-operation and the Missile Technology Control Regime (M.T.C.R.), which had been suspended after the Tiananmen incident of 1989 and only resumed in October 1994;
7. put off a planned visit to Beijing in June by John Holum, Director of the U.S. Arms Control and Disarmament Agency, for talks on weapons proliferation and nuclear energy;
8. put off a planned visit by Thomas McNamara, U.S. Deputy Assistant Secretary of State for Political and Military Affairs in July.

There were also repercussions for U.S. commercial interests. A U.S. company, Greiner International, said it had been on the verge of concluding a US$35 million contract in June 1995 to provide equipment and engineering services for a new airport in Nanjing. But in a clear retaliation against the United States for granting Lee's visa the business went instead to a British rival, Siemens Plessey Systems. A source at China's State Planning Commission "acknowledged privately that a decision was taken in Beijing to withhold the contract from Greiner because of the Lee visit".[8] At the same time, American car companies Chrysler and Ford lost a contract to Germany's Daimler-Benz to build a US$1 billion plant in Nanfeng, Guangdong Province. The same German company also won a US$50 million joint-venture contract to make buses in China.

Response to Taiwan

China's response to Taiwan reflected its disappointment, confusion and anger. At first, it directed its anger only at the United States with what appeared to be only a routine protest to Taiwan. While accusing Taiwan of setting up obstacles to rapprochement, the spokesman for the Chinese government at the same time urged Taiwan to accept the offer by President Jiang Zemin to hold talks on ending hostility, and called on Taiwan to lift a decades-old ban on official contacts and the three direct links with China. It emphasized that it was expecting "to intensify exchanges and mutual trust between two sides".[9] China's A.R.A.T.S. Vice-Chairman and Secretary General Tang Shubei did not even cancel or postpone his planned visit to Taiwan on 26–30 May. Nor did he cut short his visit to Taiwan. In fact, while in Taiwan, he claimed "Mr and Mrs Koo and other people at the S.E.F. will receive a friendly and polite reception in the mainland (for the second round of the Wang-Koo meeting)".[10] He also signed an eight-point agenda for the second Wang-Koo meeting, namely (1) co-operation on hijacking and fishing disputes; (2) agreement on the protection of Taiwanese investment in the mainland; (3) bilateral non-governmental trade and intellectual property right protection; (4) bilateral cultural, educational and press exchange; (5) bilateral agricultural exchange; (6) bilateral exchange of science and technology; (7) bilateral exchange of tourism; and (8) other important issues in bilateral relations.[11]

It was only after Lee's provocative speech at Cornell University that China responded with sharp criticism and moved to "punish" Taiwan. On 16 June, it announced that it had suspended the second round of the Wang-Koo meeting, scheduled for 20–23 July, and the preparatory talks scheduled for 27 June-1 July, until such time as Taiwan ceased activities aimed at promoting its independence. It cancelled a planned trip by its business leader Zheng Hongye, Chairman of the China Council for the Promotion of International Trade, which would have been the first visit by a Chinese business leader to Taiwan since the lifting of a four-decade-old Taiwanese ban on such visits. It also ruled out a meeting between Jiang Zemin and Lee Teng-hui unless it took place within the mutual understanding of the "one China" principle. It criticized Taiwan's new U.N. bid as "trading money for principle", "creating two Chinas" and "an insult to the U.N. whose membership cannot be bought by money". It expressed its "strong displeasure" at Lien Chan's visit to Europe, considering it part of the diplomatic offensive by Taiwan. While in Prague, China's Deputy Education Minister Wang Mingtou cut short his visit and refused to sign a bilateral student-exchange agreement in protest at Lien Chan's visit there.[12] It called Canada's decision to allow a visit by Hsu Li-teh a "grave incident" and made representation to the Canadian government to protest. As the Canadian ambassador John Paynter was out of the country, the chargé d'affaires Kenneth Sunquist was summoned and a complaint was lodged.

The most dramatic action China took was to launch "missile tests" and military exercises near Taiwan, and to assemble troops in Fujian Province directly across the strait from Taiwan between July 1995 and March 1996.

Missile Tests and Military Exercises

From 21 to 26 July 1995, a surface-to-surface missile test, code-named "95–*Ziqiang*", was conducted in a sea area north of Taiwan by the third division of the Second Artillery Corps of the Chinese People's Liberation Army (P.L.A.), directly under the Central Military Commission (C.M.C.). Since June 1994, the P.L.A. had conducted at least 10 missile tests and drills in the East and South China Seas, but they had never been so close to the Taiwan Strait. This test was only 50 kilometres from Taiwan-controlled Pengchia Yu Island and 150 kilometres north of Taipei (see Map 1). Six surface-to-surface missiles were test-fired. According to *Tokyo Shinbum*, two missiles were fired from the Xinjiang Autonomous Region, two from Jilin Province and two from Jiangxi Province.[13] According to *Jane's Defence Weekly*, the six missiles were four CSS-6 [*Dongfeng*-15/M-9] and two CSS-5 [*Dongfeng*-21] ballistic missiles.[14]

The second missile and artillery test, code-named "95–*Zizhu*", was conducted from 15 to 25 August by the P.L.A. Navy's East China Sea Fleet, the Navy's air force, and the Second Artillery Corps. The test site was about one-sixth the size of Taiwan, in a sea area 136 kilometres north of Taiwan (see Map 1). The military exercises deployed C201, C101 and C801 missiles, navy vessels, including *Jianghu*-class destroyers, live artillery shells, ship-to-ship and ship-to-air missiles, and navy war planes, including *Jian*-7 fighters, firing air-to-air missiles.[15] They conducted cruising manoeuvres and tactical-formation training.

In mid-October 1995, the P.L.A. conducted combined air and sea exercises, with rocket and missile launches from navy vessels, flyovers by fighter planes

Map 1: The P.L.A. Missile Test Sites
(July & August 1995 and March 1996)

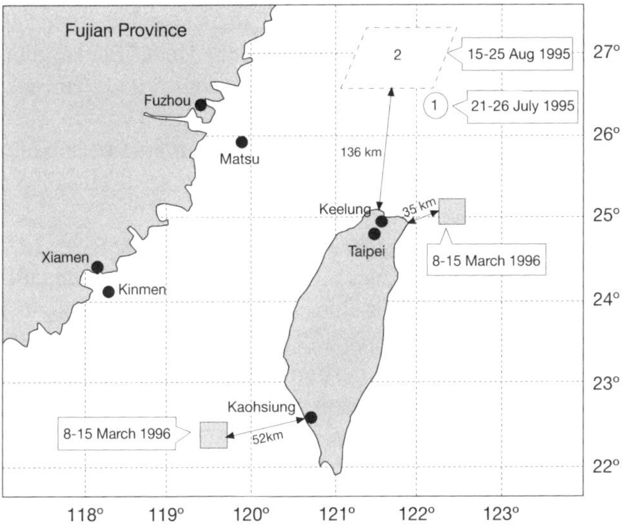

Source: Free China Journal (Taipei), 8 March 1996, p. 1.

and helicopters, as well as manoeuvres by a nuclear submarine in the East China Sea.

From 22 to 25 November 1995, the P.L.A. held an amphibious exercise around Dongshan Island, which is located south of the two shores of the Taiwan Strait and is the second largest island of Fujian Province, covering an area of 194 square kilometres. Its topography, terrain, weather and water conditions closely resemble those of Taiwan. The exercise was part of an annual training programme, but China used it as another stern warning to Taiwan. The exercise involved 2,000 ground, naval and air troops as well as armed police and people's militia. Civil vessels were also mobilized.

This exercise was different from previous ones in three ways: (1) the armed police participated; (2) most of the new equipment in active service since the 1980s and 1990s was mobilized in the Dongshan exercise, including Russia-made Su-27 fighters, which were the most advanced in China's airforce, and a new-type barrier-breaking, mine-sweeping device, the GSLIII rocket mine-sweeping vehicle; (3) some 100 admirals, colonels and experts marshalled soldiers for battle on the sea and in the air, and studied new tactics and new knowledge between September and October. They pursued three-dimensional offensive and defensive maritime training on the basis of new equipment and technology. The results were partly implemented in the Dongshan exercise in November.

The largest military exercises were held from 8 to 25 March 1996. They drew much more attention, not only because of their size and timing, i.e. around Taiwan's presidential election, but also because the United States sent two aircraft carrier battle groups to the Taiwan Strait to "observe" the exercises.

The exercises were under the command of General Zhang Wannian, Vice-Chairman of the C.M.C. and Head of the Headquarters for Operations against Taiwan [*dui tai junshi zhihuibu*], which had been set up in 1995 during the Taiwan Strait crisis.

Both the Nanjing and Guangzhou military regions (there are seven military regions in China) were then under the command of the Headquarters. During the exercises, the two military regions moved their crack units to Fujian and Guangdong provinces to be reorganized into a field army group facing Taiwan. It was reported that the troops taking part in the military exercises also included crack units from various field group armies of other military regions, including a crack division of the "elite" 38th Army.

It was in fact a three-round exercise. The first round, conducted from 8 to 15 March, was ground-to-ground "missile launching training". The missiles were launched into two box-shaped splash zones (see Map 2):

One splash zone of the missiles was located 20 to 40 nautical miles off north-east Taiwan, close to the port of Keelung, and the other was 30 to 50 nautical miles off Kaohsiung on the south-west coast. Both zones covered some 500 square nautical miles.

The P.L.A. fired four unarmed ballistic missiles which all landed exactly within the two "target boxes". Three splashed down in the "target box" off Kaohsiung. Another landed in the "target box" off Keelung.

The second round, conducted from 12 to 20 March, was naval and air exercises with live ammunition (see Map 2).

The third round was due to begin on 18 March, but in fact did not start until the following day because of poor weather. It was a large-scale joint ground, sea and air exercise around Pingtan Island, which is Fijian's largest island and the largest live-fire field, topographically similar to Taiwan (see Map 2).

According to the public notice issued by China, the sphere of the joint ground, sea and air exercise started from Nanri Island in the south and ended in the sea area opposite Jiangtian in the north, covering a sea area of approximately 6,000 square kilometres. It was only 30 kilometres away from the Taiwan-controlled Mazu Islands [Matsu].[16]

The exercises tested the combat readiness of the following: control of sea and air, high-speed ferrying of troops, landing of armoured infantry, establishing a beachhead, mechanized parachute assault, multi-layer artillery barrage, breakthrough by strong assault force, three-dimensional deep-thrust, breaking

Map 2: Sites of the P.L.A. Missile Test and Military Exercises in March 1996

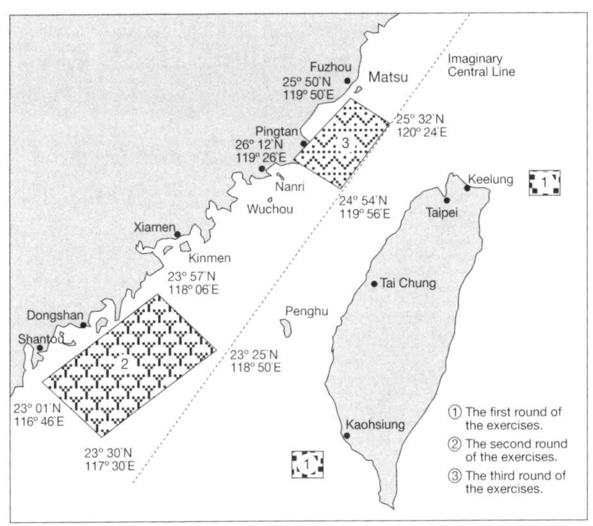

Source: Youth Daily News (Taipei), 16 March 1996, p. 1.

Note: The first "box zone" was a sea area formed by a line connected by four points at 25 degrees 13 minutes north and 122 degrees 20 minutes east, 25 degrees 13 minutes north and 122 degrees 40 minutes east, 24 degrees 57 minutes north and 122 degrees 40 minutes east, and 24 degrees 57 minutes north and 122 degrees 20 minutes east.

The second "box zone" was a sea area formed by a line connected by four points at 22 degrees 38 minutes north and 119 degrees 25 minutes east, 22 degrees 38 minutes north and 119 degrees 45 minutes east, 22 degrees 22 minutes north and 119 degrees 45 minutes east, and 22 degrees 22 minutes north and 119 degrees 25 minutes east.

resistance and attacking in depth and electronic interference. The landing exercise was conducted in harsh weather with support from the air force, destroyers, guided-missile destroyers, escort vessels, minesweepers, submarine chasers, landing ships and support vessels.

These exercises were aimed at making preparations for a forced amphibious landing, sea and air blockade and seizure of islands under certain conditions. They added muscle to the Chinese pressure on Taiwan, an island heavily dependent on foreign trade, by extending two virtual pincers near its two major ports on either side. The exercises ended just two days after Taiwan's presidential election.

Warning China of "grave consequences" arising out of its "risky" acts (in the words of U.S. Secretary of State Warren Christopher), the United States deployed the guided missile cruiser *Bunker Hill* around the Taiwan Strait to monitor incoming Chinese ballistic missiles in the area, as well as assembling off Taiwan its largest fleet in East Asia since the end of the Vietnam War in 1975: two aircraft carrier battle groups.

The *Independence* battle group included a *Forrestal*-class carrier, the *USS Independence*, which was commissioned in 1950 and carried about 75 warplanes. Other members of the battle group were the destroyers *O'Brien* and *Hewitt*, the guided missile frigate *McClusky*, the oiler *Pecos* and the guided missile cruiser *Bunker Hill*.

The *Nimitz* battle group included the nuclear-powered carrier *USS Nimitz*, the cruiser *Port Royal,* the destroyers *Callaghan* and *Oldendorf*, the frigate *Ford* and the replenishment ships *Willamette* and *Shasta*.

The United States also deployed three nuclear-powered attack submarines. The submarines *Columbus* and *Bremerton* were part of the battle group around the aircraft carrier *Independence*. A third nuclear submarine, the *Portsmouth*, was deployed to support the carrier *Nimitz*.[17]

During China's March 1996 exercises, the *Independence* was located about 110 miles east of Taiwan in international waters outside areas designated by China as target regions for missile firings and live-ammunition drills while the *Nimitz* was on its way from Japan to join the *Independence*.

War Zone, Warnings and Verbal Attacks

While these exercises near Taiwan were underway, China also set up a war zone and issued stern warnings to intensify pressure on Taiwan.

In November 1995, China made known that it had set up the "Nanjing War Zone" within the Nanjing Military Region. The military region and the war zone were two different terms for largely the same administrative unit in the P.L.A. army. According to Beijing's explanation, a "war zone" was an operational region set up to realize a strategic plan and implement a strategic task, and it sometimes broadly referred to the region where a war was fought. Therefore, the "war zone" referred to the established unit in the military region that was assigned to carry out a definite military task. The Nanjing Military Region was called the "Nanjing War Zone" when a specific military task was given.

The adoption of the "war zone" terminology suggested that China could mobilize troops not only within the Nanjing Military Region but also from other military regions, which were temporarily assigned by the C.M.C. to the command of the war zone. In particular, the air force, which was under the direct command of the P.L.A. Air Force Headquarters, and the naval force, i.e. the East China Sea Naval Fleet, which was under P.L.A. Navy's direct command, the missile force which was under direct command of the P.L.A.'s Second Artillery Corps and the armed police corps were temporarily put under the command of the war zone during the Taiwan Strait crisis. This staunch combat force could be put into quick and co-ordinated action. Procurement, including from civilian sources, of weapons, ammunition, food and medical supplies, warehouses and hospital facilities, which were spread around the various military regions, could also be co-ordinated.

The Nanjing War Zone was responsible for operations against Taiwan. It was divided into two sub-zones: the first one, serving as the forefront, comprised Fujian Province and Jiangxi Province. The second one, the rear support, consisted of Jiangsu Province, Zhejiang Province and Anhui Province.

Within the Nanjing War Zone, the Headquarters for Operations Against Taiwan [*dui tai junshi zhihuibu*] was set up to be in charge of the study of military strategy, deployment of forces and overall planning for military exercises. Its commander was C.M.C. Vice-Chairman Zhang Wannian. The first deputy commander was Chief of General Staff Fu Quanyou, and the deputy commander was Deputy Chief of General Staff Qian Shugeng. Its 19 members included Kui Fulin, Deputy Chief of the P.L.A. General Staff; Zhou Ziyu, Deputy Director of the P.L.A. General Political Department; Liu Shunrao, P.L.A. Air Force Deputy Commander; He Pingfei, P.L.A. Naval Deputy Commander; and generals and officers from Nanjing and Guangzhou Military Regions as well as the East China Sea Naval Fleet.

One office and five groups were set up under the headquarters. Fu Quanyou was appointed the office director and Qian Shugeng was appointed the first deputy director in charge of routine work. The five groups were Investigation and Research, Intelligence, Work, Operational; and Liaison.

According to C.M.C. Vice-Chairman Liu Huaqing, the headquarters had four functions:

1. To maintain a grasp of the military trends of Taiwan's three services and study the military situation in the Taiwan Strait.
2. To be responsible for making proposals to the C.M.C. on military strategy and principles targeting Taiwan.
3. To be responsible for making plans for military exercises in the Taiwan Strait and the Nanjing War Zone.
4. To be entrusted with the command of implementing war preparations and operations targeting Taiwan in an emergency.[18]

At the same time, China reminded Taiwan that it had not abandoned the option to use force to recover the island in the event of Taiwan's independence and foreign intervention in Taiwan, and remained ambiguous about what it meant by listing "Taiwan's independence" and "foreign intervention in Taiwan" as two situations in which it would use force. In other words, whether the condition of "Taiwan's independence" only referred to a formal or declared independence, exclusive of a de facto independence or a further drift towards a formal independence was left open, as was whether Taiwan's de facto official relations with foreign countries, foreign arms sales to Taiwan and the dispatch of U.S. aircraft carrier battle groups could be interpreted as "foreign intervention". Apart from these two conditions, the Chinese reiterated, though occasionally and privately, other situations where force would be used, i.e. (1) large-scale social turmoil against mainlanders by local people in Taiwan; (2) the development of nuclear weapons in Taiwan; and (3) too long a delay in reunification.

China warned: "If things develop to a stage that forces us to take those measures we don't want to, we will absolutely not hesitate ... If it should ever, unfortunately, come to a military confrontation between the two sides (China and Taiwan), the P.L.A. must take decisive measures and end that unfortunate situation in the shortest time."[19]

At the same time, China, through a series of articles, meetings and academic symposiums, violently attacked Taiwan's efforts to gain independence, and Lee in particular, accusing him of being a "traitor" to "be dumped into the garbage bin of history".

However, all this only amounted to "verbal attacks and military threats", and did not carry any intention to wage a real war on Taiwan to force reunification. Therefore, despite taking a strong public position, Beijing made a point of ensuring things would not get out of control. For example, when students in several Chinese universities sought to organize demonstrations to protest against Lee Teng-hui's U.S. visit, Beijing was careful not to mobilize them and even advised them not to demonstrate for fear of triggering off mass student protests. In universities such as Beijing University, the Chinese People's University and Nanjing University, authorities only allowed students to organize demonstrations against Lee within the campus grounds.

Notes

1. *Strait Times* (Singapore) (hereafter cited as *ST*), 24 July 1995, p. 36.
2. *ST*, 25 October 1995, p. 29.
3. Ibid.
4. *ST*, 27 June 1995, p. 5.
5. *ST,* 22 September 1995, p. 14.
6. "China: Li Peng Tells Bush of Problems with Bilateral Ties, Comments on Population Issue", Reuters, 12 September 1995.
7. *ST,* 10 June 1995, p. 1.
8. *ST,* 7 July 1995, p. 16.
9. *ST,* 23 May 1995, p. 15.
10. *ST*, 28 May 1995, p. 1.
11. *Lianhe Zaobao* [United Morning News] (Singapore), 29 May 1995, p. 1.

12. *ST*, 21 June 1995, p. 13.
13. *Lianhe Zaobao*, 10 August 1995, p. 16.
14. Duncan Lennox, "Iraq: Ballistic Missiles", *Jane's Defence Weekly*, from Reuters, 17 April 1996.
15. *Lianhe Zaobao*, 24 August 1995, p. 18.
16 "Taiwan: Beijing 'Military Observer' – China's Army Will Ignore 'Foreign Forces'", *Wen Wei Po* (Hong Kong), 16 March 1996, p. A1.
17. "USA: 3 U.S. Attack Submarines to Operate Near Taiwan", Reuters, 14 March 1996.
18. "China: Hong Kong Journal Examines Chinese Military Pressure On Taiwan", *Hsin Pao* (Hong Kong), from Reuters, 3 January 1996.
19. "China: Beijing Warns against Interference", *SCMP*, from Reuters, 19 December 1995. "China: Chinese President Reportedly Calls for Fleet Alert Against Taiwan", Kyoto News Service, from Reuters, 8 January 1996.

Part II

China vs. the United States over Taiwan

3

U.S. China Policy:
Facing a Rising China[1]

The Taiwan Strait crisis of 1995-96 was not an accident. It should be examined in the broad framework of post-Cold War international politics, in which the United States, China and Taiwan, in the process of bargaining over Cold War dividends and redefining their positions in the new strategic structure emerging in the Asia Pacific, had unavoidably come into conflict.

Lee Teng-hui's United States visit was obviously not simply a personal trip. It reflected Taiwan's intensified effort to change the status quo in the strategic structure in the Asia Pacific that had been in place for the previous two decades during the Cold War. Taiwan felt that it had been deprived of its former international status as member of the United Nations, as well as diplomatic recognition by the United States and most other countries, because of U.S. efforts to seek China's strategic support at the expense of Taiwan. The collapse of communism in Europe and the former Soviet Union dramatically reduced China's strategic weight in the eyes of the United States and encouraged Taiwan's eagerness to redress what it perceived to be the wrong it had suffered during the Cold War.

To China, Taiwan's efforts posed a serious threat not only to stable China–United States relations but also to the established strategic structure in the Asia Pacific, which already accepted the "one China" principle, a condition China insisted on for every country wanting to establish diplomatic relations with it. Taiwan's efforts were also a serious threat to China's vision of the future strategic structure in the Asia Pacific which, as China firmly demanded, should not go against the "one China" principle.

China also wanted to reap dividends from the Cold War. As a matter of fact, China had played a significant role in containing Soviet expansion and in its collapse. In hindsight, without China's de facto strategic alliance with the United States and its efforts in forming an international anti-hegemonic united front in the 1970s–80s, the Soviet Union would not have collapsed so easily. The United States would have spent much more time licking its wounds after the Vietnam War and would not have been in a position to deal Moscow any heavy blows. Moreover, the whole of Southeast Asia would not have been so stable following the shock of the U.S. withdrawal from Vietnam.

During the Cold War, China tried to exploit its strategic weight to get concessions out of Washington over Taiwan. The Taiwan issue was raised during the talks for the China–United States rapprochement of 1972 and China–United States normalization of 1979. In the 1980s, Beijing once again tried to persuade Washington to help solve the Taiwan issue. On one occasion on 19 December 1984, Deng Xiaoping asked the British Prime Minister, Margaret Thatcher, to tell the U.S. President, Ronald Reagan, that he hoped to see co-operation between the United States and China for the resolution of the Taiwan issue during Reagan's second term as president. In July 1985, during his visit to the United States, Chinese President Li Xiannian made the same request, which was repeated later on numerous occasions, such as during Deng's interview with an American correspondent on 2 September 1986, during Premier Zhao Ziyang's talk with U.S. Defence Secretary Caspar Weinberger on 9 October 1986 and during C.M.C. Vice Chairman Yang Shangkun's visit to Washington in May 1987. However, the United States only glossed over the issue in the 1970s as discussed in Chapter 1. In the 1980s, it refused to help on the grounds that the Taiwan issue should be settled peacefully by the Chinese on both sides of the Taiwan Strait and that it would not get involved.

The end of the Cold War did not leave China well-compensated for its role in the collapse of the Soviet Union. Instead it was subject to economic sanctions, diplomatic isolation and political bashing from the United States. China had not received such treatment since the early 1970s.

The U.S. hostility could partly be attributed to the Chinese military crackdown of the student demonstration at Tiananmen Square in 1989. However, this alone could not explain the U.S. China policy totally. The United States was actually trying to expand its "leadership" in world affairs. A rising China after the Cold War was viewed by many as posing a challenge to U.S. leadership. This concern accounted largely its new China policy and consequently its Taiwan policy. It is simplistic to view the granting of Lee Teng-hui's visa for his "private visit" as simply a misstep by the Clinton Administration or congressional demagoguery. The Taiwan crisis of 1995-96 was only the tip of the iceberg. It reflected a broader and deeper conflict of interest between the two powers. Therefore, in examining all the factors which led to this crisis, we should, instead of merely focusing on cross-strait relations, also look at the strategies adopted by the two powers vis-à-vis each other against a broader background of post-Cold War international politics.

The Rise of China and U.S. Concern

Since 1989 China–United States relations have been marked by tension over many issues. The Chinese military crackdown of the student demonstration in Tiananmen Square in 1989, significant though it was, has not been the only source of tension. Various sanctions against China were imposed by the Bush Administration following the Tiananmen incident, but the majority of the clashes have taken place since mid-1993 under the Clinton Administration. This suggests that the tensions cannot be simply attributed to different conceptions of democracy and human rights, different ideologies and different political and social systems which, as a matter of fact, had existed long before. Nor could they have arisen from trade disputes, intellectual property right (I.P.R.) protection and controversial trade practices, which in most cases are technical issues and could thus be restricted to business circles rather than politicized. Obviously, geostrategic concern over a rising China also cuts deeply into overall U.S. diplomatic thinking.

Like many other countries, the United States took the view, shortly after the Tiananmen incident, that it would not be long before the Beijing government collapsed because of extremely adverse domestic and international difficulties. At the very least the government would be long preoccupied with the job of maintaining internal stability. Therefore, for a time, the United States shifted its focus to Japan, perceiving it to be a rising power which might challenge the United States in the next century. After 1989, Japan featured prominently in discussions and received considerable attention. China was only perceived as a threat when, to the surprise of many, it did not collapse but, on the contrary, registered double-digit GNP growth in 1993. While its annual average growth during 1980–90 was 9.0 per cent, it grew 11.7 per cent during the period of the Eighth Five-Year Plan from 1991 to 1995.[2] Its foreign trade rose by an annual average of 19.5 per cent to US$1,014.5 billion during the period. As a result, its position in the world trade league table rose from fifteenth to eleventh. Its foreign exchange reserves rose from US$11.1 billion in 1990 to US$73.6 billion in 1995 (over US$100 billion for 1996 and over USS$140 billion for 1997 and 1998).[3] In those five years, it approved 229,800 foreign-funded projects and used US$114.7 billion foreign investment, making it the leading developing nation in terms of overseas investment.[4]

The average growth rate of China's GNP was 6.3 per cent during 1950–80, and 9.0 per cent during 1980–90 (while the average GNP growth of the world was 3.0 per cent). The growth was expected (before the onset of the Asian financial crisis in July 1997) to be 9.3–10.2 per cent for the period 1990–2000; 8.0–8.7 per cent for the period 2000–10, and 7.0–7.8 per cent for the period 2010–20. If the expected growth rate is correct, its GNP by 2020 will be 10 times that of 1990 in constant price. This means that by 2010 China's economy as a whole will be the third largest.[5] James Wolfensohn, president of the World Bank, noted in September 1995: "Our statistics show that by the year 2010 China will be the largest economic power in the world ... maybe a little longer .... They will have 8 to 10 per cent growth in the next five years".[6] At the World Economic Forum in Davos in 1996, many delegates expected that between 2015 and 2020 China would replace the United States as the world's largest economy.[7] These popular assessments (at least before the Asian financial crisis) influenced strategic thinking in terms of China by some Americans.

China's foreign trade has been growing faster than its GNP since it began its economic reform programme in 1978 when its total volume of foreign trade was only US$20.65 billion. In 1993, it reached US$195.8 billion, with the average annual growth rate topping 16 per cent. In 1994, its exports were US$120 billion and imports US$114.8 billion, making it the third largest developing country exporter of manufactured goods.[8] In 1995, the total volume of China's imports and exports reached US$280.85 billion, an 18.6 per cent increase over 1994, with exports at US$148.77 billion (22.9 per cent more than 1994) and imports at US$132.08 billion (a 14.2 per cent increase over 1994).[9] The structure of China's exports also changed. In 1995, manufactured products accounted for 85.6 per cent of total exports, up 11.1 percentage points from 1990.[10]

China has made spectacular strides in economic development, making its target more easily attainable. By the end of 1995, China had achieved its target of quadrupling its 1980 GNP five years ahead of schedule. In the 5th Plenum of the 14th Central Committee of the C.C.P. in September 1995, China set its economic growth for 1996 to 2000 at 8 per cent. This was aimed at quadrupling its 1980 per capita GNP by 2000. It plans to double its GNP in ten years from 2000 to 2010 with an annual growth rate of 7.2 per cent. Should China be able to continue at this rate of economic growth into the twenty-first century, its production could rival Japan, the United States or Western Europe. Former U.S. Secretary of State Henry Kissinger said that China "is on course to emerge as an extraordinary superpower within 20 years."[11]

Then U.S. strategic thinking about China began to shift. By 1993, the United States began to seriously consider the implications of a rising China. The United States, almost for the first time in decades, began to view China warily as a serious long-term global competitor. In the 1970s and 1980s, the United States saw China as its strategic partner, though a convenient one, in counteracting Soviet military power. At times during this period, U.S. officials griped to their Chinese counterparts that they were not spending enough money or devoting enough attention to modernizing the P.L.A. Now, they were concerned about China's rising military power.

Though few believed that China would be able to pose a serious military threat to the United States for another 10 to 15 years, there was considerable concern that it had the potential to threaten U.S. global interests in future. Some

Americans proposed containing this rising China. This view was not only reflected in discussions in prominent newspapers and journals but also supported by quite a few U.S. officials and China experts (though some of them revised their views afterwards). For instance, U.S. Assistant Secretary of State for East Asian and Pacific Affairs Winston Lord once cautioned in early 1995 that China might turn into a Soviet-style adversary in the next century and this merited a new policy of containment.[12] Harvard University Professor Ezra Vogel observed: "China is now just starting out as a growing power, just as Japan and Germany were growing powers at the beginning of this century. ... It's the role of all of us to see we have a stable system that tries to encourage China and yet *tries to prevent it from going too far*."[13] A *Time* magazine essayist Charles Krauthammer declared that, just as Washington moved to check Soviet expansion in the Cold War, "containment of such a bully (China) must begin early in its career".[14] Influential journalists and newspaper commentators like Richard Bernstein and Ross Monroe, in their book *The Coming Conflict with China,* presented a picture of a coming war between China and the United States. Similar views about the threat China posed could be found in almost all the politically influential newspapers and journals in the West.

China's Vulnerabilities

Although its ascent may continue, China lacks three critical determinants needed to achieve superpower status: a favourable *security surplus*; military and economic *hard power*; and political, social and intellectual *soft power*.[15]

A Security Surplus: Safe at Home and in the Neighbourhood

To become a world power, a country needs guaranteed stability on its borders. This enables it to project and sustain control and influence beyond its borders. Geographic location is an important aspect of security. The United States, for example, which has a huge security surplus, shares borders with only two countries, both weaker than itself, and is protected by two vast oceans from threats by other major powers.

China, in contrast, has about two dozen neighbours with which it shares either land or sea borders. At least four of these nations have a population of more than 100 million: Russia, Japan, India and Pakistan. These countries would pose serious geopolitical constraints should China seek to become a dominant global power. Even the Chinese on Taiwan have strenuously resisted China's reunification efforts, and the Taiwan issue itself may occupy China for some time and sabotage the momentum of modernization. The posture of other neighbouring powers is no more encouraging.

The North-Eastern Flank: Japan and the Two Koreas

Because of enmities and tragic confrontations in the past, the Japanese and Chinese tend to see their countries as competing in a zero-sum game. Unfortunately, there is no evidence yet that they will be able to turn their bilateral relations into a win-win situation in the future. Although Japan and China have much to gain by working together, and much to lose in confrontation, few people in either country realize that a stronger China undermined by a hostile Japan — or vice versa — could lead to another tragedy for both countries.

Even if Japan did try to end this traditional animosity and move to ally itself with China, the United States would very likely oppose the shift. U.S. strategists prefer to see a continued U.S. military presence not only in Japan, but also on the Korean Peninsula — even, as U.S. Defence Secretary William Cohen once noted, if Korea is reunified. This preference has less to do with U.S. concern over regional contingencies than with its persistent East Asia strategy to prevent either China or Japan from achieving regional dominance, and, more importantly, to prevent the two — perhaps with other countries in the region — from forming an East Asian power bloc.

The Korean Peninsula serves as another security constraint for China. A major flare-up there could trouble China's relations with its major trading partners: the United States, Japan and South Korea. In the long term, Korean nationalism is worrisome to Beijing. Relations with North Korea have been problematic in the past; for example, in 1994, North Korea laid territorial claim to part of a crater lake (called *Tian Chi* in Chinese) on Mount Paektu inside China.[16] China has also had territorial disputes with North Korea over some islands in the Yalu River, and with South Korea over islands in the Yellow Sea. Chinese strategists are worried that a reunified Korea, if reunification were achieved under U.S. guidance and protection, would not enhance China's security and that a sudden surge of Korean nationalism would have strategic implications for China.

The Northern Flank: Russia and Mongolia

The current rapprochement between China and Russia may aim at twenty-first-century strategic co-operation, but it will hardly lead to a firm long-term alliance in the absence of an excessive U.S. threat. Russia is unlikely to give China sufficient top-of-the-line weapon systems and technologies to help it achieve even regional military dominance. China's motivation for the partnership lies less in building an offensive alliance against Washington than in cushioning itself against U.S. pressure and protecting itself against radical nationalism that has the potential to erupt after a political crisis in post-Yeltsin Russia.

Strong nationalism in Mongolia could also mean trouble for China. Dealing with Mongolia has been a challenge for China for two thousand years, and ethnic separatism in China's Inner Mongolia region has been supported by some Mongolian organizations. The pan-Mongolian movement made its presence known in the first world conference of Mongolian peoples held in Mongolia in 1993, and Beijing has accused Washington of supporting the movement in order to split China.[17] In a published appeal in the *Il Tovchuu* newspaper in Mongolia in 1996, some nationalists called for global pressure on Beijing to free ethnic minority dissidents detained in Inner Mongolia, and they urged "the peoples of Inner Mongolia, Tibet, and Xinjiang to fight for freedom and independence".[18] Although the Mongolian government has not publicly supported these organizations so far, it nevertheless tolerates them, and Mongolia is now seeking to further strengthen its ties with the United States and Japan to balance China's increased power.

Islamic Influences and Tibet in the West

Instability and ethnic separatist tendencies are even worse in Tibet and Xinjiang than in Mongolia. In Xinjiang, the movement by Islamic fundamentalists to turn the area into an independent Republic of East Turkistan has its appeal, as evidenced in Uighur riots and in shootings and bombings in recent years. Strong cultural links with some Islamic Central Asian countries, and their reported tacit political support of the independence movement, make the threat to stability in Xinjiang even more potent.

Tibet will be a nagging problem for Beijing for a long time. Unlike the Manchurians who ruled China from the mid-seventeenth to early twentieth century, but accepted the Chinese culture and were finally assimilated into it, the Tibetan culture will remain distinctive, independent and even somewhat exclusive. Xinjiang attracts many Han Chinese migrants because of its geographical accessability, favourable climate and generally higher living standards. However, most Han Chinese migrants find it very hard to stay in Tibet for long, mainly because of its harsh high plateau conditions. The proportion of minority population in Xinjiang dropped from 93.3 per cent in 1949 to 61.9 per cent in 1996, mainly due to massive Han Chinese migration,[19] whereas in Tibet, many Han Chinese stayed there only temporarily. The number of Han Chinese in Tibet is not clear as many Han Chinese still officially register themselves in Tibet although they no longer live there. What is more, it will take quite a long time before China's economic boom expands to the far-flung area of Tibet. In the meantime, regional economic disparity will add to social and political uncertainty in Tibet.

If the power and influence of Islamic nations increases dramatically in the future, it is doubtful whether China will be able to build an alliance with them easily. China is likely to resist joining an Islamic confrontation of the West: for its continued modernization it may be necessary for China to continue to rely on the West as a main source of funds, high technology and export markets for a long time. China's only strategic motive in developing future relations with Islamic nations would be to fend off excessive U.S. pressure by threatening to exploit strategic vulnerabilities of the United States. However, if U.S. pressure on China were to recede, China would probably position itself independently between the West and the Islamic world.

The Chinese, in general, are more familiar with the achievements of the West than with those of the Islamic world, and they are more receptive to Western than Islamic culture. Psychologically, culturally and politically they are not well prepared for a close strategic relationship with Islamic countries. Trends in Chinese religious conversions and Chinese study abroad help illustrate this.

In the thirteen hundred years since Islam came to China, there have been few Chinese (Han) conversions. For historical and geographic reasons, Islam has been mainly accepted by minorities in the Xinjiang area (i.e. the Hui, Uygur, Kazak, Uzbek, Kirgiz, Tajik, Tatar, Dongxiang, Baoan and Salar). They were exposed to Islam before Confucianism and they lived near other Islamic people and far from the centres of Chinese civilization. In 1991, the Muslim population in China totalled more than 17 million (concentrated in Xinjiang) and since then it has remained roughly the same.

In contrast, Protestant Christianity came to China in the nineteenth century, and Catholicism, despite previous intermittent forays into China, only began to spread widely after the Opium Wars of the 1840s and 1850s. By 1949, there were 700,000 Chinese Protestants. Under the Communist regime, especially during the Cultural Revolution, these numbers dropped, but since China opened up to the outside world in the late 1970s, conversions have increased dramatically. By 1995, there were 6.5 million Chinese Protestants and 4 million Catholics. By 1997, the number of Protestants had risen to about 10 million.[20] Compared with the Chinese Muslims in Xinjiang, these new Chinese Christians are younger, better educated and more widely exposed to various cultures. Their choice reflects a Chinese preference for Western civilization.

Similarly, the overwhelming majority of overseas Chinese students, both government-sponsored and self-funded, choose to study in the West. The trend in Chinese emigration is the same. And scholars in China's think-tanks and research institutes prefer to do research on the United States and other Western countries; few study Islamic states and societies.

These cultural realities suggest that there is little economic, cultural, psychological or political basis for China to pursue a close, long-term strategic alliance with Islamic nations. Even if a tactical alliance were formed because China felt cornered by the West, the alliance would likely be short-lived.

On its western flank, China is actually more concerned with internal stability, potential Islamic infiltration and expansion and possible entanglement in a major war between India and Pakistan or in the Middle East. At the summit between Chinese President Jiang Zemin and U.S. President Bill Clinton in June 1998, China agreed not to provide nuclear and missiles technologies to Iran. This concession was partly a result of U.S. pressure, but also perhaps more importantly, because of China's belief of Iran's covert provision of the Islamic independence movement in Xinjiang. On grounds of these suspicions, Beijing keeps a watchful eye on Iran's covert provision of scholarships to young Chinese people (mostly of Hui descent) for studies in Tehran.[21]

Obsession with the Islamic independence movement in Xinjiang explains China's long-standing friendship with Pakistan. Pakistan, because of its need for China's strategic support to balance India's power, not only seeks to constrain India's geopolitical expansion, but also works to check outside support for Xinjiang's Islamic independence movement. As the main backer of the Taliban, who continue to dominate Afghanistan, Pakistan can also make it difficult for Islamic separatists in Xinjiang to acquire arms that originate from or move through Afghanistan.

A firm alliance between India and China seems out of the question due to historical distrust, territorial disputes, cultural disparity and geopolitical competition. This mutual antipathy was well illustrated when India justified its surprise nuclear weapon testing in 1998 by branding China as a primary potential threat. The testing suggested that India's bitter defeat in the border war with China in 1962 still cuts deeply and that India has since been making a tenacious but quiet effort to overtake China in terms of wider power and influence.

At China's southern flank also stands the Association of Southeast Asian Nations (ASEAN), which seeks a balanced position between China and the West and between China and Japan rather than an alliance with China. Strong nationalism makes ASEAN sensitive to any hint of Chinese dominance, and some ASEAN countries have either regional geopolitical ambitions or a deep-seated suspicion of China and of ethnic Chinese minorities in their own countries.

Apart from these regional geopolitical constraints, China's rise has aroused strong suspicion and resistance in the West. China's continued ascent will likely be very much constrained by the geopolitical distribution of power both inside and outside the Asia-Pacific region. Although these regional constraints are subject to change, the countries around China cannot change their political and strategic fundamentals overnight to become its allies. For a long time to come, many of China's neighbours may continue to find their economic interests closely linked with the United States and seek closer identification with the United States than with China. Thus, regional geopolitical constraints for a rising China will remain strong.

No Leading "Hard Power"

China lags far behind developed countries in terms of military and economic power which are necessary components of being a dominant world power, and as such constitute "hard power".

Military Power

With its very low level of technology, the Chinese military has a long way to go before it possesses the capabilities needed by a world power. Right now, China cannot even establish air superiority around its borders or naval supremacy along its coast. The most advanced operational fighter in China's air force is the Russian Su-27, of which it has only a few dozen. These Su-27s are not a sure match for the F-16s the United States has sold to China's Asian neighbours, fall short of the Su-35s which Russia sold to India and pale in comparison to Japan's FX and F-15. The performance of China's own air fighters, such as the J-8II, cannot match that of the Su-27. Its J-10s and FC-1s, even when operational, will hardly change the balance of air power with other major powers such as the United States and Russia. It will also be very difficult for China to acquire a reasonable degree of naval capability before at least 2020. First, the navy's air defence, command and control, intelligence, electronic warfare, logistics and anti-submarine capability need to improve significantly.

Despite impressive progress in missile technology, China's aerospace industry as a whole remains underfunded and not particularly advanced. Its efforts in computer science, and consequently China's capability for strategic information warfare, started much later than in developed countries.

China has reportedly focused its military research and resources on a few directed and non-directed energy weapons projects, such as electro-magnetic pulse (E.M.P.), laser guns, microwave beam weapons, particle beam weapons, millilitre wave weapons, computer virus planting, etc., to enhance its capability for strategic information warfare. Attainment of a few such weapons, even if successful eventually, is at best "asymmetrical war" as coined by Richard Armitage, former U.S. assistant secretary for defence, or "acupuncture war" [*dian xue zhan*] as the Chinese call it.[22] It is not equivalent to a general and massive enhancement of comprehensive military, industrial and scientific power to a level of world leadership. What is more, while China may be developing a few of these weapons, Western countries may be developing more and better weapons given their more advanced industrial and scientific basics.

For some years to come, China's military modernization will continue to be plagued by a wide range of problems, including supply controls, prohibitive costs, low absorptive capacities, managerial and administrative roadblocks and bureaucratic and political in-fighting. The process will be painful and slow. China's weapon supply is likely to be limited by the international situation and its domestic economic situation will also limit weapon procurement. With large numbers of outmoded and obsolete weapons, a critical need for greater reform — especially in state-owned enterprises — and the huge cost of military research and development and technology, China lacks the resources to quickly and comprehensively upgrade its weapon systems to match those of the West.[23]

Even if it had the necessary financial resources, China would still find it difficult to catch up with the West. China's various internal systems constrain further rapid development in such areas as the economy, science and technology and defence. These internal systems will take a long time to reform.

Economic Power

China's economic growth has been impressive but these figures should not be used to exaggerate China's power and influence in the world economy. The figures do not show the whole picture, nor do they necessarily reflect proportionally increased productivity or technological advances. Currently China's labour productivity is among the lowest in the world, and it is only a fraction of that of the United States. According to the Institute of Management and Development's *World Competitiveness Yearbook 1996*, the United States ranked eleventh in the world in terms of overall productivity (US$58,028 GDP per person employed) while China ranked forty-fourth (US$1,106). For production in manufacturing, the United States was fifteenth (US$40,601 manufacturing value added per manufacturing worker) while China was thirty-ninth (US$1,404). For agricultural productivity, the United States ranked eighth (US$29,544 value added per active person) while China came in forty-second (US$244).[24]

China's economy has maintained fast economic growth for nearly 20 years. During this time, the growth in investment and capital has been several times that of economic growth. Labour productivity and the rate of return on capital have not risen significantly. In certain industrial and business sectors, they have actually declined.[25] It is not difficult for a country to have high economic growth with huge increases in investment. But it is not easy to raise rates of return of capital and labour productivity. The latter shows the maturity and strength of an economy while the former implies economic vulnerability and dependence as shown by the financial crisis which hit some East Asian economies in the late 1990s.

A case in point is China's seemingly rapid growth of exports, its "big leap forward". According to the United States, only 20 per cent of Chinese exports to the United States are directly shipped to the United States, with the remaining 80 per cent diverted through a third place, mainly Hong Kong.[26] According to the Trade Statistics Subgroup of the Trade and Investment Working Group of the China–United States Joint Commission on Commerce and Trade, the average rate of value-adding of Chinese exports to the United States via Hong Kong was 40.7 per cent in the two years of 1995 and 1996, which was far above the re-export value-adding rate under general circumstances. If this value created in Hong Kong and other third places were excluded, China's export volume would be lower than its growth figures suggest. What is more, the rules of origin which are currently adopted by both China and other countries to calculate external trade also result in an exaggeration of China's export growth. Goods determined as originating in China are recorded as imports from China, regardless of whether they are actually exports via a third place or whether the goods have acquired added value in that third place.

Processing trade expansion is a major factor behind China's export growth in the 1990s. Total export volume rose to US$151.1 billion in 1996 from US$62.1 billion in 1990, up 16 per cent per year on average. In the period, processing trade soared from US$25.42 billion to US$84.33 billion, an annual rise of 22.1 per cent. In the 1990–96 period, the ratio of processing trade to overall Chinese exports rose from 41.0 to 55.8 per cent, and even topped 70 per cent in its share of Chinese exports to the United States in 1996. The bulk of the sector has developed since the mid-1980s when developed countries started to move their labour-intensive industries or production procedures to China in a bid to cut production costs. Those processing trade products are primarily sold to their traditional overseas markets via entrepot trade through Hong Kong but, according to the rules of origin, are calculated as part of China's exports even though much of the profit is made by Hong Kong and foreign investors in joint ventures in China.

At present, China's influence in the global market remains insignificant. Unlike a world power, it does not use investment, high-technology products and control of a leading industry to dominate sectors of the world market. Instead, its economic importance lies mainly in its import market and in foreign investment in its industries. Its export growth depends to a significant degree on foreign investment and cheap labour rather than on high technology and higher efficiency. It is notable that in the first 11 months of 1996, foreign-funded enterprises were responsible for 41 per cent of China's total export trade and 53 per cent of its imports.[27]

This does not place China in a strong bargaining position. Its imports and exports now account for more than half of its GNP. More than 30 per cent of China's exports went to the United States in 1994 compared with just 10 per cent in 1985,[28] making Chinese goods more dependent on the U.S. market and the international market than ever before. In fact, it is more accurate to say that foreign countries now have more influence in China's economy than vice versa. China's economic growth increasingly depends on support from the global economy which may not be a sure thing in future for economic, political or strategic reasons.

Whether China will have any dominance in the international market in the future is also questionable. Its economic growth so far has been less on the basis of enhanced productivity through high technology than on high consumption of energy and other resources, high foreign investment and cheap labour costs. Although it is reasonable for a developing country like China to use its large population to comparative advantage to develop mainly labour-intensive industries before moving on to the next stage of enhancing its productivity through capital-and-technology-intensive industries, its low productivity labour-intensive industries will not automatically or easily evolve into high productivity, high technology industries.

These characteristics of China's economy also mitigate smooth, dynamic growth in the future. It is possible that the current economic meltdown in Southeast Asia could be repeated in China, in one form or other, as its economy becomes increasingly influenced by international capital and markets. As it moves toward full integration in international capitalist markets, China is simply not in the driver's seat.

China's future economy will also be compromised by widespread environmental degradation, a huge — and still growing — population and an increasingly distorted population structure, unstable political and social institutions, continued losses by state enterprises, growing unemployment, an inadequate infrastructure, growing regional and individual disparities in income, incomplete agricultural reforms, a shortage of skilled labour and the absence of legal and institutional frameworks needed for a modern market economy.[29] China's past economic growth has been more dependent on resource use than on enhancing productivity through high technology, and it is likely to run out of steam unless it acquires and exploits high technology.

President Jiang's recent earnest call to develop science and technology in China reflects this challenge. However, China is faced with a more daunting task than is commonly realized, because its current low productivity in these areas is more a problem of distorted, unproductive systems than of limited resources for research in science and technology.

In fact, China has a very impressive number of professionals. In 1995, there were 19.13 million in its state units alone (5.63 million engineers and technicians,

540,000 agricultural technical staff, 3.04 million medical staff, 300,000 scientists and 9.63 million teaching staff). Not counting medical and teaching staff, there were at least 6.47 million professionals in science and technology or, on average, almost 18 per cent of state employees. However, despite these figures performance was far from satisfactory.[30]

A survey by China's National Commission of Science and Technology shows that nearly half of the research institutes and organizations in China published no research papers in 1995. Since China has about 5,000 research institutes and organizations, each with an average of 125 scientists and researchers, this means nearly 2500 research institutes and organizations with 310,000 scientists and researchers did not even publish one research paper for the whole year.

The survey also found that only 5 per cent of the research institutes and organizations produced scientific output that reached the "national level" (the top rank), while the scientific output of another 15 per cent reached the "ministerial level" (the second rank). This means that 4,250 research institutes and organizations with 530,000 scientists and researchers failed to produce scientific output worthy of even the second rank.

A third finding of the survey was that on average there was only 0.09 invention patent for each of the research institutes and organizations.[31] This means that there was only one invention patent for 11 research institutes and organizations, or about 1390 scientists and researchers in 1995.

A fourth finding demonstrates that in 1995, 97 per cent of the total 5,000 research institutes and organizations used inventions or new technologies in no more than 10 "diffusion projects" (projects that help more companies to use more advanced technology and new inventions). In other words, each "diffusion project" took at least 13 scientists and researchers on average. This diffusion rate is even less impressive given that these "diffusion projects" also include each repeated usage of the same new technologies by various state or non-state units both at the same levels and at different levels.[32]

It is obvious that this poor performance by China's science and technology sector cannot be accounted for simply by lack of resources. There are evidently huge institutional and systemic constraints. These constraints explain why China has been very slow to absorb foreign technology to achieve major technological breakthroughs, even though it has spent heavily — through direct government purchases and joint ventures — to import advanced equipment and production lines. It also explains why, despite an increasing number of scientific and technological achievements in laboratories, the successful innovation rate is only around 10 per cent. Less than 10 per cent of patented new technology was used in actual production in 1991–95.[33]

To address these institutional and systemic constraints effectively will take much longer than it will to devote more resources to scientific and technological development. Failing that, it will be hard for China to raise its scientific and technological levels, and hence its productivity, to achieve a dominant world position. We should also bear in mind that China is still far from completing its transition from a command economy to a market economy, a transition which is not only arduous and risky, but which also requires time to reach the stability necessary for long-term, sustained, and powerful economic growth.

No Leading "Soft Power"

No nation becomes a world power without having "soft power" as well as "hard power". Soft power includes political, social and intellectual power, and encompasses the following elements: (1) open, stable, durable and absorbent domestic political, social and economic arrangements; (2) strong cultural, political and moral appeal and cohesion; (3) intellectual leadership; (4) strategic foresight and diplomatic skill; (5) effective governance, both domestically and internationally, including effective mobilization of national and international resources (especially non-military resources, such as manipulation through international organizations and regimes, rules and norms, and through management of international capital flow); (6) an educated, culturally strong populace; and (7) a high standard of living and life style.

China has far to go before it can lay claim to such soft power. Economic and military power cannot substitute for a strong political and social infrastructure. Given the current fragility of China's domestic political and social systems (compared with the mature liberal democracy of the United States), excessive expansion abroad would only lead to disaster. This institutional fragility at home will severely undermine any attempt China makes to become a world power.

The rising nationalism and cohesion of the Chinese since the early 1990s should not be viewed as a full endorsement by the people of their current government by Beijing. Rather, it reflects resentment of foreign pressure on China and the shabby treatment of China, as well as concern that Soviet-style chaos would follow a sudden collapse of the government.

A careful examination of rising Chinese nationalism, such as that found in the popular *A China That Should Say No,* shows that the Chinese people do not resent having human rights and democracy issues raised. Rather, they resent what they view as a de facto U.S. containment of China's rise through the use of these issues. The Chinese criticize U.S. "soft containment", but they also object to the pervasive corruption at home, and many of them believe that China lags behind Western countries in its protection of individual human rights and in democratization. Opinion polls in China from 1995 through 1997 showed that a high percentage of young people considered the United States the nation most hostile to China, but a high percentage also considered the United States the most desirable place to visit and study in.[34]

This point is also reflected in the large number of Chinese students and scholars who choose to stay overseas when their studies are finished, especially in the United States. According to official Chinese figures, more than 300,000 Chinese students went abroad for education between 1979 and 1998 and so far, only a third of them have returned home.[35] Out of the 154,000 privately-sponsored Chinese students abroad (between 1978 and 1997), only 5,000, or 3.2 per cent of them, returned.[36] Many government-sponsored students and scholars returned either because they were on short-term visits (too short to find jobs and scholarships to continue to stay abroad and too difficult to extend or change their student visas because they were sponsored by the government instead of privately). Other reasons include family obligations (most of them have families in China to go back to), or because of financial penalties (those failing to return, forfeit a surety deposit, now generally RMB50,000), assured high positions on their return or because they want to return before they go abroad again as privately-sponsored students.

If China cannot attract its own best young talent to return, how can it attract the best foreign talent, as the United States has done, to serve the country? This capability is one manifestation of a country's soft power. China's general standard of living is only part of the problem. China has not built a satisfactory merit system or appealing political and social environments. Although living standards will rise as economic modernization succeeds, even with economic prosperity, it will take time to build the kind of systems that attract and reward indigenous and foreign talent. Until then, China cannot lead in a world of high technology. China has proved that it has strong national cohesion in times of national crisis, such as during foreign invasions or threats, or during natural disasters such as the massive floods of the Yangtze River in 1998. However, this cohesion in difficult times has no bearing on China's ability to attract elite talent in times of peace.

If China's appeal to its own people is limited, then its appeal to other countries, and thus its ability to form power blocks with other countries, is very much compromised. The United States has such an ability: its diplomacy of human rights and democracy is used as much to enhance its own soft power and reduce China's as it is out of true concern and belief.

China's official communist ideology, although different from classic Marxism or Stalin-style communism, limits the country's appeal not only to Western countries but also to its Asian neighbours. What China now practices is not communism or even socialism in the strict sense, but until it revises or replaces its official ideology with something more appealing (such as a revised Confucianism), China will have difficulty enhancing its internal cohesion and attracting other countries to unite around it.

Weak international intellectual leadership is another soft-power shortcoming. In its economic obsession, China has paid significant attention to science and technology at the expense of social science research, including international studies. The overwhelming majority of government-sponsored students and scholars sent abroad study science and technology. For reasons ranging from de facto discouragement to the politicization and consequent press control of different academic views, few scholars specialize in the social sciences. Among those who do, many give up their low-paying research work and turn instead to business. There is a serious "brain drain" in China, not only to other countries, but also from the social sciences to natural science, technology and business studies, as well as from intellectual research to commercial activities. For obvious commercial reasons, many of the country's most talented young people, if they do not go overseas, choose to stay in joint ventures or foreign companies in China rather than in research institutes. This will have an adverse effect on China's continued rise in the long term.

Weakness in social science research is also prominent in China's international studies, especially the study of other countries, particularly if they are far from China and have unfamiliar cultures. This lack of sophistication in international relations partly accounts for China's frequent failure to demonstrate intellectual leadership, diplomatic creativity and initiative in international affairs. It also partly accounts for China's tentativeness and clumsiness in exploiting international norms, rules and organizations to its own advantage. Without these international coalition-building skills, China will be unable to skilfully exploit multilateral arrangements to achieve its diplomatic goals or organize a well co-ordinated, large-scale, multinational operation as the United States did in the Gulf War of 1991. China may win some diplomatic skirmishes, but it will have difficulty building lasting strategic alliances.

One manifestation of its weakness in diplomacy is China's frequent failure to anticipate a problem — as, for example, when it was caught unprepared by Taiwan President Lee Teng-hui's United States visit in 1995. More often than not, China's diplomatic efforts resemble a fire engine kept on the run, using counterproposals and countermeasures to try to douse "fires" set by others. More of China's diplomatic proposals and decisions should focus on seeing potential problems ahead of time and taking the initiative to address them first.

Diplomatic skill is essential for a world power. With such skill, China could turn regional geopolitical constraints, or deficits, into strategic assets and dramatically increase its strength. Many Chinese officials and strategists still fail to recognize this point and tend to attribute their lack of capability solely to economic and military weakness. They fail to see that this soft power is not automatically derived from hard power. As a result, China often acts largely on its own, as it has traditionally, without being able to skilfully exploit the strength of international organizations and international regimes. The more

China operates in such manner, especially on behalf of its economic and military modernization, the more suspicious its neighbours will become about its intentions, and the more its rise will intensify regional geopolitical constraints.

The China Challenge

China is still far from possessing the leading hard and soft power needed to become a global leader, and its security surplus and continued ascent could be very much constrained by the geopolitical distribution of power in the Asia-Pacific region. Why, then, are many strategic thinkers, especially in the United States, preoccupied with a rising China?

Many other countries are economically or militarily powerful, are almost as large as China, or have risen rapidly in recent decades, yet they do not elicit the same concern. China is viewed as a serious challenge because it represents a combination of these "undesirable" factors. In addition, with its independent and comprehensive industrial, economic, military and scientific systems, China would be difficult to bring under foreign control, but, could easily assume a distinctive political role in the world. China is often viewed as one of the countries in the world that has the potential (regardless of its intentions) to displace U.S. leadership in world affairs.

However, this challenge from China is, for the time being, only a remote possibility and a manageable one. Not only will China's rise be slower and more difficult to sustain in the future, but a "hot" confrontation would neither succeed in crippling China nor in replacing the current style of government with one of Western-style liberal democracy. It would, however, serve to make China more cohesive (often the case when a nation is faced with foreign intervention and invasion). A confrontation would cost the United States more than it can afford. China is not expanding outside its national borders as the Soviet Union did, and it generally keeps a low profile. It is largely focused on its domestic modernization, and its current international behaviour is no worse than that of other big powers. Given the huge commercial opportunities in the vast Chinese market, the United States would find it difficult to rally allies for a direct confrontation. On the other hand, if the United States took unilateral action, it would be weakened and vulnerable to other competitors. Moreover, the commercial opportunities in the booming Chinese market may benefit the United States more than other countries and perhaps even more than China itself. In that market, the United States may be able to garner enough resources to maintain its world leadership for much less than it would otherwise cost. Thus, Washington's plan is to enhance its own strength in the Asia Pacific should a rising China or other powers assert themselves in the region and pose a challenge to U.S. world dominance.

The "Hand-Shaped" Asia-Pacific Strategy

So what is the U.S. strategy in the Asia Pacific? As I see it, the U.S. post-Cold War global strategy is a two-ocean strategy, simultaneously reaching across both the Pacific and Atlantic oceans to assert world leadership. This strategy resembles a human figure, with the United States as the head, the rest of North and South America as the body and two arms extending across the two oceans to hold leadership in Eurasia. Controlling the Eurasian continent (or the "grand chessboard," as Zbigniew Brzezinski, former U.S. national security adviser, called it[37]) is fundamental to U.S. strategic interests if the United States is to retain its sole superpower status in the coming century.

In the U.S. Asia-Pacific strategy, the hand reaching toward China has the following five "fingers": United States–Japan relations; United States–Australia relations; United States–Korea relations; United States–ASEAN relations; and United States–Taiwan relations. These five "fingers" are positioned first, to prevent the formation of a strong East Asian power bloc, either through domination by a major local power such as China or Japan, or by a cohesive and exclusive East Asian community; second, to push China further away from major sea-lanes crucial to U.S. military and commercial security; and third, to wear out any local challenger by entangling it in local geostrategic constraints while attempting to influence desirable political changes from the inside.

Although Washington has recently been talking more about building multilateral arrangements in the Asia-Pacific region, in reality it has not shifted its emphasis from bilateral relations. When the United States and Australia renewed their defence alliance in July 1996, they issued a joint declaration describing the two countries as natural allies in a new security partnership for the twenty-first century. William Perry, then U.S. Defence Secretary, referred to this relationship as the "southern anchor" of the U.S. strategy in the Asia-Pacific region.[38]

This strategy also has a "northern anchor" as noted by Perry: United States–Japan security relations. In April 1996, U.S. President Clinton visited Tokyo to issue a joint declaration with Japan renewing the two nations' defence alliance; in 1997, Japan and the United States revised the 1978 Guideline of United States–Japan Defence Co-operation in an attempt to revamp their strategic relationship and widen potential military co-operation. These moves intensified the deep-rooted suspicion and competition between China and Japan, and without co-operation between the two, it would be impossible to have an East Asian power bloc.

United States–Korea relations are also of tremendous long-term importance in this strategy. In 1997, U.S. Defence Secretary William Cohen acknowledged as much when he stressed that U.S. troops in both Japan and South Korea should stay there, even if North and South Korea reunify.[39] Indeed, it would be much more difficult for the United States to withdraw its military presence from Northeast Asia, either in Korea or Japan, than from its Southeast Asian bases, such as those in the Philippines. Conflict is potentially more volatile and destructive in Northeast Asia than in Southeast Asia and, more importantly, a cohesive East Asia power centre is far more likely to start from Northeast Asia than from Southeast Asia. Without Northeast Asia, an East Asian power bloc is impossible. North Korea's military capability may be growing, but it has been purposely exaggerated to justify the U.S. military presence and its Theatre Missiles Defence (T.M.D.) plan in East Asia.

The strategic finger of United States–Taiwan relations has also worked well so far. Relations between mainland China and Taiwan took a sudden downturn following Lee Teng-hui's United States visit in 1995. As far as the United States is concerned, Washington is unlikely to overlook the strategic value of Taiwan by supporting an early and smooth reunification of Taiwan and mainland China.

The hand-shaped strategy has succeeded, so far, in helping to prevent the creation of an exclusive regional power bloc in East Asia. Thanks to the recent financial crisis in East Asia and the consequent overwhelming influence of the International Monetary Fund and the United States in countries such as Thailand, Indonesia and Korea, the "five fingers" have been further strengthened.

The introduction of the T.M.D. plan in East Asia is not only an attempt on the part of the United States to upgrade its traditional military industry to an information-based weaponry system, thus maintaining a clear edge (and profit) in the forthcoming strategic information warfare competition, but is also an effort to reinforce and further institutionalize these three "fingers" in Northeast Asia (United States–Japan, United States–South Korea and United States–Taiwan).

The rhetoric of "the China threat" also serves U.S. strategic purposes well. It is not intended to present China as an immediate threat or to push for military confrontation, but rather to heighten suspicion of China by other countries, thus discouraging the formation of a regional power bloc in East Asia and undercutting China's security surplus.

In its examination of a rising China in the early 1990s this chapter has laid the foundation for a better understanding of the U.S. Asia-Pacific strategy after the Cold War and the U.S. Taiwan policy. It also provides a basis for the discussion in the following chapter of China's behaviour following Lee Teng-hui's United States visit, its efforts between 1997 and 1999 to improve relations with Washington and its current Taiwan policy.

Notes

1. This chapter is an elaboration of an article by the author entitled "China and the United States: Asymmetrical Strategic Partners" published in *The Washington Quarterly* 22, no. 3 (summer 1999): 147–64. The author thanks *The Washington Quarterly* for its permission to use it in the book.
2. *Liaowang* [Outlook] (Beijing), 25 December 1995, p. 1.
3. Xinhua, "China's GNP Grows By 75% During 1991–95", Reuters, 6 March 1996.
4. Xinhua, "Trade Accounts For Nearly 50 Percent China GDP", Reuters, 4 March 1996. Figures are from China's State Statistics Bureau.
5. See the article by a well-known Chinese economist in *Lianhe Zaobao*, 6 July 1995, p. 24.
6. *ST*, 22 September 1995, p .17.
7. Robert Gottliebsen, "China and World Population Are the Dominant Issues", *Business Review Weekly*, from Reuters, 4 March 1996.
8. Faust and Kornberg, *China in World Politics*, p. 88.
9. CCTV (overseas) News Program, 2 February 1996.
10. Xinhua, " Trade Accounts For Nearly 50 per cent China GDP", Reuters, 4 March 1996.
11. "Kissinger Says China Key to Stable Asia", Reuters, 21 March 1995.
12. *ST*, 29 September 1995, p. 1.
13. "U.S. Starting To View China As Potential Enemy", *Los Angeles Times*, Reuters, 16 April 1995. Emphasis added.
14. "USA: China and the US: The New Cold War", Reuters, 31 August 1995.
15. Joseph S. Nye Jr. uses the term "soft power" in his book *Bound to Lead*. However, I use the term more broadly than he does. "Hard power", as used here, refers to military and economic power, while "soft power" encompasses political, social and intellectual power.
16. "North Korea-China Border Dispute over Paektu Possible", *Choson Ilbo* (South Korea), from Reuters, 13 March 1995.
17. Kyoto News Service, "Chinese Document Reportedly Says U.S.A. Has 'Evil' Influence on Mongolia", Reuters, 2 June 1994.
18. Irja Halasz, "Mongolian Rights Activists Denounce China Arrests", Reuters, 28 February 1996.
19. Liu Guoning, *Xinjiang Tongji Nianjian* 1997 [Xinjiang Statistical Yearbook 1997] (Beijing: China Statistics Press, 1997), pp. 47–53.
20. For the figures, please see three white papers released by the Chinese government: Information Office of the State Council of the P.R.C., *Freedom of Religious Belief in China* (Beijing: Information Office of the State Council of the P.R.C., October 1997), pp. 1–2; Bureau of Religious Affairs of the State Council of the P.R.C., *Religions and Freedom of Religious Belief in China* (Beijing: Bureau of Religious Affairs of the State Council of the P.R.C., July 1995), pp. 1–3; Information Office of the State Council of the P.R.C., *Zhongguo de Renquan Zhuangkuang* [The Human Rights Situation in China] (Beijing: Information Office of the State Council of the P.R.C., October 1991), pp. 41–42.

21. *Lianhe Zaobao*, 10 September 1998, p. 18. The word "covert" is used because, going against normal practice in China, Iran chose not to involve or even inform Chinese governmental and educational institutions about the recruitment of Chinese students. What made Beijing more suspicious was that Iran in many cases approached individual Chinese young people with offers of scholarships, rather than generally inviting students to apply for scholarships.

22. See Lin Chong-ping, *He Ba* [Nuclear Dominance] (Taiwan: Minshen Publishing House, 1998), pp. 1–32.

23. For a detailed discussion of China's military modernization, please see Bates Gill, "Determinants and Direction for Chinese Weapons Import", *Pacific Review* 8, no. 2 (1995): 359–82.

24. Institute of Management and Development, *World Competitiveness Yearbook 1996* (Lausanne: Institute of Management and Development, 1996), pp. 496, 498 and 500.

25. Zhang Xiaoming, "Lessons China Can Learn from Asia's Crisis", *ST*, 16 October 1998. The article was originally published in Chinese in *China Economic Times*, 9 October 1998.

26. Xinhua, "China Issues White Paper on Trade Balance with USA", Reuters, 24 March 1997.

27. Jim Parker, "China Faces Hard Road to World's Top Economy", Reuters, 21 April 1997.

28. "Trade Peace", Reuters, 4 March 1995.

29. Australian Department of Foreign Affairs and Trade, *China Embraces the Market: Achievements, Constraints and Opportunities* (Canberra: BHP Australia, 1997).

30. He Xianghao, *Diyi Dongli: Dandai Zhongguo de Keji Zhanlue Wenti* [The Primary Momentum: China's Science and Technology Today] (Beijing: Jinri Zhongguo Publishing House, 1998), p. 25.

31. Ibid., pp. 25–26.

32. *Zhongguo Keji Xinxi* [China Information of Science and Technology] (Beijing), no. 4, 1996. He, op. cit., pp. 25–26.

33. Ibid., pp. 35–36.

34. For example, see Daniel Kwan, "Charm Bid Stepped Up Ahead of Jiang Visit", *SCMP*, 6 October 1997.

35. CCTV (overseas) News Program, 30 October 1998.

36. The data was released by China's Education Minister Chen Zhili on 24 November 1998. See Mary Kwang, "China's Footloose Students Abroad", *ST*, 25 November 1998.

37. Brzezinski Zbigniew, *The Grand Chessboard: American Primacy and its Geostrategic Imperatives* (New York: Basic Books, 1997).

38. Stephen Hutcheon, "Chinese Critic Says US Was the Target", *The Age* (Melbourne), 9 August 1996, p. 8.

39. Charles Aldinger, "Japan: U.S. Troop Cut Could Spark Asia Arms Race — Cohen", Reuters, 8 April 1997.

4

China's U.S. Policy:
To Avoid a Head-on Collision

Taiwan in China's Overall Development Strategy

To understand why Beijing felt so slighted by Lee Teng-hui's United States visit in 1995, we should first of all examine the importance of the Taiwan issue in China's overall development strategy.

In my view, China's basic overall development strategy since 1978 has been to build a booming coastal economy in the south first, i.e. Shenzhen, Xiamen and other special economic zones in the south. This southern coastal economy would be positioned to obtain foreign capital and high-technology from the world market, while at the same time its influence would extend inward to other coastal regions in the north as well as middle and far-flung regions to bring about a nation-wide, mutually supplementary and wave-like economic development. The purpose of this would be to build strong, comprehensive and well co-ordinated industrial, scientific and agricultural bases for China's sustained development into the next century.

In order to extend outward, China needs a strong "small triangle" made up of the southern coastal economy as well as Hong Kong and Taiwan. Developments in Hong Kong and Taiwan will make or break China's future development. Initially they will serve as two pillars in the "small triangle". And, post-reunification, they will form a bigger "nucleus" which will greatly boost China's economy and status in the world.

In a talk on 23 October 1993, Chinese President Jiang Zemin called for the reunification of Taiwan's economy and the mainland's "solid industrial technologies", saying that if Taiwan joined hands with the P.R.C., "none in the world could bully us".[1] By the end of 1995, the combined foreign currency savings of Taiwan, China and Hong Kong topped US$210 billion, overtaking Japan as the largest.[2] The combined amount of foreign trade registered by Taiwan, Hong Kong and China in 1996 totalled US$890 billion, coming in third after the United States and Germany, with aggregate exports and imports reaching US$450 billion and US$440 billion respectively, both at the third-highest levels.[3]

Since the late 1970s, China has been trying to tap fully Hong Kong and Taiwan's resources for its economic modernization. According to official Chinese sources, by 1995, the investment by businessmen from Hong Kong, Taiwan and Macao comprised about 70 per cent of total foreign investment in China,[4] with much going unreported. Hong Kong and Taiwan are viewed as two the "feet" of the "China bird" which will allow it to take off (China's geographical shape resembles a bird). China does not want to see its modernization "hopping" along on only one foot (Hong Kong): it wants the use of both feet.

China's deep suspicions of the U.S. Taiwan policy stem from its belief that this policy aims to prevent the "China bird" from flying high by holding one of its feet. Similarly the last British Governor of Hong Kong, Chris Patten's political reform there was perceived by Beijing as an attempt to hold down its other foot in order to sabotage China's rise.

The Chinese Reading of U.S. Motivation

Given Taiwan's strategic importance and the deep suspicion that exists between Beijing and Washington, many Chinese do not believe the decision to grant a U.S. visa to Lee was a misstep by the U.S. administration under congressional pressure. Rather, they see it as a reflection of a broader U.S. strategy to contain China after the Cold War. Since the early 1990s, the United States has allowed visits by the Dalai Lama and Taiwan's president, upgraded its relations with Taiwan, mended relations with Vietnam and stiffened the resolve of some Southeast Asian countries in their dispute with China over the Spratly islands. It has roared like a lion over human rights violations in China, but squeaked like a mouse about Russian attacks on Chechnya and human rights violations by some its allies. It has enhanced its security co-operation with Japan, South Korea and Australia. It has continued to impose economic and high technology sanctions on China. It sabotaged China's bid to host the 2000 Olympics and frustrated China's attempts to enter the World Trade Organization (W.T.O.) earlier as a full member.

Under these circumstances, it is not difficult for Chinese leaders to believe that the policy of the United States is to contain China. The U.S. Taiwan policy has consequently been perceived, as President Jiang Zemin once noted, as supportive of Taiwanese independence in order to divide China.[5]

Chinese strategists believe the U.S. strategic intention behind its Taiwan policy is to separate Taiwan from China in order to prevent China from becoming a strong rival to the United States. This effort, whether successful or not, is likely to be a big headache for China. If Taiwan successfully resists Beijing's attempt to reunify either by maintaining the status quo of de facto independence or by becoming independent formally, it would most likely side with the United States, rather than China. This would not only add to China's strategic worries but might also be used to encircle China with a chain of islands, from Japan and South Korea to the north, to Taiwan island and down to the Spratly islands in the South China Sea. Locked within this island-chain China would have little prospect of becoming an ocean power in the next century and its booming coastal economy would face constraints.

On the other hand, to forcibly reunify with such an unco-operative and U.S.-backed island would cost China dearly in terms of its modernization effort, international image and regional stability. From this perspective, every dollar from U.S. arms sales to Taiwan not only brings huge commercial returns to the United States but also increases the potential cost to China. Even if it reunified with the mainland, Taiwan would be a political burden rather than an asset. Thus, although the United States might fail to prevent reunification it would achieve the strategic purpose of preventing China from becoming too strong a competitor, or at least delaying its rise, without having to confront China face-to-face on the battle field which would cost the United States too dearly. What is more, before reunification takes place the Taiwan issue is a valuable trump card which can be used to influence Chinese diplomatic behaviour. As this is a very sensitive issue for China, it is an obvious point of leverage. For example, in business negotiations with certain countries China has sometimes had to make more concessions in exchange for their acknowledgement or reiteration of the "one China" policy, the promise not to sell arms to Taiwan, or not to allow visits to their countries by senior officials from Taiwan. Some countries have also managed to get huge "economic assistance" from both sides by shifting or threatening to shift their diplomatic relations between the P.R.C. and the R.O.C.

At worst, this may be a figment of the Chinese imagination. However, over and above the ideological commitment behind U.S. support of Taiwan, the strategic importance of Taiwan cannot be said to be non-existent. Since the end of the Cold War, China has seen an alarming trend in United States–Taiwan relations through increased U.S. arms sales, the upgrading of its relations with Taiwan in 1994 and the granting of a visa for Lee's United States visit in 1995. At the same time, it has also seen an increasing trend towards formal independence on the part of Lee Teng-hui's government in Taiwan. This has prompted the Chinese into strong action to stop the dangerous trend.

U.S. Arms Sales to Taiwan

U.S. arms sales to Taiwan have continued despite the shift of U.S. diplomatic recognition from the R.O.C. to the P.R.C. in 1979. The 17 August 1982 communiqué between China and the United States limited the ceiling of both quantity and quality of U.S. arms sales to Taiwan to levels not exceeding previous sales. However, both the quantity and quality have increased, especially since the end of the Cold War. In late 1992, the Bush Administration announced its decision to sell 150 F-16 aircraft fighters to Taiwan. In terms of quality, the F-16s far exceeded any weapons sold by the United States to Taiwan before and the decision was made before China's decision to buy any Su-27s from Russia.

Subsequent U.S. arms sales (before 1995) included, for example, modified air defence systems (M.A.D.S.), also known as the "*Patriot* PAC-2 plus", *Hawk* missiles, including the setting up of missile maintenance centres and related military communications equipment, *Stinger* anti-aircraft missiles and the *Avenger* mobile anti-aircraft defence missile system (capable of launching eight *Stinger* missiles from two reloadable pods). Other weapons "leased" by the U.S. to Taiwan include armed helicopters, such as OH-58D *Kiowa Warrior* helicopters and *Super Cobra* attack helicopters, anti-electronic-interference equipment, AGM-84A *Harpoon* missiles, launchers for *Hellfire* anti-tank missiles and *Knox* class anti-submarine frigates. The U.S. arms sales continued after the Taiwan Strait crisis of 1995–96.

Apart from selling the "hardware" to Taiwan, the "software", i.e. the technology to make these weapons, intelligence sharing, military training and logistical services, was also transferred from the United States to Taiwan.

The United States Upgrades Relations with Taiwan

The United States also took steps to upgrade its "unofficial" relations with Taiwan. In September 1994, after summing up a year-long review of United States–Taiwan relations, President Clinton announced that he had approved the first adjustments in U.S. Taiwan policy in 15 years. Officials of U.S. commercial and cultural agencies, such as the Commerce Department, would now be able to visit Taiwan or meet Taiwanese counterparts in their U.S. offices in an open manner. Officials may in the future include cabinet level officials. State Department officials up to under-secretary rank, who were previously barred from meeting Taiwanese officials, may now do so as long as they hold commercial or other non-political portfolios. However, these meetings would continue to be "unofficial" and held outside the White House, the State Department and the Pentagon.

Taiwanese leaders (the vice-premier and above) would still be barred from visiting the United States, but would be allowed to transit on U.S. soil, if necessary staying overnight if their air schedule required. Taipei's senior officials would be allowed to hold talks in Washington on an "unofficial" basis, with the exception of the Foreign and Defence ministers. The United States would not back Taiwan's campaign to enter the United Nations, but would support its entry into other non-statehood-defined international bodies such as the General Agreement on Tariffs and Trade (G.A.T.T.). Although the review would pave the way for more senior U.S. officials to visit Taipei on trade-boosting missions, these visits would be decided "on a case by case basis". Taiwan would be allowed to change the name of its U.S. office from the Co-ordination Council for North American Affairs, to the Taipei Economic and Cultural Representative Office.[6]

Lee is Granted a U.S. Visa

After the United States announced it would upgrade its relations with Taiwan, Lynn Pascoe, head of the American Institute in Taiwan or Washington's "unofficial ambassador" to Taipei, paid an official visit to President Lee Teng-hui in his office for the first time in 15 years. He also visited Premier Lien Chan and Foreign Minister Fredrick Chien at their offices. The U.S. Secretary of Transportation, Federico Pena, visited Taiwan in December 1994, becoming the most senior U.S. official to visit Taiwan in 15 years. Taiwan's senior officials also made a number of transit stopovers in the United States. Nevertheless, Taiwan was "not fully satisfied" because its president and premier still could not visit the United States.

Assured by U.S. officials that Washington was unlikely to take the further step of agreeing to a visit by Lee Teng-hui, Beijing did not make a fuss. Some people in the P.L.A. believed that the United States would not stop short of allowing visits by Taiwan's higher officials, including Lee, if no strong action was taken to dissuade Washington from making such a decision. However, many people in the Ministry of Foreign Affairs held the view that the United States would not break its word and go that far.

So when the United States agreed to Lee's visit within days of U.S. Secretary of State Warren Christopher's assurance that Lee Teng-hui would not be given the visa, Beijing was shocked. What bothered Beijing was not only the breaking of a promise but also what it saw as an alarming trend of Congress and the Administration working together more closely to play the Taiwan card against China.

The Congress resolutions on the visa were not binding. However, the president went ahead to grant Lee the visa. Even though at the time U.S. overseas missions were unable to issue visas because of the government shutdown (due to tensions between the White House and Congress over the budget) Washington made an exception for Lee.[7]

Some analysts argued that the president might have been hoping to take the steam out of other contentious anti-Beijing legislation that was circulating in Congress. Without the Lee decision, Congress might have approved an act which would have upgraded the U.S. mission in Taiwan to an official level. However, China did not seem to buy that argument. As Chinese official journal *Liaowang* pointed out:

> Whenever the views expressed by the U.S. Congress are in agreement with those of the Administration and the latter feels it to be inconvenient to express them or act upon them, the Congress will volunteer to play the role of charging fighter while the Administration pretends to be an unwilling partner, being carried forward [by the Congress], murmuring complaints in order to deceive. It was so when the U.S. government decided to sell 150 F-16s to Taiwan in 1992. And last year [1994] when the U.S. government upgraded its relations with Taiwan. And this year [1995] when it granted a visa to Lee Teng-hui.[8]

The Chinese noted that if Congress was doing something which really went against the will of the White House, the Clinton Administration would have put up more of a lobby against it than it actually did. The Chinese take on the situation was supported by a group of visiting American congressman, Republican Representative Dennis Hastert of Illinois, who insisted that congressional pressure had nothing to do with Clinton's decision to grant Lee the visa.[9] A year later, a *Washington Post* report was published which claimed that the White House had agreed to Lee's visit as early as April 1995, before Christopher's assurance to China that the visa would not be granted. This reinforced the view of some, although not all Chinese, that the visa decision, to use the words of Foreign Minister Qian Qichen, was "a carefully planned political act aimed at splitting China and advocating 'two Chinas'".[10]

This Chinese perception of the U.S. strategic intention of keeping Taiwan separated from China looms large in its Taiwan policy. In a talk with Wang Daohan, chairman of A.R.A.T.S., in October 1996, I asked him whether at the first Wang-Koo meeting in 1993 China had foreseen that cross-strait relations would retrogress so much. He said that China had never expected cross-strait relations to proceed smoothly. But that China had expected international powers (i.e. the U.S. or Japan) to rock the boat rather than Taiwan. Such a view has been repeatedly voiced in interviews I have had with other Chinese officials.

This helps to explain why Beijing initially (i.e. from 22 May when the United States announced its visa decision to 9 June when Lee made the speech at Cornell University) targeted its anger almost solely at the United States. It believed that the United States intended to drive a wedge between China and Taiwan to sabotage the momentum of cross-strait relations two months ahead of the second Wang-Koo meeting.

For this reason Tang Shubei did not cancel or postpone his visit to Taiwan in May despite the U.S. visa announcement days just before and while in Taiwan he proceeded to invite Koo to the second Wang-Koo meeting. Tang could not have done so without a clear nod from President Jiang Zemin. Chinese strategists told me that Jiang personally instructed Tang to go to Taiwan as scheduled. Later, as will be explained in detail in Part III of this book, Lee's Cornell speech among other things caused Beijing to change its perception of Lee and redirect its anger towards Lee.

Why China Responded So Strongly

Alarmed by the trend in the United States–Taiwan relations since the end of the Cold War, China felt that it had to do something to stop or at least slow down the momentum. The President of the China Society for China–United States Relations, Zi Zhongjun, was concerned that there "could be a domino effect on the upgrading of Taiwan's relations, not only through U.S. actions but also those of other countries."[11] The U.S. Assistant Secretary of State, Winston Lord, accused Beijing of "over-reacting" to Lee's visit.[12] However, the Chinese felt that it was precisely because they had not reacted strongly enough to earlier "hostile" U.S. actions against China that the United States did not know how far they could push China. If China's response had been stronger, for example, when the United States upgraded its relations with Taiwan in 1994, when Lee had made "private" or "vocational" visits to some Southeast Asian and West Asian countries before 1995, and when Taiwan's Deputy Premier Hsu Li-teh's attended the Asian Games in Hiroshima (Japan) in October 1994, the White House would have thought twice about granting Lee the visa. If they did not react strongly, Lee might similarly visit Japan where he had studied at university for an alumni reunion. Shortly after Lee's visit to the United States, Philippine President Ramos invited Lee to visit his country for a second time. Gestures like this confirmed China's fears of a growing trend and prompted China to take decisive action.

The Director of China State Council's Taiwan Affairs Office, Wang Zhaoguo, noted that Taiwan "dares to push for the island's independence because it has the tacit support of the United States and Japan".[13] If China's reaction stopped the United States from going too far in supporting Taiwan's drift towards independence, Japan and most of the international community would follow suit. And without strong international support, Taiwan is less likely to gain independence.

Chinese domestic politics have also played a part in this and are examined in detail in Part III of this book. In short, the Chinese felt they had been unfairly treated by the West, counting among their humiliations the *Yinhe* Freighter incident, their failed bid to host the 2000 Olympic Games, their thwarted attempts to enter the W.T.O. as a founding member and various U.S. sanctions (either actual or threatened ones). Their pent-up frustration and anger at what they saw as China-bashing by the West at last erupted. China's message to the West was that they should "not take its previous restraint in its diplomacy as a sign of frailty". Chinese leaders were well aware that although they could not afford to express outrage on issues such as the W.T.O. and other trade disputes because of the price they would pay in terms of actual economic benefits, on this issue they could do so with impunity. The clear U.S. double-crossing in this case would make it difficult for other countries to blame China, which was reacting to rather than initiating the trouble.

China was also aware that there were differences between the U.S. Congress and the Administration over Lee's visit to the United States. There were even differences between the State Department and the White House. The former insisted that Lee's visit should take the form of a "transit stay" while the latter insisted that Lee should be granted a "private visit". Some State Department officials who were familiar with Chinese politics anticipated a strong Chinese response, in contrast to those in Congress who did not believe that this would be the case. These State Department officials were actually very cautious and made some effort to limit the publicity and impact of Lee's activities during his visit in the United States. China's strong response gave them grounds to stand up against pressure from Congress.

Why China Exercised Such Restraint

Yet, China's response towards the United States was mostly symbolic and stopped short of blatant retaliation. Beijing remained clear-minded enough not to jeopardize its overall interests by sidelining China–United States relations. In this respect, Beijing was mindful of its overall national strategy of prioritizing modernization. How China read the international situation in the 1990s also played a role.

To Avoid Conflict in an Unsettled World

China takes the view that the world at present is a far more complex place than it was during the Cold War. Whereas the rigid bipolar international structure and high tension between the then two superpowers during the Cold War created a narrow but largely predictable spectrum of policy choices, nowadays the former rules of bipolarity that guided state behaviour no longer exist. Non-structural factors such as domestic politics, territorial and ethnic disputes, differences over democracy and human rights, environmental issues, etc., have assumed a more important role in shaping state policy priority and consequently international politics. Policy choices of one state have become more unpredictable. The ending of the Cold War has brought about the readjustment and reorganization of international structures. The bipolarity in the Asia Pacific has given way to "a situation of several powers of the United States, Russia, Japan, A.S.E.A.N. and China, which are relevantly independent and *mutually constraining*".[14]

Mindful that yesterday's friend could be today's rival, each country is keeping a close watch on the new fluid situation and making corresponding changes in policy towards other countries while developing its own comprehensive national strength. China, therefore, has neither the intention nor the capability at this moment to lead other countries to challenge the leading position of the United States. Such an effort would force the United States, which is watching out for new competitors after the collapse of the former Soviet Union, into a premature confrontation with China. This would jeopardize China's modernization efforts at home and enhance suspicions among other Asian countries about China's rise. Such a confrontation would also quickly turn the "unsettled" international power structure to a settled one that would be very unfavourable for China. In this fluid situation, inactivity is better than activity and a low profile is better than a prominent one. Deng Xiaoping explained this point on 24 December 1990:

> In the present international situation, there are too many unpredictable factors and contradictions that are becoming sharper and sharper. They are more complicated and messier than in the past when the two superpowers contended with each other. How should one act in this situation? No one has a good idea. Some third world countries want China to be their head. However we should under no circumstances attempt that. *This is a fundamental state policy. We cannot afford to play the role of the head.* We do not have that capability. *There is not even a single benefit in being the head.* Many initiatives will be lost as a consequence (of being the head).[15]

These remarks by Deng reflect the basic line of China's current foreign policy, which is, as Deng himself put it, "observing the situation with cool-headedness, keeping a low-profile and avoiding head-on confrontation to enhance flexibility and improving relations with neighbouring countries to fend off U.S. pressure". Thus China laid down its guidelines for China–United States relations as "enhance trust, reduce trouble, develop co-operation and refrain from confrontation". It is clear that the essence of China's foreign policy has been to avoid confrontation with the United States.

With the bitter memory of the high price it paid for its high profile against the United States in the 1950s–70s and against the Soviet Union in the late 1950s–80s, China is unwilling to play the role of a "hero" in confronting the United States. Not only will China not get "even a single benefit" from it, but it will also be perceived as a rising security threat by the United States as well as by its Asian neighbours. China wants to avoid a head-on collision with the United States, and to keep any military conflict as far away as possible from East Asia so as not to jeopardize economic and political stability there.

Three Hot Curves and Four Hot Spots

In China's view, there are three "hot curves" in the world, i.e. points for major military conflict: (1) the Middle East; (2) the former Soviet Union and areas around it in East and South Europe and Middle Asia; and (3) South Asia (between India and Pakistan). There are also four "hot spots" around China in East Asia, namely Nansha (the Spratly) Islands, Taiwan, Diaoyu (Senkaku) Islands and the Korean Peninsular. China considers that as long as China can avoid a head-on collision with the United States, refrain from being dragged into actual military clashes in the three "hot curves" and carefully handle the four "hot spots", its modernization efforts have better prospects of success.

How Can China Fend Off the United States?

With determination, China should succeed in keeping out of any military action in these trouble spots. A more difficult task for China is to fend off the "comprehensive engagement" by the United States, which Beijing views as "engaging China in all the issues with well-measured pressure in order to obtain more Chinese concessions and/or find a point for breakthrough". This is not something which can be avoided by simply trying to keep a low profile. The United States, confident after the collapse of the Soviet Union, will continue to seek to "engage" China no matter how unwilling the latter is.

This situation has prompted China to adopt a strategy, which can be best described in Chinese as *mianli cangzhen* [hide needles in cotton]. While seeking improved relations with Washington (i.e. the "cotton"), it also takes a stand whenever appropriate to remind Washington that if cornered, it also has the means to hurt U.S. fundamental interests (i.e. the "needles"). This strategy is likely to make Washington hesitate about coming down too hard on China. Chinese leaders have on many occasions reminded their American visitors that China and the United States are both big countries which have important roles to play in the stability of the future world. Their hidden message is clear: China is not merely asking Washington to give it due respect as a major power, but is warning Washington that its current supremacy may not last forever. The day may come when the United States needs China's strategic support in world affairs. If Washington goes too far now, in time when it needs strategic co-operation, the Chinese may not be as forthcoming as they were in the early 1970s and 1980s.

With this understanding, the reported Chinese sale of missiles and nuclear technology to some countries is better interpreted as planting "needles" to remind Washington that China, as a nuclear-armed power, could also do massive damage to U.S. global interests if cornered.

This Chinese strategy of "hiding needles in cotton" is obviously more to avoid confrontation with the United States than to provoke it. China did not intend to carry out any actual military attacks on Taiwan let alone on the United States when it carried out military exercises in the Taiwan Strait 1995–96, but sought to send a clear and strong message on the Taiwan issue, as well as stop or slow down Taiwan's further drift from China.

China thought that its previous mild response had led both Lee Teng-hui and the United States to believe that it would not do more than make a routine protest at Lee's United States visit. Many Taiwanese officials had expected this before Lee's United States visit. China's concern was that if it continued to make only routine protests, neither the United States nor Taiwan would take it seriously later on. If other countries took the lead from the U.S. visa decision there might be a chain-reaction, which would be a diplomatic disaster for China. Only strong action would halt this potential problem.

However, Beijing wanted to achieve this without seriously and irrevocably damaging its relations with the United States. It was aware, especially after Taiwan's presidential election in 1996, that people in Taiwan generally did not accept the Chinese proposal of "one country, two systems" for reunification. On the contrary, they supported their government's push for more international space. China believed that the key to halting Taiwan's drive for independence lay in China–United States relations rather than with the people of Taiwan. If relations between the United States and China were stable, it would not be in Taiwan's interests to push aggressively for independence. In Beijing's view, one important reason for Taiwan's push was the antagonism between China and the United States since the Cold War and the fact that the United States now viewed China as a major future challenge rather than a strategic partner. It was also aware that within Taiwan there was popular support for any efforts to expand Taiwan's international profile. Under these circumstances it would be better to stabilize and improve China–United States relations before working on Taiwan. China believed that improved China–United States relations would make other countries hesitate before challenging China on the Taiwan issue (such as inviting Lee for a visit) or other issues. Thus the international environment would be more stable and the conditions for China's modernization more favourable. For this reason, China has put more effort into working on the United States than on Taiwan.

Chinese Reconciliation

Following Lee's United States visit in early June, China cut or suspended many of its contacts with the United States, demanding that Washington adopt practical and effective measures to redress the consequences of Lee's visit. Despite the moratorium, Chinese Foreign Minister Qian Qichen went ahead with a previously arranged meeting with U.S. Secretary of State Warren Christopher in Brunei in June 1995. However, Christopher did not accede to the Chinese demand that the United States should promise not to allow a second visit to the United States by Lee Teng-hui. He only agreed verbally to review applications on a case-by-case basis and that any future visits would be "private and unofficial".

In August 1995, in a move towards reconciliation, China received the U.S. Under-Secretary of State, Peter Tarnoff, for a two-day visit to Beijing, where he met Qian Qichen and Vice-Foreign Minister Li Zhaoxing. Another sign of a thaw in frosty China–United States relations came when P.L.A. General Li Xilin, commander of the Guangzhou Military Region, attended a ceremony in Honolulu held by the U.S. Defence Department, marking the fiftieth anniversary of the end of World War II.

In the same month, China expelled, rather than jailed, a Chinese American, Harry Wu, or Wu Hongda, to pave the way for U.S. First Lady Hillary Clinton to attend the United Nations Conference on Women in September. Also in the same month, two U.S. air force officers, Colonel Joseph We Chan, the air force liaison officer at the U.S. Consulate-General in Hong Kong, and Captain Dwayne Howard Florenzie, his deputy, sneaked into a number of restricted military zones in China's south-east coastal areas and acquired secret information by photographing and videotaping. They were caught red-handed. However, with only a routine protest, China expelled them within 24 hours without allowing the incident to further strain the already tense China–United States relations.

In September, China clarified that its ambassador to the United States, Li Daoyu, would return to his Washington office. This decision cleared the way for a new U.S. ambassador to take up his post in Beijing. In late September, China ended a three-month delay and approved President Clinton's choice of former senator James Sasser as ambassador to Beijing.

Apparently China wanted its ambassador back — a crucial step for the meeting between President Jiang Zemin and President Bill Clinton during the United Nations General Assembly session in October 1995. China had been lobbying hard for such a meeting and was hoping for a formal summit. Although Jiang and Clinton had met several times at international conferences, such as in Seattle in November 1993 and in Jakarta in November 1994, there had never been a formal summit. The United States repeatedly refused to set up such a meeting. President Clinton also turned down Jiang Zemin's request during the World War II commemoration ceremonies in Moscow. Nevertheless, Jiang Zemin persisted in requesting for a meeting with President Clinton while attending the United Nations' fiftieth anniversary celebrations in New York in October 1995. This time, although Jiang was refused a state visit to the capital Washington, he was allowed a working visit to New York. Instead of refusing to meet President

Clinton unless he was assured of the ceremonial courtesies to which he was entitled, Jiang agreed to a working visit to New York instead of a state visit. This took place in October 1996.

In December 1996, Chinese Defence Minister Chi Haotian went ahead with a visit to the United States which had previously been called off in the aftermath Lee's United States visit. This took place, despite the U.S. Defence Department's announcement, just days before the visit, of a US$63 million contract for Taiwan missiles.

Other reconciliatory gestures from China included acceding to the U.S. request to release from prison, albeit on "medical" grounds, Wei Jingsheng, Wang Dan and other prominent dissidents. China also agreed to sign (on 16 March 1998) and actually signed (on 5 October 1998) the Covenant on Civil and Political Rights. It cancelled deals with Iran for a pair of 40-megawatt heavy water reactors. It promised for the first time on 23 September 1997 not to sell Iran the C-801 and C-802 cruise missiles. It also co-operated with Washington on several other issues such as nuclear non-proliferation and the nuclear test ban, the Indian and Pakistan nuclear tests, the Korean Peninsula, etc. These reconciliatory initiatives led to the two Jiang-Clinton summits in October 1997 and June 1998 which greatly improved China–United States relations.

Fence-Mending

Chinese strategists generally believe that the United States has "*liang chong xing*" (dual characters). On the one hand, it is concerned about the long-term strategic implications of a rapidly rising East Asia (at least before the 1997 economic meltdown of East Asia economies) and rising China. And on the other hand, at least under the present circumstances, it prefers stability in East Asia and in United States–China relations, from which it stands to benefit more, both economically and strategically, than if it keeps violently "rattling the cage" (in the words of U.S. House Speaker Newt Gingrich). It is also in U.S. interests to keep Taiwan's push for independence from getting out of hand and upsetting stability in East Asia. To both Beijing and Washington, the Taiwan issue is not, and should not develop into, the most urgent and dominant issue. Therefore neither wants to see its foreign policy agenda hijacked or set by Taiwan.

It is evident that, the Clinton Administration did intend to mend fences with China. At the height of tensions President Clinton and his aides downplayed reports about the likelihood of a military conflict between Beijing and Taipei, and resisted pressure from Congress for a tougher policy. They did not plan to change their "comprehensive engagement" policy. They reiterated Washington's commitment to the "one China" policy and called on leaders of both sides of the Taiwan Strait to resolve their disagreements peacefully.

Indeed, the United States did send its aircraft carrier *Nimitz* across the Taiwan Strait in December 1995 and positioned the *Nimitz* and *Independent* aircraft carrier groups near the Taiwan Strait during China's March 1996 military exercises. However, this did not mean that Washington was gearing up for a major military confrontation. First, it was clear that the stepped-up Chinese military exercises amounted to psychological warfare and posed no imminent military threat to Taiwan. There were no more than 150,000 Chinese troops stationed across the Taiwan Strait (not enough for a serious occupation), and only a small proportion of them were actually mobilized in all the exercises. Second, before the March 1996 exercises started, China sent Liu Huaqiu, Director of the Office of Foreign Affairs of the State Council, to Washington to assure the United States that the exercises were just that. He stayed there as a "hot line" for senior U.S. officials so as to avoid any misunderstanding that might lead to military clashes.[16] Third, Chinese President Jiang Zemin revealed later that before starting the March 1996 military exercises, China warned Washington that they would suffer the consequences if their warships passed through the Taiwan Strait again (as they had in December 1995).[17] The U.S. warships instead positioned themselves 110 miles east of Taiwan in international waters and outside areas designated by China as target regions for missile firings and live-ammunition drills. According to other Chinese sources, before starting the military exercises, fourteen P. L. A. submarines, including nuclear ones, deliberately "disappeared" from their home harbours. The U.S. aircraft carriers consequently moved even further back.

Another story is that after Liu Huaqiu arrived in Washington to act as a "hot line" during the March 1996 P.L.A. exercises, the U.S. government did not seem to be in a hurry to have a serious meeting with him. However, as soon as China fired its first missiles, he was urgently called (on 7 March 1996) to meet U.S. Defence Secretary William Perry, Secretary of State Warren Christopher and National Security Adviser Anthony Lake who notified Liu of the potential "grave consequences" for Chinese actions. The unexpectedly high accuracy rate of the Chinese missiles seemed to take the Americans by surprise. In interviews I conducted, I ascertained that this time, the P.L.A. had placed a "new device" in its missiles which made them much more accurate than those used in its July 1995 "missile tests". These missiles posed a much more serious threat to the U.S. aircraft carrier groups. Perhaps it was concern for the safety of its soldiers that made Washington so serious.[18]

All this points to the fact that Washington sent its aircraft carriers to the Taiwan Strait convinced that it was highly unlikely that U.S. troops would get militarily involved. It was more of a gesture for international and domestic political consumption. This also debunks the theory that the P.L.A. did not launch an actual military invasion because of the presence of the U.S. aircraft carriers. From the beginning, the P.L.A.'s purpose was to wage psychological warfare and the presence of U.S. aircraft carriers was aimed at the intended psychological effect of the military exercises on Taiwan's presidential election.

In May 1999, three years after the P.L.A.'s March 1996 exercises, Taiwan claimed that due to poor weather, the P.L.A. had changed its plans for the third round, and instead of occupying some small islands off Taiwan, it undertook a simple military exercise around China's Pingtan Island.[19] On the one hand, with no evidence to back it up, this allegation is unconvincing. If China had planned a military occupation of some small islands off Taiwan, the Western media is bound to have exposed it by now. But there have been no reports or even rumours over the past three years. On the other hand, even if this story is true, it also supports my argument that it was the weather and not the presence of U.S. aircraft carrier battle groups which persuaded the P.L.A. to relocate its exercises. Moreover, the U.S. aircraft carriers had come even though a P.L.A. occupation of Taiwan or large scale P.L.A. invasion was unlikely.

China had actually anticipated a more belligerent response from the United States. Before the March exercises, Chinese strategists had listed in an internal report three possible scenarios:

1. The United States sends aircraft carriers *across* the strait again;
2. The United States positions aircraft carriers *near* the strait;
3. The United States positions aircraft carriers *in* the strait, directly separating the troops on the either side of the strait.

In the event of the last scenario, China insisted that missiles should be fired as originally planned, even if this meant firing over the U.S. aircraft carriers.[20]

Instead of being confrontational, the Clinton Administration actually took steps to alleviate tensions in China–United States relations after Lee's United States visit. The Secretary of State Warren Christopher held a series of meetings and consultations with Chinese Foreign Minister Qian Qichen in Brunei and New York to discuss ways to stabilize relations. During these meetings and consultations, the United States indicated that it had fully recognized the seriousness and sensitivity of the issue of visits by Taiwanese leaders. It also repeatedly reiterated its continued implementation of the "one China" policy, its commitment to the maintenance of non-official relations with Taiwan, its willingness to abide by the three China–United States joint communiqués and its opposition to the stance of "two Chinas" or "one China, one Taiwan", and to Taiwan's U.N. membership. It also expressed its intention to have more high-level contacts with senior Chinese leaders.

It promised, albeit verbally, that future visits by Taiwanese officials to the United States would be "completely private, very few" and limited to "purely personal reasons such as medical treatment", and that pronouncement of political speeches in public would be prohibited. Washington also listed some requirements for transiting Taiwanese high officials: (1) they could stay no longer than 24 hours; (2) they were prohibited from any public activities; (3) they were not allowed to make any public statements or give press conferences.[21] The United States subsequently applied these conditions to transit visits by Taiwan's Premier Lien Chan and Vice President Li Yuanzhu on their respective trips to Dominica in August 1995 and Haiti in February 1998.

In late August 1995, the U.S. Under-Secretary of State, Peter Tarnoff, made a fence-mending visit to Beijing. In September, the U.S. First Lady, Hillary Rodham Clinton, attended the United Nations Women's Conference in Beijing. In mid-October 1995, the U.S. Commerce Secretary, Ron Brown, visited Beijing. In November 1995, the U.S. Assistant Secretary of Defence, Joseph Nye, visited Beijing to resume military contacts with the P.L.A.

In the following year, President Clinton, Secretary of State Christopher, and Defence Secretary Perry made a number of speeches which further demonstrated U.S. intentions of improving relations with Beijing. In a series of meetings between Christopher and Qian Qichen in the Hague, Jakarta and Beijing, the two sides quickly reached agreement over disputes concerning the Chinese sale to Pakistan of "magnetic coils" that could be used in the production of enriched uranium and the intellectual property rights issue. The two sides also made arrangements for exchange visits of senior officials and agreed to set up three ministerial-level joint committees later in the year to discuss matters related to trade, science and technology and the economy.

In May 1996, President Clinton announced the extension of China's Most Favoured Nation (M.F.N.) trade status for another year without conditions. In July 1996, U.S. National Security Adviser Anthony Lake visited Beijing to lay the groundwork for the first exchange of state visits by the presidents of the two countries since the late 1980s. No U.S. president had visited China since President George Bush in early 1989 and no Chinese President had paid a state visit to the United States since former President Li Xiannian's visit in 1986.

While in Beijing, Lake met Chinese President Jiang Zemin, Premier Li Peng, Foreign Minister Qian Qichen, Defence Minister Chi Haotian and Director of Foreign Affairs Office of China's State Council Liu Huaqiu. Lake was also scheduled to go to Shanghai to meet Wang Daohan, chairman of A.R.A.T.S. which handles relations with Taiwan in the absence of official relations. Though the visit was cancelled at the last moment due to the weather, Lake nevertheless announced that the United States would promote cross-strait dialogue.

This was an interesting gesture on the part of the United States. In the early 1980s, the Reagan Administration had given Taiwan six promises. Among them was not to interfere in cross-strait affairs by pressing Taiwan to talk with China. Washington had kept to this promise except when, in 1987, the U.S. Secretary of State, George Shultz, caused serious concerns in Taiwan by showing willingness to promote cross-strait talks. Lake's gesture and remarks thus crossed the boundaries the second time.

Over that year, other high ranking U.S. officials visited China including Joseph Stiglitz, chairman of the U.S. Presidential Council of Economic Advisers and White House economic adviser, in August 1996. Most prominent was the meeting between President Clinton and President Jiang Zemin at the A.P.E.C. summit in Manila in November 1996 when Clinton presented the idea of establishing a "co-operative partnership" with China.

In 1997, the Clinton Administration launched a major lobbying campaign to persuade Congress to continue China's M.F.N. trading status. Soon after the establishment of the second Clinton Administration, the new U.S. Secretary of State, Madeleine Albright, made her first visit to Beijing in February, followed by Vice President Gore's visit in March, which was the highest level visit since the 1989 Tiananmen incident. The two sides reached an agreement on the exchange of presidential visits. According to the agreement, President Jiang Zemin was to pay a formal state visit to the United States in late 1997 and President Clinton would visit China the next year. Other high ranking U.S. officials visiting China included U.S. Chairman of the Joint Chiefs of Staff, General John Shalikashvili, in May 1997, the highest-ranking U.S. military official to visit China since 1985. The U.S. House Speaker Newt Gingrich also visited China.

Washington also moved on two fronts to defuse the Taiwan situation. On 11 March 1996, National Security Adviser Sandy Berger and Under-Secretary of State, Peter Tarnoff, summoned Taiwan's national security adviser, Ting Mou Shih, and advised Taiwan to cool its independence drive because U.S. military support was not going to be a blank cheque.[22]

In 1997, for the first time, U.S. State Department spokesman, James Rubin, announced what later became widely known as the U.S. "three nos" policy towards Taiwan. This was that the United States did not support Taiwanese independence, did not support a "two China" or "one China, one Taiwan" policy, and would not back Taiwan's admission to any international body based on statehood. At the Chinese request that the United States repeat the formula at the highest level, Secretary of State Madeleine Albright reiterated these points at a 30 April 1997 news conference in Beijing, in reply to an unrelated question on Taiwan,[23] as did President Clinton in reply to a question on Taiwan in a radio question-and-answer programme during his visit to Shanghai immediately after his summit with Jiang in June 1998. In the two Jiang-Clinton summits in 1997 and 1998, the two sides announced they were working together towards a constructive strategic partnership.

Trends and Impact

In terms of the grand strategic visions of the two countries, the United States and China should work together to build a strategic partnership in the twenty-first century. However, any trend in this direction could be affected by domestic politics and ideological and nationalistic zeal on both sides.

The "five fingers" in the U.S. "hand-shaped" Asia-Pacific strategy have been strengthened through such events as the revision of the 1978 United States–Japan security guidelines, the North Korean missile/satellite launch in 1998 which indicated that country's growing military capability, the 1995-96 Taiwan Strait crisis and the Asian economic meltdown which began in July 1997. The formation of a strong East Asian power bloc seems unlikely in the foreseeable future. So, with its limited security surplus and its limited hard and soft power, China's growth need not alarm the United States.

In any case, China is not the sole or even the most serious problem the United States faces in the coming century. One strategic implication from the Asian financial crisis is that finance kills. In this sense, China is not yet a serious threat, either in the sense of the U.S. traditional security or financial security.

The greater challenge for the United States will be a general and relative erosion of its power, which is likely to result from the massive and rapidly growing costs of maintaining leadership in a world of increasing uncertainty and volatility. This calls for a change of leadership style: a departure from the rigidity of previous dominant world powers, in favour of a more flexible balancing act through accurately identifying critical international issues and state relations and positioning itself accordingly.

As the international situation has become increasingly fluid, Washington should avoid getting bogged down on one issue, as this will jeopardize its capability to reposition itself quickly to address other issues. Therefore, it does not make strategic sense for Washington to be so rigid with China on the Taiwan issue, as this compromises its positioning on other international issues. This should not be seen as a favour to China because it serves U.S. national interests both globally and in the Asian Pacific region.

In the long run, a co-operative China that is rising at a reasonable pace is not only desirable but also necessary to broad U.S. global and regional interests. Having China co-operate as a strategic partner, at least on certain issues, will enhance U.S. strategy. China and the United States are likely to share many common strategic interests for a long time to come. Premature and rigid identification of China as a permanent foe would lead to a hardening of political alignments and reduced strategic flexibility, and in the long run, this would be dangerous.

It has become obvious that although Japan is an international player, Washington cannot count on it as the major stabilizer in East Asia. Politically and strategically, Japan does not and will not possess the kind of importance that China has and will have. Even in terms of economic importance, China is gradually catching up and will eventually overtake Japan. History shows that even with the United States–Japan Security Treaty, Asia's stability could not have been as easily maintained without the co-operation of China. Examples include the Korean War in the 1950s, the Vietnam War in the 1950s–70s, and the China–India border war in 1962. China could be the major stabilizer in East Asia if it acted in partnership with the United States, and not only could it help stability in East Asia (Northeast and Southeast Asia), but it could also be a key player in resolving potential crises in Russia, East Europe, South Asia and Middle Asia. Japan may be used by the United States to constrain China if necessary, but it cannot provide major stabilization for the region.

In the grand two-ocean strategy the United States has for the chessboard of Eurasia, U.S. strategic performance in Europe would be severely constrained without a stable East Asia, where a United States–China strategic partnership can serve as the major stabilizer, or "anchor," as Brzezinski has pointed out.[24] In the "unsettled middle" between rising China and expanding Western Europe, the role of the United States as sole superpower is bound to be called into question. Washington needs strategic co-operation from Beijing for a stable East Asia as a stepping stone to extend its influence across the "unsettled middle" of Eurasia. If the "middle" remains unsettled, the leading position of the United States in world affairs in the next century cannot be guaranteed. This perhaps is what a "constructive strategic partnership" means to Washington (Washington came up with the term "strategic partnership" to which Beijing added the word "constructive"): that China accepts U.S. leadership in world affairs in exchange for U.S. acceptance of certain Chinese strategic interests in their mutual strategic co-operation for East Asian stability. If China cannot be won over as a partner, it could prove to be a high barrier to U.S. efforts to extend its strategic influence to the critical "unsettled middle" of the "grand chessboard", especially with the uncertainty in Russia.

China is now aware that the leading position of the United States in the world is beyond challenge for a long time to come. Few Chinese believe that China will have the capability to challenge the United States even within the next fifty years. Before it has acquired such capability, there is little strategic rationale for China to challenge U.S. leadership despite its political rhetoric. China's angry response to the United States following the U.S. decision to give Lee Teng-hui a visa in May 1995 and the U.S.-led N.A.T.O. (so-called mistaken) bombing of the Chinese Embassy in Belgrade in May 1999 was obviously not a challenge to U.S. leadership. It was more a reflection of strong Chinese feelings in the face of unexpected hurt and loss of national dignity.

Some Chinese believe that with this partnership with the United States, China may have more breathing space to concentrate on its pressing domestic reform. And others hope that the United States may eventually treat China as a major strategic stabilizer in East Asia with a role more important than Japan's.

But the question is whether the United States has enough political tolerance of a country whose current political and social systems are so different from its own. Will its ideological zeal blind it to the advantages of the grand strategic design? Will U.S. domestic politics hijack foreign policymaking, threatening U.S. global strategic interests?

The Clinton Administration seems to have embraced such a grand strategic vision. In 1997–98 it repeatedly claimed it would make an effort to build a "constructive strategic partnership" with China. However, domestic politics and the ideological zeal of some elements of Congress and the mass media have exerted mounting pressure on President Clinton's China policy. They first made use of the reported Chinese political donations for the 1996 U.S. presidential election to attack Clinton's China policy as being influenced by Chinese money (these reports have subsequently been proven to be misleading).[25] Then, in early 1999, the Chinese nuclear spying case brought accusations that the Clinton Administration's pro-Beijing policy had been at the expense of U.S. national security.[26] They also exaggerated the threat and number of China's missiles deployed in its military exercises around Taiwan to justify covering Taiwan with the T.M.D.[27] Moreover, they have introduced legislation, the Taiwan Security Enhancement Act, which will enhance military co-operation between the United States and Taiwan.[28] Increasing pressure has also been brought to bear on the Administration to continue to submit to a UN resolution in 1999 condemning China for human rights violations, despite the refusal by U.S. allies to support the U.S. initiative.

While domestic politics and ideological zeal in the United States may pull United States–China relations off the track towards a constructive strategic partnership, rising Chinese "nationalism" (so-called in the Western press) or "patriotism" (so-called in the Chinese press) is also exerting strong pressure on Chinese leaders who prefer to maintain a low profile international policy to avoid serious clashes with the United States.

After the 1989 Tiananmen incident, a very high percentage of Chinese could have been considered pro-American. And in 1991, the Gulf War attracted much popular support of the United States among the Chinese. Some Beijing residents even went to the United States embassy to donate money in support of U.S. military action. This was in sharp contrast to the nation-wide Chinese outcry against the U.S.-led N.A.T.O. bombing of Yugoslavia over the Kosovo issue in 1999. Some Chinese students volunteered to go to Yugoslavia to fight N.A.T.O. after the Chinese Embassy in Belgrade was bombed in May 1999.[29]

In a matter of a few years, what the United States had hoped would be a "peaceful evolution" of the Chinese people has turned into what I would call a *peaceful re-evolution.* Many "pro-Americans" have revised their perceptions of a benign United States. They consider the United States more interested in weakening China than in championing human rights and democracy in China. An opinion poll conducted in 1995 showed that over 80 per cent of Chinese youth considered the United States to be the most unfriendly country to China. This percentage increased when the United States dispatched its aircraft carriers to the Taiwan Strait in March 1996 and when the Chinese Embassy in Belgrade was bombed in 1999.

This surging "nationalism" is less the product of China's propaganda than the fruits of "China bashing" in Western countries. It is noteable that Chinese students in the United States, where there is little "Chinese communist propaganda", are often more nationalistic than they were before they left China for the United States, and certainly more nationalistic than those who remain inside China.

Since 1989, Chinese people in general, both overseas and in China, have been upset by several incidents such as the *Yinhe* freighter incident,[30] the annual U.S. threat to withdraw the M.F.N. trading status from China, the U.S.-orchestrated international opposition to Beijing's bid to hold the 2000 Olympic Games, the hardening of the U.S. position on the terms for China's entry into the G.A.T.T./ W.T.O. despite Chinese concessions, and the U. S. support of Taiwan's resistance against earlier reunification with China. These events, together with China-bashing in the Western press, have convinced more and more Chinese people that the West is not only targeting the Chinese government but also the Chinese nation, and seem to be aimed less at improving the Chinese human rights record and democracy but more at weakening both China's hard power and soft power to protect Western global and regional interests.

The Chinese book, *A China That Should Say No*, published in 1996 by some young people who did not have any government connections, clearly showed this strong resentment among ordinary Chinese people. Although this resentment ebbed when efforts on the part of both President Jiang and President Clinton in 1997–98 culminated in their two summits, intensified China-bashing by right-wing U.S. conservatives from mid-1998 stoked up nationalistic sentiment once again. Things came to a head when the U.S.-led N.A.T.O. force bombed the Chinese Embassy in Belgrade on 8 May 1999, provoking strong protests by tens of thousands of Chinese students and others in more than 20 cities.

Clearly, this Chinese "nationalism" is not expansionist. It is more a righteous indignation at the loss of national dignity in what they believed to be a calculated N.A.T.O. bombing of the Chinese Embassy and well-organized China- bashing by some U.S. politicians ahead of the 2000 presidential election. This "defensive nationalism" is different from "aggressive nationalism" which is based on racial supremacy, supreme military and economic strength, commercial greed, or religious/ideological zeal. It is therefore likely to wane if the United States takes a more benign attitude toward China.

If the on-going China-bashing orchestrated by right-wing U.S. conservatives goes to extremes, it will correspondingly invite surging Chinese nationalism. These two trends, if allowed to get out of control, will derail the development of the "constructive strategic partnership" between the United States and China.

As for Taiwan, whether China and the United States succeed in becoming such partners or not, it will face greater challenges ahead, although of a different nature. This point will be discussed in Part IV.

If it ever comes into being, how long could such a "constructive strategic partnership" last? It is possible that Washington has proposed such a partnership only out of strategic expedience, a temporary palliative for China so that it will not make trouble in East Asia while the United States is focusing on the "unsettled middle" of the Eurasian continent. It is the U.S. assessment that before 2015 there is no power in the world, including China, that can pose a serious military challenge to the United States. The United States is making the best use of this period of time to fix its "strategic nuances" one by one and to set up and strengthen the global strategic infrastructure for the future before it meets any serious challenger.

Within this strategic vision, the United States aims to complete its dominance of the Eurasian continent by fixing the "unsettled middle" first. This is the strategic rationale for its military operation in Kosovo over and above the concerns about Serbian ethnic cleansing that it uses to justify its military operation there. If the Kosovo operation is successful, the United States will be better positioned to intervene in Russia should problems arise there after Yeltsin.

However, what will the United States do once it has established dominance in the "unsettled middle"? Chinese strategists are concerned that it may turn next to the Korean Peninsular and the Taiwan problem in East Asia.[31] In other words, the United States may then extend its "five fingers" towards China until it collapses. U.S. Secretary of State Madeline Albright's proposal regarding N.A.T.O.'s strategic reorientation for the twenty-first century has added to China's concern. In November 1998, she stated that, in the future, N.A.T.O. must be able to protect its expanded borders and "security" from threats posed by the proliferation of weapons of mass destruction, disturbances among minority nationalities and regional conflicts.[32] Such N.A.T.O. military operations outside its borders would not require U.N. approval. China is concerned that this would enable N.A.T.O. to deploy "peacekeeping troops" in an Asian country and intervene in Taiwan, Tibet, Xinjiang and the Nansha (Spratly) Islands, justified by its proclaimed concern about ethnic turmoil and regional conflict there.

If the Beijing leadership begins to consider this alarming scenario seriously, readjustment and even reorientation of its strategy is likely. This change, whatever it is, will affect China–Taiwan relations in the coming years, as will be discussed in Part IV.

Notes

1. "Jiang Zemin Calls for Increased Economic-Industrial Co-operation with Taiwan", Reuters, 25 October 1993.
2. CCTV (overseas) News Program, 16 January 1996.
3. Central News Agency, "1996 Taiwan–HK–Mainland Foreign Trade World's 3rd-Largest", Reuters, 19 May 1997. Figures are from Taiwan's Board of Foreign Trade.
4. *Liaowang*, no. 44 (1995), p. 14.
5. *ST*, 26 August 1995, p. 17.
6. For the U.S. decision to upgrade its relations with Taiwan, see "China: Beijing Condemns Interference", Reuters, 9 September 1994.
7. "USA: US to Risk New Visa Storm", Reuters, 6 January 1996.
8. *Liaowang*, no. 25 (1995), p. 44.
9. *International Herald Tribute* (hereafter cited as *IHT*), 9 June 1995, p. 1.
10. *ST*, 1 October 1995, p. 1.
11. *ST*, 25 October 1995, p. 29.
12. *ST*, 1 June 1995, p. 12.
13. "Taiwan: US, Japan Backing 'Helping Taiwan's Independence Push'", Reuters, 30 January 1996.
14. Chen Qimao, "*Guanyu Zai Yatai Diqu Jianli Zhenzhi Xinchixu De Tansuo*" [Probing into Establishing a New Political Order in Asia Pacific], *Guoji Wenti Yanjiu* [International Studies] (Beijing), no. 1 (1992), pp. 1–8. Emphasis added.
15. Deng Xiaoping. "*Shanyu Liyong Shiji Jiejue Fazhan Wenti*" [Be Good at Using Opportunities for the Development], in *Deng Xiaoping Wenxuan* [Selected Works of Deng Xiaoping], vol. 3, (Beijing: People's Press, 1993), p. 363. Emphasis added.
16. For a detailed story about Liu's mission to Washington and his talks with U.S. officials, see *The Washington Post*, 21 June 1998, p. A01. Also gleaned from my interviews with Chinese officials and strategists in both Beijing and Shanghai in 1996.
17. Jiang Zemin told Liang Su-yung, former speaker of Taiwan's Legislative Yuan, this during his visit to Beijing in 1998. See *Lienhe Zaobao*, 14 October 1998, p. 13.
18. For the urgent U.S. request to meet Liu by Perry, Christopher and Lake, please see Barton Gellman, "U.S. and China Nearly Came to Blows in '96", *The Washington Post*, 21 June 1998, p. A01.
19. See *Chung Yang Jih Pao* [Central Daily News] (Taipei), 7 May 1999.
20. From my interviews in Beijing in 1996 .
21. *Lianhe Zaobao*, 13 September 1998, p. 22.
22. Barton Gellman, "Reappraisal Led to New China Policy", *The Washington Post*, 22 June 1998, p. A01.
23. Ibid.
24. Brzezinski, *The Grand Chessboard*.
25. The probe into the reported Chinese political donations was orchestrated mainly by the Republicans after losing the presidential election in 1996. It focused on the Democratic Party and Clinton's presidential campaign. After two years of investigation, the lawyers and investigators concluded in a report published in *The New York Times* in December 1998 that the probe had found no indication that the president and his party knew Chinese businesses or officials were behind any of the donations. The Chinese donations were aimed at gaining access to American high technology, not at

influencing the outcome of particular contests. It also said that based on inference and evidence including bank records, telephone calls and witness statements, the probe found that the Chinese were seeking to enhance the political standing of U.S. campaign fund-raisers, to give them clout in arguing for favourable policies on trade and technology. (See "'Gifts' for US technology", *SCMP*, 16 December 1998.) Before the ruling, however, the Republicans had launched a high profile campaign to question President Clinton's political integrity and his China policy.

26. The United States learned in 1995 that China had made an unusually rapid leap in nuclear warhead development. A 1988 Chinese document, obtained by U.S. intelligence, and close analysis of Chinese weapons tests prompted U.S. officials to suspect China had developed a warhead similar to the W-88 miniaturized warhead developed at Los Alamos Laboratory in the United States. A Taiwan-born American scientist, Lee Wen-ho, working in the laboratory has been the target of an F.B.I. investigation since 1996.

    The timing of the U.S. media "discovery" of the case was surprising as the suspect in the case had been under F.B.I. investigation since early 1996. By early 1999 when the U.S. media accused Lee of spying for China, no strong evidence to support such an accusation had been found and therefore no legal accusation had so far been lodged against Lee. Lee denied being a spy. Instead, he claimed to be a loyal American who had repeatedly co-operated with federal investigators on the trail of real Chinese agents. Richard Baum, a China scholar at the University of California, Los Angeles, noted: "What is extraordinary is not the fact that some Chinese nationals snoop around American research labs trying to pick up technical information on the cheap, but that some American journalists, politicians and congressional aides seek to portray such activity as a massive, co-ordinated Chinese government assault on American security. They whip up a red scare that is far out of proportion to the problem's actual dimensions and then use the resulting, self-generated hysteria as a club with which to attack the Clinton presidency." (Tom Plate, "Keep a Level Head over Engagement with China", *IHT*, 13 March 1999).

27. They first claimed that the "Chinese government has deployed more than 120 ballistic missiles, and possibly as many as 200, on its side of the Taiwan Strait." Such a deployment — at least a doubling of the previous number of missiles massed on China's southern coast — would be sure to fuel calls in the United States for including Taiwan in the T.M.D. On 12 February 1999, Pentagon spokesman Navy Captain Michael Doubleday contradicted this by declaring that "China has not increased the number of missiles aimed at the island in five or six years and has not seen any increases since an early 1990s build-up." *The Los Angeles Times*, 11–12 February 1999.

28. "Helms Says 'Over My Dead Body' to Taiwan Sales Cut", Reuters, 14 April 1999.

29. John Leicester, "China Students Wish to Fight NATO", The Associated Press News Line (hereafter cited as AP), 14 May 1999.

30. In late July 1993, the United States, based on its intelligence information, claimed that the Chinese freighter *Yinhe*, headed for Iraq, was carrying prohibited chemicals that could be used by Iraq for chemical weapons. It sent warships and helicopters to tail the *Yinhe* all the way in case it dump the chemicals at sea to destroy the evidence and finally forced it to dock at Dubai on 4 September. However, the Americans did not find the chemicals. The Chinese people were angry because, first, it was an a

matter of national dignity that its freighter had been harassed in such an insulting manner at high sea. Second, at the time of writing (late 1999) the United States had not yet offered any compensation for the freight delay and port fees incurred when *Yinhe* was forced to dock at Dubai for American inspection. Third, without apology, the United States claimed that they reserved the right to do it again in similar circumstances.

31. See Yan Xuetong's public lecture in Singapore, *Lianhe Zaobao*, 17 May 1999, p. 14.
32. "China: Perceived NATO Threat", *Oxford Analytical Daily Brief (c)*, 12 March 1999.

Part III

China vs. Taiwan

5

On a Collision Course

Having discussed China–United States frictions over Taiwan, Part III of this book now examines the development of relations between mainland China and Taiwan particularly between 1995 and 1998. Developments in cross-strait relations since late 1998 to 1999 and future prospects will be discussed in Part IV.

This chapter looks at the evolution of both China's perception of Taiwan and Taiwan's position on reunification before the 1995–96 Strait Crisis to help explain how China and Taiwan got onto a collision course and why China has come down so hard on Taiwan.

China's Perception of Taiwan[1]

The sharp response by Beijing to Lee's United States visit reflected a fundamental change of its perception of the position of Taiwan leaders on reunification, and consequently a major change in its Taiwan policy.

When Chiang Kai-shek and Chiang Ching-kuo were in power in Taiwan from 1949 to 1987, Beijing never suspected them of seeking Taiwan's independence. Mao knew his old rival too well to be disturbed by the thought of Chiang Kai-shek seeking Taiwan's independence. He considered Chiang's resistance as only an unwillingness "to confess to being defeated" or a "matter of face", not an intention to seek Taiwan's independence. On the contrary, the two Chiangs suppressed those who advocated independence no less harshly than they did communists in Taiwan. Very often they strenuously resisted what they suspected to be a U.S. effort to split Taiwan from China permanently. As a matter of fact, in private many Chinese officials and scholars highly respect the two Chiangs as national heroes as far as reunification and maintaining China's territorial integrity are concerned. They regard them as having strong patriotism. As for their close alliance with the United States against Beijing, this is seen as a strategy for survival and common ground in an ideological commitment against communism, but never against reunification.

It is now widely reported that in the 1950s and 1960s, Chiang Kai-shek tried to maintain secret channels with Beijing for negotiation and that he sent his own men to Beijing several times for secret discussions with leaders about reunification. It is not clear how many times the two sides contacted each other for reunification talks but there is no doubt that such contacts did take place. This was confirmed by Qiao Shi, chairman of the Standing Committee of China's N.P.C. in December 1995.[2] My interviews in China and the latest Chinese official publications also confirm this. At the very least, it is certain that there was a secret channel and visits by Cao Juren are not in doubt. Between 1956 and 1965, Cao travelled several times between Taiwan and the mainland. His trips finally resulted in six mutually-agreed conditions for reunification in 1965, namely:

1. Chiang Kei-shek returns to the mainland with his subordinates and settles in any province of China except Zhejiang Province. Chiang would remain the leader of Kuomintang.
2. Chiang Ching-kuo would be the governor of Taiwan Province. Taiwan would retain what it has had for 20 years with the exception of rights over diplomatic and military affairs, and, at Beijing's request, tillers would have their own land. This agreement would be re-negotiated after 20 years.
3. Taiwan would not receive any aid from the United States. If there were any financial difficulties, Beijing would provide the same amount of financial aid that the United States used to provide.
4. Taiwan's navy and air force would be reorganized under Beijing's control. Its infantry would also be reorganized and reduced to four divisions with one division stationed in the Jinmen and Xiamen region and three divisions in Taiwan.
5. Xiamen and Jinmen would be merged as one free city standing between Beijing and Taipei as a buffer and liaison zone. The commander of the army division in this area would also be the mayor of the city. The commander would have the rank of lieutenant general and should be acceptable to Beijing politically.
6. The official ranks and salaries of all the civil officials and military officers in Taiwan would remain the same and the living standard of people in Taiwan would not be allowed to go down.

Based on these six conditions, Chiang agreed to negotiations in 1965.[3]

There were also other secret channels which helped this breakthrough in 1965. For example, in October 1958, Zhang Shizhao, who enjoyed personal relations with top leaders in both Beijing and Taipei, went to Hong Kong to pass two proposals from Beijing to Chiang through K.M.T.'s connections in Hong Kong. The first one was that at a minimum the two sides should start building initial contacts such as direct post and telecommunications, followed by direct flight and sea transportation links, either officially or through private organizations. The second one was that Taiwan should have its own government, army and party organizations, which would be financially assisted by Beijing, but under the condition that Taiwan accept itself as part of the P.R.C.[4]

As Taiwan did not respond to these two proposals, in another secret meeting with "special guests" from Taiwan in 1960, Chairman Mao and Premier Zhou Enlai put forward a plan of *yi gang si mu* (one principle and four points) for negotiation. The principle was that Taiwan must return to China. And the four points were:

1. After Taiwan's return to China, Chiang would retain all rights over the arrangement of key local government and military personnel except diplomatic rights which would be handed over to the central government in Beijing.
2. The central government would provide financial support if necessary for the army, government and economy in Taiwan.
3. Social reform in Taiwan would not be embarked upon immediately, but would be postponed for when conditions were ripe, with respect to Chiang's views and after consultations with him.
4. Each side should refrain from any behaviour that would be harmful to the unity of the other side.[5]

These proposals were actually an embryonic form of the "one country, two systems" formula which Deng put forward publicly in the early 1980s.

With the onset of the Cultural Revolution, contact between the two sides was terminated. Given what was happening in China, Chiang was understandably unwilling to continue with the process and Beijing was too preoccupied with its internal chaos to give proper attention to the matter.

The process was restarted when Deng resumed power of the C.C.P. in the late 1970s. From then on, Beijing took the initiative on many occasions to bring about peaceful reunification with Taiwan as discussed in Chapter 1. This effort received a favourable response from Chiang Ching-kuo in the 1980s, according to Qiao Shi who related this in a conversation with Professor Wang Chi of U.S. Georgetown University. In the conversation, Qiao Shi also disclosed that Beijing and Taipei had discussed ways to reunify when Chiang Ching-kuo was alive.[6]

According to other Chinese sources, Chiang Ching-kuo and Beijing kept secret and informal channels open for initial contacts over several years in the 1980s. In 1987, Chiang finally made an important step towards negotiation on reunification. However, this process stopped almost as soon as it started. One reason is that Chiang Ching-kuo died early the following year. Another is that, according Chinese sources, the Americans intervened. Washington at that time sent C.I.A. officials to Taiwan to investigate the reported secret contact between Beijing and Taipei and had talks with Chiang Ching-kuo. After the C.I.A. officials left, Chiang said to the people around him, "We are still a colony". If it did not succeed in terminating the process, the American "concern" must have at least made Chiang more cautious than before.

These claims should not be dismissed as groundless, especially as the contacts were confirmed by Chairman Qiao Shi, a high-ranking leader. Although the details remain vague, it is a clear fact, verified by other sources,[7] that Chiang did make efforts to contact Beijing and that Chiang and Washington did not enjoy good relations. Chiang was constantly on guard against U.S. support of local pro-independence or other power groups out to weaken or overthrow him. The United States also intervened during the transition period in Taiwan politics in the late 1980s.

Moreover, while Chiang Ching-kuo was attempting to establish contact with Beijing, he took several steps which lead to a thaw in cross-strait relations. One of them was to allow people in Taiwan to go to the mainland to visit their relatives, though via a third place such as Hong Kong. And it is partly for this reason that Beijing has a high opinion of Chiang, and views him as doing his bit to prevent Taiwan's independence.

After Chiang Ching-kuo's death in January 1988, Beijing put its hope on Lee Teng-hui to continue the process, as shown in the two telegraphs to Taiwan by then C.C.P. General Secretary Zhao Ziyang. The first one was sent on 14 January 1988, addressing to the K.M.T. Central Committee. While expressing condolence to Chiang's death, Zhao hoped that "the new Taiwanese leader ... would carry further the recent favourable developments in the cross-strait relations".[8] The second one was sent on 8 July 1988, addressed to Lee directly. While expressing congratulation to Lee assuming chairmanship of the K.M.T. at its 13th National Congress, Zhao reaffirmed his hope for Lee to make efforts towards reunification.[9]

In mid-1991, the anxious Beijing made an open appeal for such negotiation by issuing a three-point "7 June Talk". The statement was a milestone in the evolution of China's Taiwan policy. It was issued in the name of the Office for Taiwan Affairs of the Central Committee of the C.C.P. The main points are: (1) earlier authorization of relevant departments and organizations for the three direct links and cross-strait exchanges; (2) earlier talks between the C.C.P. and the K.M.T. for a formal termination of the cross–strait hostility, leading to gradual reunification. Under the One China Principle, other issues could also be discussed. People from other parties and circles in Taiwan may also be invited for the discussion: (3) The C.C.P. welcomes visit by K.M.T. leaders or persons authorized by the K.M.T. Central Committee. The C.C.P. is also willing to visit Taiwan if invited.[10]

Taiwan did not respond to the appeal of the "7 June Talk" until two years later at the first Wang-Koo meeting in Singapore. At a dinner, Tang Shubei, Vice Chairman and Secretary General of A.R.A.T.S. asked why Taiwan let the chance of negotiation slip by not responding to the "7 June Talk", his S.E.F. counterpart Qiu Jinyi (in Chinese *pinyin*) answered that the proposed negotiation was on a party-to-party basis (i.e. C.C.P. vs. K.M.T. instead of government vs. government). Therefore, it could not be accepted. And Taiwan decided not to respond.[11]

By then, Beijing had become uneasy about Taiwan's position on reunification. At the end of 1991, Chinese President Yang Shangkun changed the wording in an internal document from "placing our hope on the government of Taiwan and placing our hope on the people in Taiwan", to "placing our hope on the government of Taiwan but more hope on the people in Taiwan". Clearly, Beijing had become suspicious about the "government of Taiwan".

According to Xu Jiatun,[12] in a personal talk between Deng Xiaoping, the then premier Zhao Ziyang and himself in the mid-1980s, the three concluded that the reason for Chiang Ching-kuo's refusal of Deng's "one country, two systems" proposal was because of the "loss of face" involved, i.e. the R.O.C. government would be reduced to a local government after reunification. From late 1989, Beijing began to feel uneasy about Lee's position on reunification.[13]

This uneasiness was, at this stage, mainly based on the facts. First, there had been no personal relations between Lee and Chinese leaders as there had been between the two Chiangs and many Chinese leaders in Beijing. Beijing was therefore not as sure about Lee's true character as they had been about the two Chiangs. Second, Lee was a native-born Taiwanese (although his ancestral home is in China: Yongding, Fujian Province) and had never lived in the mainland. He might not have such strong personal feelings towards the mainland as the two Chiangs had had. Third, Lee's lack of enthusiasm for reunification talks stemmed from his anti-communist ideology. Fourth, some even thought that Lee could not afford to go too far on the reunification issue because he was still weak compared with other veteran K.M.T. leaders. Though they were not sure of what Lee would do once he consolidated his position in K.M.T., they warned against a premature judgement of Lee at that time.

Based on this perception, Beijing did not try to influence the internal transitional politics of Taiwan in the early 1990s in the belief that there was no fundamental difference between Lee and Hao Po-tsun or any of the other veteran K.M.T. leaders who were engaged in a fierce power struggle with Lee for the

K.M.T. leadership. Both Lee and Hao were strongly anti-communist, and therefore held similar views about conducting reunification talks immediately. It was purely a power struggle, not a struggle between those who were for Taiwan's independence and those who were for Taiwan's reunification. Now Beijing has realized that Lee's antagonism towards reunification was not simply a matter of being anti-communist like Hao, nor was it because of internal politics, but because of his own personal beliefs. This makes Lee different from Hao.

In the informal meetings between A.R.A.T.S. and S.E.F. in 1992, especially the one in August, where Taiwan's insistence on "*yi ge zhong guo, ge zi biao shu*" [One China but free interpretations] made China suspicious of Lee's real intention on reunification. Whereas its previous uneasiness about Lee was largely because of lack of personal information, contact and therefore understanding, now it felt that it had somewhat, through these informal meetings, sounded Taiwan out of its true position on reunification. This marked a significant milestone in China's perception.

Before an S.E.F. negotiation team went to Beijing in 7–11 April 1993 to finalize the details for the forthcoming first Wang-Koo meeting, the Taiwan government, through the M.A.C., announced on 3 April a five-point instruction (actually 5 No's) to limit the function of the negotiation team, namely (1) No political issues should be involved; (2) No contact or meeting with high mainland government officials; (3) No discussion on direct two-way investment; (4) No discussion on what the S.E.F. is not authorized for; and (5) No formal signing on any agreements.[14] In the early morning of 11 April when the S.E.F. team had finished its negotiation with the mainland side and was ready for the farewell meeting with their host Wang Daohan, the M.A.C. phoned this team at their hotel, ordering it to withdraw one agreement, which was already agreed upon and duly recorded in the meeting minutes, i.e. that the Wang-Koo meeting should be regularized for once a year. The M.A.C. even said that if China did not agree to this, Taiwan would rather cancel the forthcoming Wang-Koo meeting.[15]

Annoyed as he was, Wang Daohan still accepted this sudden change of mind and went for the first round of the Wang-Koo meeting in Singapore on 27 April 1993, where, in order to make it a success, he put aside political issues to concentrate on practical matters. Despite the public celebration of the great success of the Wang-Koo meeting on surface, Chinese leaders felt, but had not yet determined, that there was something wrong with Taiwanese leaders. While China claimed the meeting as a step of historical importance, heading towards reunification, Taiwan also claimed it as a step of historical independence, but in its illustration to the world of Taiwan and China being two equals and China being, as a matter of fact, divided and separately administered.[16]

By 1993, Beijing had also noticed that the tendency towards independence in Taiwan had accelerated alarmingly with the mushrooming of many independence organizations and the return of many Taiwan independence figures from overseas. For the first time they were tolerated by the government when they actively campaigned for Taiwan's independence. Some Chinese strategists suspected Lee of protecting and encouraging this independence trend. However, it seemed that at that time Beijing had not yet reached a consensus on Lee. One reason was that Lee's true colours had not been revealed. While encouraging this proclivity for independence under the name of "democratization", Lee also pushed for the first round of the Wang-Koo meeting in 1993, which Beijing eagerly viewed as a breakthrough in cross-strait relations. However, with hindsight, Lee's intention in pushing for the Wang-Koo meeting was to mislead Beijing into thinking that he was for reunification and that the increasing trend towards independence in Taiwan was not something that Lee advocated but which he was unable to stop. Lee's tactics worked to the extent of making Beijing hesitate about putting its weight behind Hao in the power struggle between Lee and Hao for K.M.T. leadership in 1993.

Another factor that accounted for Beijing's expectations on Lee is the secret communications between Lee and Chinese leaders. Before his death in early 1988, Chiang Ching-kuo had agreed to send a 5-men group to visit the mainland for secret talks on reunification. After Lee took over the power in 1988, though he did not send the 5-men group, he kept some secret channels between Beijing and Taipei. For example, Nan Huai-chin, a respected senior historian and philosopher in Hong Kong, had arranged for the secret meetings between the two sides in Hong Kong. Beijing first sent Jia Yibin, a member of the Standing Committee of the Chinese People's Political Consultative Conference to see Nan on 31 January 1988, with its wishes to meet Lee. On 21 April 1989, together with Yang Side, director of China's Taiwan's Affairs Office and representative of Chinese President Yang Shangkun, Jia went to see Nan again in Hong Kong. Yang Side asked Nan to pass Beijing's sincere wishes for cross-strait talks to Lee Teng-hui through Nan's former students Su Chi-cheng and Cheng Shu-min, both were Lee's confidants.

Nan went to Taiwan and met Lee in 1990. In December 1990, Su Chi-cheng, Lee's secretarial chief, went for a secret meeting with Yang Side in Hong Kong. The next year, for several times in Hong Kong, Beijing, Shanghai and Zhuhai, Su Chi-cheng and Cheng Shu-min secretly met officials from Beijing. They included Wang Daohan, Yang Side and Xu Mingzhen. In August 1992, Xu Mingzhen visited Taiwan with the excuse of visiting his relatives there. Thereafter, he also made several visits to Taiwan.

In these secret communications, to show his "sincerity", Lee once told emissaries from Beijing that if Beijing did not like the K.M.T. he would work to cripple it. If it did not like Hao Paocun, he would make an effort to "pull him down". It seemed that Beijing was somewhat taken by Lee, partly because of his secret communications and partly because, as some people speculated, Lee once joined the Communist Party in Taiwan.[17]

However, Lee was only successful in this respect once. When he tried it for the second time, i.e. he attempted to use the prospect of the second round of the Wang-Koo meeting in July 1995 to make Beijing acquiesce to or at least tolerate his U.S. visit and the Cornell University speech, he failed. Taiwan thought that Beijing would be only too eager to participate in another breakthrough in cross-relations through the Wang-Koo meeting and for that reason would also be more likely to accommodate Taiwan's wishes. However, Taiwan was wrong this time.

By this time Beijing had come to see that Lee wanted the second round of the Wang-Koo meeting, not so much to achieve a breakthrough in cross-strait relations as to use it as a bargaining chip to get Beijing to accept his "pragmatic diplomacy". Beijing was not willing to pay such a high price for the second round of the Wang-Koo meeting which, in its view, was not only beneficial to China but also to Taiwan. The second round was expected to solve some pressing technical problems such as protecting Taiwanese investments in the mainland and Taiwanese business interests in Hong Kong before Hong Kong's return to China in July 1997. What is more, Taiwan's independence was not something Beijing would ever agree to exchange for anything.

It should be pointed out that despite some suspicions, Beijing was for a long time unwilling to come to a final conclusion that Lee was totally in favour of Taiwan's independence. Beijing expected Lee to be accommodating on the reunification issue, despite evidence after 1993 to the contrary. By August 1993, with Beijing standing idle, the so-called "main-streamers" under Lee finally tipped the balance of power in the K.M.T. Although these main-streamers had successfully phased out most of the K.M.T. leaders who advocated reunification, Beijing had still pinned its hopes on Lee as the person with whom it was prepared to negotiate reunification.

Nevertheless, there were some strategists who began to have deep suspicions about Lee. From 1994, Beijing began to suspect that Lee was not what they had perceived him to be. Once he had gained firm control of the K.M.T. without any serious political rivals, he was confident enough to disregard Beijing's reaction. Feeling secure in his position, Lee began to show his true colours, shocking Beijing into reconsidering its perception of him. Lee's "pragmatic diplomacy", such as the bid for U.N. membership, intensified. Most of his trips overseas to push for "pragmatic diplomacy" in one form or another took place after 1993, such as his trips to the Philippines, Indonesia, Thailand as well as several African and Latin American countries in 1994, and to the United Arab Emirates and Jordan in 1995.

As he gained confidence Lee became more outspoken about his personal beliefs on reunification and in his verbal attacks on Beijing. He called Chinese leaders "a group of bandits and hooligans" in a presidential office press release at the Lake Incident of 1994, causing great offence[18]. Chinese leaders were even more offended when, in May 1995, he mocked the P.R.C.

by calling it the son and the R.O.C. the father.[19] Chinese strategists told me that after reading the report on Lee's derogatory father-and-son expression, Qiao Shi wrote on the report: "*Ci ren tai xiao zhang* [This man is too arrogant]".

However, the two most significant events which proved to be turning points in Beijing's perception of Lee were his conversation with Japanese writer Ryotaro Shiba in May 1994 and his Cornell University speech in 1995.

Lee's conversation with Japanese writer Ryotaro Shiba shocked many people in Beijing who had previously pinned hopes of reunification on Lee. In the conversation, Lee strongly and clearly expressed his determination to lead Taiwan away from the mainland, his preference for Japanese culture over Chinese culture and his unwillingness to see a strong and united China ("a Chinese empire", to use his own words) in the future. Many people in Beijing realised that this was the real Lee and that China had been fooled from the very beginning by Lee's sweet-talking.

However, Beijing made no moves to change its fundamental policy with regard to Lee. There were a few reasons for this. First, some people doubted that Lee, despite his personal inclination toward independence, had the determination and capability to push for Taiwan's independence. Thus the drift towards independence, though still annoying to Beijing, would likely be slow and manageable and therefore not worthy of any dramatic reaction for the time being. Second, some were unwilling to confess they had erred in their judgement of Lee, either because of the political implications for their positions or because it made a mockery of all the work they had done in past years. They warned that it was dangerous to jump to conclusions about Lee too soon, and that what Lee had done up to that point did not demand a fundamental change in China's Taiwan policy. Third, some believed that Lee had acted within the context of the political and social situation in Taiwan and that any other politician in Lee's position would have done the same in order to survive politically. Nevertheless, they had some reservations about what Lee had said and considered that this was going a bit too far.

There were also other viewpoints and therefore no consensus was reached to push for a major policy change like that following Lee's United States visit in 1995. For example, the P.L.A. and some other elite think-tanks warned in 1994 that Lee and Washington would go further and faster in their co-operation to reach the first target in Lee's "pragmatic diplomacy", i.e. his visit to the United States. However, the Ministry of Foreign Affairs considered this unlikely before the U.S. announcement that it would grant Lee a visa for his United States visit in May 1995.

Nevertheless, Chinese President Jiang Zemin went ahead with an eight-point proposal on 30 January 1995, calling for a termination of hostilities across the strait and the first meeting of leaders of both sides. Why did Beijing make such a proposal despite its suspicion of Lee? First, China's Leading Group of Taiwan Affairs, encouraged by the breakthrough in the first Wang-Koo meeting in April 1993, had started preparing the new guidelines for reunification on 30 June 1993. It was finished in November 1993, before the Bogor A.P.E.C. meeting. However, Beijing chose not to announce the proposal in 1994 because of the change in the political situation in Taiwan: By the end of 1993, most of the pro-reunification K.M.T. leaders had been phased out and the K.M.T. was dominated by "mainstreamers" who opposed reunification. Cross-strait relations were also seriously strained following the Lake Incident and Lee's interview with Japanese writer Ryotaro Shiba in 1994. By the time the proposal was announced in early 1995, Beijing did not have very high expectations of Lee, but wanted to put a stop to the deterioration in cross-strait relations. Moreover, announcing the proposal would keep the initiative in Beijing's hand. Beijing's thinking was that even if the eight-point proposal failed to achieve its purpose, it would likely serve as a brake to slow down the pace of Taiwan's drift towards independence. Also some Chinese leaders still had lingering hopes that Lee would turn around and wanted to put him under "further observation". One of China's top Taiwan specialists, Li Jiaquan, noted that even at that time Beijing's approach was to "cure the sickness to save the patient".[20]

Beijing anticipated three possible responses from Taiwan to Jiang's eight-point proposal: (1) warm; (2) lukewarm; (3) cold. The first one was considered unlikely and the last one undesirable. It hoped to get a lukewarm response. But what Beijing got was worse than cold in the form of Lee's six-point response in April 1995, followed by Lee's visit to the United States which was given high publicity and treated as a de facto state visit. In his public speech at Cornell University, Lee vehemently advocated "popular sovereignty" and the "R.O.C. in Taiwan" and declared he would "challenge the impossible". Taiwan's subsequent actions included an intensified U.N. bid, a visit to Europe by the Premier three days after Lee returned, a planned visit to Canada by the Deputy Premier, and Lee's instruction to "make full use of the excellent situation" following his visit to "go all out" to expand Taiwan's international space. All this sent a strong message to Beijing that Lee not only personally favoured Taiwan's independence but also had the determination to go through with it.

Beijing suspected that Washington had tried to sabotage the improvement in cross-strait relations by driving a wedge between China and Taiwan through its visa decision. So prior to Lee's speech in the United States, it had chastized only the United States. However, articles criticizing Lee were prepared in early June 1995 but were not allowed to be published because Beijing wanted to wait and see what Lee would do and say in the United States first. Every word of Lee's speech at Cornell University and his behaviour in the United States were quickly relayed to the anxiously waiting Chinese leaders, who then decided to take decisive action against Lee. Reports and articles criticizing Lee were finally allowed to appear in all major newspapers in China. As the Chinese saying goes, once the water is spread on the ground, it is difficult to take it back.

In contrast to their erstwhile belief that international forces were the only threat to China's reunification, Beijing now saw that Lee himself was a threat. In Beijing's view, Lee's determination, whether intentionally or unintentionally, helped "international forces" contain China.

The idea of "Chinese helping foreigners to contain China" angered the Chinese. This, together with the realization they had been fooled and ridiculed by Lee, fuelled popular resentment against Lee. Internal political strife and a flurry of policy debates about Taiwan and U.S. intentions followed. It would have been surprising if China had not reacted strongly.

At the Central Meeting in Beidaihe in July 1995 the decision to hold military exercises was taken. It was decided to hold one initially to test Lee's response. As it turned out, Lee took an uncompromising stance. Beijing therefore decided to maintain the pressure by holding more.

It can thus be seen that what determined China's harsh response towards Lee was not its resentment of Taiwan's model of democracy and direct presidential election but its discovery of the true Lee Teng-hui and its concern over his determination to "go all out" for independence. This explains why China did not react before Lee's visit to the United States, despite Taiwan's democratization. Obviously, with China's change in perception following Lee's United States visit, went its change in perception of Lee's true intentions behind the direct presidential election, "democratization" and the constitutional reform.

Thus, the interpretation that China's military exercises in 1995–96 were targeted against democracy rather than Taiwan's drift towards independence is apparently incorrect, even though it is true that Beijing would not accept Taiwan's model of democracy.

Taiwan's Position on Unification

Taiwan under both Chiang Kai-shek and Chiang Ching-kuo held a consistent position that Taiwan was as much Chinese territory as mainland China and that there was only one China and this China was the R.O.C. not the P.R.C. This position began to change after Lee took office.

In the late 1980s, Lee Teng-hui still proclaimed: "One China is the supreme principle". On 23 February 1988, he still insisted on a "one China policy, not a two Chinas policy".[21] But in 1990, Lee raised the notion of "one China, two governments". His own words were "One country, two governments. This is a fact."[22] In its "Guidelines for National Unification" of February 1991, Taiwan held that "there is only one China". But for the first time, it introduced the notion of "one China, two equal political entities". Beijing and Taipei reached vocal consensus on the "one China" principle in a meeting between A.R.A.T.S. and S.E.F. in March 1992 and reaffirmed this in the first round of the Wang-Koo meeting in 1993. This principle was then explained in three sentences: The first two were that there is only one China in this world; and Taiwan is part of China. However the two sides had different versions for the third sentence. For Beijing, it read "the P.R.C. is the sole legitimate government of China" while for Taipei it read the R.O.C. Taipei later claimed that the "two sides agreed to disagree on one China", and had settled for *"yi ge zhong guo, ge zi biao shu"* [one China but free interpretations]. However, Beijing denied that it had ever allowed any "free interpretations" of the "one China" principle and claimed that it had never "agreed to disagree" on the "one China" principle. It said that in 1992 A.R.A.T.S. had made its position clear to S.E.F.: "The one China principle should be adhered to. So long as this position is claimed in talks on practical matters, [we] may not discuss the political content of this one China."[23] On 16 November 1992, in talks on practical matters, A.R.A.T.S. and S.E.F. expressed consensus on the one China principle verbally. A.R.A.T.S. announced that "both sides of the Taiwan Strait adhere to the one China principle, seeking national reunification. But the political content of the one China will not be included in their talks on practical matters".[24] However, S.E.F. maintained: "In the process of the both sides of the Strait making a common effort to seek national unification, although both sides adhere to the one China principle, they have different understanding of what is this one China."[25] So while China insisted there had only been consensus on the "one China" principle and that the content had never been discussed, Taiwan's interpretation was that "both sides agreed to disagree on one China"[26].

Shortly after issuing "Guidelines for National Unification" in 1991, Taiwan began to emphasize that "Taiwan and the mainland are both parts of China" and the P.R.C. "is *not equivalent* to China" (instead of the P.R.C. *is not* China). It would now no longer compete with Beijing for the "right to represent China" in the international arena. Instead it began to emphasize that the two parts of China should have the right to participate alongside each other in the international community as equal, prior to unification.[27]

By 1993, Taiwan's official position on sovereignty had changed to "one China but administered in different parts by the R.O.C. and the P.R.C.", insisting that Taipei had "exclusive sovereignty" over the island of Taiwan, the Penghu Islands and Jinmen and Mazu Islands.[28] At the Seattle A.P.E.C. meeting of November 1993, Taiwan's Economic Minister, Chiang Pin-kung, on Lee Teng-hui's instruction, put forward the notion of a "transitional 'two Chinas' policy heading toward unification".

By 1994, more changes had taken place. Taiwan's 1994 White Paper on cross-strait relations pointed out: "The two sides should be fully aware that each has jurisdiction over its respective territory and that they should coexist as two legal entities in the international arena."[29] Hereafter, the emphasis shifted to the "coexistence of two equal international legal entities", or "the R.O.C. in Taiwan and the P.R.C. in China", which is how Lee expressed it during his United States visit. Instead of "two equal entities" or "two equal political entities", Taiwan this time used the expression "two *legal* entities in the international arena" or "two equal international *legal* entities". Here, the very word "legal" implies "sovereignty", i.e. two equal sovereign entities. This was a total departure from what the two Chiangs had envisaged and simply impossible for Beijing to accept. Beijing viewed this position as being against the "one China" principle, while Taiwan asked China to drop its old-fashioned ideas about "one China", which, it said, was only a cultural concept and whose sovereignty could be shared by both the R.O.C. and the P.R.C. in the United Nations as equals.

In the White Paper, Taiwan categorically refused to accept, and has ever since, China's "one country, two systems" formula for reunification. It states that "Communist China's 'one country, two systems' position is the greatest obstacle to China's unification." However, Taiwan failed to put forward its own formula for reunification, stating instead that "only democracy, freedom and a system for equal distribution of wealth can solve the 'China question'".[30] By saying this, Taiwan changed its previous position that "China must respect Taiwan's democratic system" to one which listed "democracy and freedom" in China as another precondition for reunification, i.e. "democratic unification". After 1996, Taiwan emphasized that unification was only possible should China become a democracy like Taiwan in the future, i.e. one country, one good system.

Bid for U.N. Membership

With the change in its position on sovereignty and reunification, Taiwan also changed its position on the issue of whether to apply for U.N. membership. Its former position was "either the R.O.C. in and the P.R.C. out or vice versa". Now it argued for "simultaneous participation" by both the P.R.C. and the R.O.C. in the United Nations. It argued that as a country of 23 million people, the fourteenth largest trading nation in the world and the sixth largest trading partner with the United States, Taiwan should be given a seat in the United Nations. And membership of the United Nations would provide additional opportunities for greater interaction between Taiwan and China. It pointed to precedents for "parallel representation" such as East and West Germany, as well as North and South Korea. It denied this U.N. bid was intended to create "two Chinas" or "one China, one Taiwan" as Beijing had charged, and described it as conducive to the unification of China.

Taiwan's U.N. bid actually started secretly after Lee succeeded Chiang in 1988, when he instructed the Foreign Ministry to study the issue and hired a

U.S. law company for this purpose. In 1991, the United Nations section was formally set up within the Foreign Ministry.

In 1993, Taiwan made its U.N. bid openly. Since then, every year, a group of mostly Central American, Caribbean and African countries have asked the General Assembly of the United Nations to consider giving U.N. membership to Taiwan. These countries include Nicaragua, Burkina Faso, Central African Republic, Dominica, Dominican Republic, El Salvador, Gambia, Grenada, Guatemala, Guinea-Bissau, Honduras, Saint Lucia, Saint Vincent, Senegal, the Solomon Islands and Swaziland.

Nan Jin, Bei Lian, Xi He **Policy**

Meanwhile, Taiwan also adopted a new set of policies which were once described by Siew Wan-chang, later, Taiwan's Premier, in 1994 as "*Nan Jin* (go south)", "*Bei Lian* (linking north)" and "*Xi He* (peace in the west)".[31]

The *Nan Jin* (go south) policy was to expand economic relations southwards with both Southeast Asian (in a narrow sense) and (in a broader sense) Latin American and African countries in an attempt to avoid excessive economic dependence on China and to seek the support of these countries for its "pragmatic diplomacy". Taiwan adopted this policy in 1993, urging its businessmen to divert their investments away from China to Southeast Asia, with the focus on Vietnam, Indonesia and the Philippines, as well as Singapore as the potential replacement of Hong Kong for its indirect trade with China after Hong Kong's return to China in July 1997.

By mid-1995, about 70 per cent of the Taiwanese companies investing in ASEAN had done so after this policy was adopted. By the end of June 1995, 4,038 Taiwanese companies had pumped a total of US$24.7 billion into the six ASEAN countries,[32] compared to 27,000 Taiwanese companies in the mainland with a total investment of over US$24 billion. This shows that the Taiwanese investors in ASEAN countries were by and large bigger companies while those in China were mainly small businesses — a measure of the success of Taiwan's official policy to discourage big companies from investing in China.

According to the Economics Ministry regulations issued in November 1995, Taiwan adopted measures to keep Taiwan businesses with investments in China rooted on the island. Large-scale technology intensive companies seeking permission from the Taiwan authorities to build factories in China had to invest in research and development an amount equal to 3 per cent of their total pre-tax earnings. According to government figures, the industry average for research and development investment in Taiwan was 1.5 per cent. The 3 per cent requirement was expected to cut down considerably the number of Taiwan-based firms eligible to invest in China. Under the new regulations, at least 10 per cent of the staff of Taiwan-based firms had to be technical and research staff, and each firm was required to provide the government with a long-term investment plan.[33]

This "go south" policy has so far failed in its purpose of obtaining Southeast Asian countries' political support for Taiwan's return to the United Nations. Southeast Asian countries in general have a strong interest in keeping good economic relations with both China and Taiwan as well as stability in East Asia, and are therefore unwilling to involve themselves in the dispute across the Taiwan Strait. Taiwan must have been disappointed by the fact that, like many other countries, Southeast Asian countries did not offer any moral support to Taiwan when China embarked on its missile tests and military exercises in 1995–96, nor did they support Taiwan's U.N. bid. Shortly after Lee's United States visit, Philippine President Ramos invited Lee to visit the Philippines. However, he quickly withdrew the invitation and turned down Taiwan's request that he invite Lee to attend A.P.E.C. meetings in Manila. The financial crisis in Southeast Asia from mid-1997 dealt a severe blow to Taiwan's "go south" policy. Driven by economic need, many Taiwanese businessmen have shifted their business operations to the mainland.

Taiwan has managed to maintain diplomatic relations with more than 20 small African and Latin America countries. It has used its economic strength to serve its diplomacy. Lee Teng-hui made a statement in January 1993 that "We should make good use of our overseas development fund and all other possible resources to promote more pragmatic participation in world organizations. ... This will expedite our ultimate goal of returning to the United Nations."[34] This triggered Taiwan's so-called "chequebook diplomacy" (also known, among other things, as "vocation diplomacy", "alma mater diplomacy" and "transit diplomacy"). Lee denied that such spending was nothing more than "foolish handouts", choosing instead to view it as an investment in Taiwan's international standing. As he said, "Our central bank has so much in foreign reserves, so we should just go out to establish relations."[35] This effort succeeded with some countries which Lee and/or other Taiwanese high officials visited in a "private capacity".

However, Taiwan eventually realized that it was more practical to work on big powers, especially the United States, than on small countries who had little influence in the international arena. Taiwan's U.N. bid, sponsored by some 20, mostly small, Central American and African countries, was defeated every year at the U.N. Assembly's steering committee without even being put on the agenda of the U.N. session.[36] Taiwan was therefore compelled to shift its focus to working on the United States, or its *Bei Lian* policy (linking the North, or seeking support from Western countries, especially the United States). This policy had, by 1995, been successful, culminating in Lee's visit to the United States in June 1995, but at the expense of its *Xi He* policy.

Taiwan's *Xi He* policy (peace or avoid tension with China in its west) was to try to avoid high tension and military confrontation with the mainland while pushing forward its "pragmatic diplomacy" to "expand its international living space". This policy worked relatively well up until Lee's United States visit in the sense that although Beijing had become increasingly suspicious of Lee's position on reunification, the final decision to take a hard position against him had not been made. Before Lee's United States visit, quite a number of Chinese officials and strategists opted for a no-tension approach to Taiwan.

Jiang's Eight-Point Proposal

Up until Lee's United States visit, Taiwan's *Xi He* policy had been fairly successful. Lee was still careful not to seriously disturb cross-strait relations. This was demonstrated in his response to Jiang's eight-point proposal.

On 30 January 1995, the eve of the Chinese Lunar New Year, Chinese President Jiang Zemin put forward a new proposal to Taiwan:

> Reunification does not mean that the mainland will swallow Taiwan up, nor does it mean that Taiwan will swallow up the mainland. After Taiwan's reunification with the mainland, its social and economic systems will not change, nor will its way of life and its non-governmental relations with foreign countries, which means that foreign investments in Taiwan and the non-governmental exchanges between Taiwan and other countries will not be affected. As a special administrative region, Taiwan will exercise a high degree of autonomy and enjoy legislative and independent judicial power, including that of final adjudication. It may also retain its armed forces and administer its party, governmental and military systems by itself. The central government will not station troops or send administrative personnel there. What is more, a number of posts in the central government will be made available to Taiwan.[37]

He then went on to make an eight-point proposal for reunification. In brief, the main points are:

1. Adhere to the principle of one China.
2. Oppose "two Chinas" or "one China, one Taiwan".
3. Negotiate on an equal footing to reach an agreement on officially ending cross-strait hostility.
4. Chinese should not fight fellow Chinese.
5. Promote cross-strait economic exchanges and co-operation, as well as the three direct links.
6. Promote the fine traditions of the Chinese culture.
7. All parties and personages of all circles in Taiwan are welcome to exchange views with the mainland on cross-strait relations.

8. Visits by leaders of the two sides should take place. The affairs of Chinese people should be handled by the Chinese themselves.[38]

While Deng's "one country, two systems" offer in the early 1980s emphasized *the status after Taiwan was reunified*, Jiang's eight-point proposal emphasized *the way* in which Taiwan would be reunified, such as the new proposal that officially ending the hostility would be the first step towards reunification and that leaders of the two sides should meet each other. This shows that China was more realistic than it had been in the 1980s and realized that Taiwan's reunification would take more time than it had originally expected.

Lee's Six-Point Reply

Taiwan's response to Jiang's eight-point proposal was a phased one. Premier Lien Chan and some other officials initially responded to some of Jiang's points on different occasions before President Lee Teng-hui finally raised a six-point proposal as a comprehensive reply on 8 April 1995. The six points were:

1. The two sides should pursue unification based on the reality that "the two sides are governed respectively by two governments".
2. Bilateral exchanges based on Chinese culture should be strengthened.
3. Trade and economic relations to develop a mutually beneficial and complementary relationship should be enchanced.
4. Both sides should join international organizations on an equal footing and leaders of both sides should meet in a natural setting.
5. The principle of resolving all disputes by peaceful means should be adhered to.
6. The two sides should jointly safeguard prosperity and should promote democracy in Hong Kong and Macao.[39]

Beijing was disappointed. The essence of Jiang's eight-point proposal had been an invitation to Taiwan to come to the negotiating table to discuss reunification. If negotiation on reunification was too difficult, they could first discuss "an agreement on officially ending the hostilities". Given the fact that Taiwan had in fact already announced an end to hostility in 1991 when it ended the Period of National Mobilization for Suppression of Communist Rebellion, a negotiation between the two sides to reach an official agreement on ending hostilities would be easier than one on reunification.

While Jiang stressed "negotiations on an equal footing" under the "one China" principle, suggesting political (but not sovereign) equality, Lee emphasized "joining international organizations on an equal footing", implying sovereign equality and demanding China's agreement to Taiwan becoming a U.N.

member. While Jiang proposed the setting up of the three direct links at the earliest possible date, Lee said more careful studies by the two sides were necessary on the grounds that trade and transport links were very complicated issues. Lee avoided "one China" principle that Jiang emphasized, but chose to place stress on "two governments".

Lee's six-point proposal was consistent with Jiang's eight-point proposal in other aspects. However, with the key issues unresolved, China was left feeling that Lee was just shadow-boxing.[40] Still, China remained calm at Lee's reply. However, Lee's surprise visit to the United States shortly afterwards was the last straw for Beijing.

The Last Straw: Lee's U.S. Visit

What Lee said and did during and after his United States visit put an end to any lingering hopes Beijing had that Lee would at least maintain the status quo in cross-strait relations. Beijing might have had a slightly different impression if Lee had kept a low profile during his United States visit and had taken meaningful steps to work towards the second round of the Wang-Koo meeting on his return. However, instead it saw an arrogant and willful Lee, playing into the hands of the United States to contain China.

Beijing now viewed Lee's constitutional reform, the direct presidential election and Taiwan's democratization in a different light. Lee's "reform" in Taiwan started with "revising the constitution", which meant revising the R.O.C. Constitution promulgated by the Kuomintang on 1 January 1947. Both "revisions of the constitution in procedures" in 1991 and "revisions of the constitution in substance" in 1992 were conducted in the name of "democracy", using the procedures of "democratization". However, Lee had yet to make the final step of revising the part of the constitution that did not allow the sovereignty of Taiwan to be decided by popular vote. This came, nevertheless, under the guise of the "direct presidential election". It was not simply a matter of giving legitimacy to Taiwan's "president" at home and abroad, it was the key to the final step in Lee's "constitutional reform". The revised constitution would make it legitimate to choose the means of the popular vote to change the sovereignty of Taiwan, i.e. to choose Taiwan's formal independence. If this happened, Taiwan would seek foreign protection of its independence through signing military treaties with foreign powers. A U.S. military presence on the island or a revived United States–Taiwan Defence Treaty, in whatever form, would be the worst case scenario for China. China's suspicions could not be allayed by Lee's repeated assurance that he was ultimately seeking unification with China.

Lee's United States visit also intensified the deep distrust between the two sides of the Strait. On the one hand, Taiwan was suspicious of China's intention behind its "one country, two systems" formula and accused it of lacking good will. On the other hand, Lee's United States visit also gave China grounds to believe that Taiwan had neither sincerity nor good will, but was playing political tricks. Lee's response to China's conciliatory eight-point proposal to improve relations had been inadequate and all the while he had been secretly preparing his provocative visit. Lee's right-hand man, Liu Tai-ying, had come to talk to Wang Daohan in the spring of 1995 with a lot of "well-intentioned gestures and assurances". However, at the same time he had covertly paid US$4.5 million to the U.S. lobbying firm Cassidy & Associates to ensure that the U.S. Congress voted in favour of Lee's visit. It appeared to Beijing that Taiwan had asked for Chinese sincerity and yet Taiwan itself had not been sincere at all. China believed that while professing that their goal was reunification, Lee had intended to steer the island towards formal independence. Chinese official journal *Liaowang* described Lee as "pretending to prepare to advance along one path while secretly going along another".[41] With this bitter lesson still fresh in mind, Beijing was sceptical when Taiwan sent Koo Chen-fu to Beijing in October 1998 to ask for Chinese sincerity before Taiwan could agree to make further efforts to improve cross-strait relations.

China's anger should also be understood in an international context. Already annoyed by the amount of "China-bashing" going on in the West and deeply suspicious that the United States had a strategy to contain its rise, China tended to see Lee's visit as another international conspiracy against it. It felt particularly annoyed that this time it was Taiwan that had helped the "international anti-China force" to contain its fellow Chinese on the mainland. And Taiwan did so even though Lee had just (in his six-point response in April 1995) stated that "Chinese should help Chinese".

Last but not least, Lee's United States visit intensified the internal strife within the Chinese leadership, which could ill afford to appear weak on the Taiwan issue.

Notes

1. This section is an adaptation of an article by the author: "China Eyes Taiwan: Why Is A Breakthrough So Difficult", *The Journal of Strategic Studies* 21, no. 1, (March 1998): 65-78. The author thanks *The Journal of Strategy Studies* for permission to use it in this book.
2. *Lien Ho Pao* [United Daily News] (Taipei) (overseas edition), 23 December 1995, p. 1, and 22 December 1995, p. 2. Also see "Taiwan: China Fires 3 Missiles Over Taiwan, Says Report", Reuters, 25 December 1995.
3. Zhang Shan and Xiao Weizhong, *Erzhi Taiduo* [Containing Taiwan's Independence] (Beijing: China Social Publishing House, 1996), pp. 168–169. See also Zheng Jian, *Gudao Chanmeng* [Lingering Dreams over the Isolated Island] (Beijing: *Qunzhong* Publishing House, 1997), p. 373.

4. Zhang and Xiao, op. cit., pp. 167–8.

5. Ibid. Chinese President Jiang Zemin also mentioned *"yi gang si mu"* and other proposed arrangements for Taiwan's reunification in his talk with the visiting former President of Taiwan's Tsinghua University, Shen Junshan, in the early 1990s. See *Jiushi Niendai* [The 1990s] (Hong Kong), no. 8 (1996), pp. 108–9.

6. *Lien Ho Pao* (overseas edition), 23 December 1995, p. 1; and 22 December 1995, p. 2. Also see "Taiwan: China Fires 3 Missiles Over Taiwan, Says Report", Reuters, 25 December 1995.

7. For example, see Shen Cheng, *Lian'an Mishi Miwenlu* [Stories of Secret Missions] (Taipei: Shangzhou Publishing House, 1995).

8. *Renmin Ribao,* 15 January 1988, p. 1.

9. Ibid., 9 July 1988, p. 1.

10. Wang Mingyi, *Lian'an Hetan* [Peace Talks Across the Taiwan Strait] (Taipei: Caixun Publication House, 1997), pp. 39–40.

11. Ibid., pp. 36–37.

12. Xu Jiatun is a former member of the Central Committee of the C.C.P. and a former director of the China Xinhua News Agency in Hong Kong, i.e. the informal Chinese "Ambassador" to Hong Kong and now self-exiled in the United States because of the Tiananmen incident of 1989. See Xu, *Xu Jiatun Xianggan Huiyilu* [Years in Hong Kong].

13. Ibid., pp. 328; 342.

14. Wang Mingyi, *Lian'an Hetan* [Peace Talks Across the Taiwan Strait], p. 17.

15. Ibid., pp. 18–20.

16. Ibid., pp. 61–72.

17. For these secret communications and Lee's remarks, see *Chung Kuo Shih Pao,* 19 July 2000, 20 July 2000 and 21 July 2000; *Lianhe Zaobao* 20 July 2000, p. 33; "Chinese and Taiwan Officials Had Secret Talks", *ST,* 20 July 2000; Catherine Sung, "Secret Envoy Story Called a China Ploy", *Taipei Times,* 21 July 2000; and "Historic 1993 China, Taiwan Talks Took Five Years of Groundwork", AFP, 19 July 2000.

18. The Lake Incident happened on 1 April 1994, when a tourist ship *Hairui* was robbed by a group of gangsters on Qiandao Lake [Lake of a Thousand Islands] in Zhejiang Province, China. The robbers set the ship on fire and 24 Taiwanese tourists died. Before China caught the criminals and executed them in mid-May 1994, Taiwan launched a big anti-China campaign. It claimed the incident was politically motivated and accused the P.L.A. of master-minding the murder and trying to cover it up. Taiwan's M.A.C. threatened to terminate all cultural and educational exchanges with China. The D.P.P. made good use of the incident to call for the abandonment of the "one China" policy, the freezing of all cross-strait talks and the declaration of Taiwan's independence. In an official press release from the presidential office, Lee Teng-hui accused the C.C.P. of being a group of "bandits" and "hooligans". See Zheng Jian, op. cit., pp. 471–2.

19. Ibid., p. 480.

20. Li Jiaquan, ed., *Li Denghui Zhuzheng Taiwan Zhihou* [After Lee Teng-hui Stepped into Power] (Beijing: Yanshi Publishing House, 1997).

21. *"Ziwo Biaobang, Yugai Mizhang"* [A Wild Bragger and A Poor Liar], *Renmin Ribao,* 6 August 1999, p. 4.

22. *"Bo Li Denghui de 'Lianguolun'"* [Refute Lee Teng-hui's 'Two states' Theory", *Renmin Ribao*, 10 August 1999.

23. *"Yige Zhongguo Shi Wuke Zhengbian De Shishi"* [One China is an Indisputable Fact], *Renmin Ribao*, 12 August 1999.

24. Ibid.

25. Ibid.

26. Ibid.

27. Taiwan uses the word "unification" while mainland China uses the word "reunification", although in Chinese they are the same word *"tong yi"*.

28. "Taipei Denies Policy Shift to 'Two Chinas'", Reuters, 23 November 1993.

29. "White Paper on Cross-Strait Relations", Reuters, 14 July 1994. Emphasis added.

30. *Chung Kuo Shih Pao* [China Times] (Taipei), 17 September 1993, p. 4.

31. It was first raised as *"Nan Lian* (linking south), *Bei Jin* (go north), *Xi He* (peace in south)", in Xiao Quan-zheng and Li Zi-wen (in Chinese *Pinyin*), *Taiwan de Yatai Zhanlue* [Taiwan's Asia-Pacific Strategy] (Taipei: Institute for National Policy Research, 1991). In May 1993, Taiwan's then foreign minister, Qian Fu, formally adopted the expression. See *Taiwan Yanjiu* [Taiwan Research] (Beijing), no. 2 (1997). However, in 1994, Siew Wan-chang revised it to the current expression.

32. *ST*, 25 September 1995, p. 25.

33. *ST*, 27 November 1995, p. 35.

34. United Press International (Taipei), 1 January 1993, quoted from Faust & Kornberg, *China in World Politics*, p. 43.

35. *ST*, 5 April 1995, p. 11.

36. *ST*, 22 September 1995, p. 3.

37. Xinhua, "China: President Jiang's Speech on Reunification", Reuters, 31 January 1995.

38. Ibid.

39. *Lien Ho Pao*, 4 April 1995.

40. For further reading regarding China's dissatisfaction with Lee's reply, see *Liaowang*, no. 23 (1995), pp. 19–20; and "Wen Wei Po Editorial on Lee Teng-hui's Reply to Jiang Zemin's Speech", Reuters, 13 April 1995.

41. *Liaowang*, no. 32 (1995), p. 9.

6

Bark without Bite

Despite China's strong displeasure over Lee's United States visit, its military exercises were only intended to be symbolic. To explain this, this chapter examines China's military capability, especially its air force, navy and ground troops, and its overall strategy before finally explaining the rationale behind its actions.

The P.L.A. Capability

In 1995, the P.L.A. had 2.2 million ground troops out of a total of about 3 million military personnel, up to 8,000 main battle tanks, 2,000 light tanks, 4,500 armoured infantry fighting vehicles and personnel carriers, 14,500 towed artillery pieces and 3,800 multiple-rocket launchers. The P.L.A. Navy had 52 submarines, 18 destroyers, 32 frigates and about 870 patrol and coastal vessels. Its naval air force had 855 shore-based combat aircraft and 68 armed helicopters. It also had a marine force of 5,000 and 25,000 coastal defence troops. The Chinese Air Force had about 4,970 combat aircraft. By comparison, in 1995, Taiwan had an army of 240,000 with 570 main battle tanks and 905 light tanks. Its navy consisted of 4 submarines, 22 destroyers, 16 frigates and 98 patrol and coastal vessels. The Taiwanese Air Force had 430 combat aircraft. If the P.L.A. controlled the air and sea, the massive P.L.A. ground forces would overwhelm Taiwan's troops. However, the question is, could the P.L.A. indeed gain such control?

Air Force

In 1995, the P.L.A. air force (P.L.A.A.F.) had the third largest fleet in the world, but most of their equipment was obsolete, largely consisting of outmoded combat aircraft such as the Nanchang J-5, Shenyang J-6, Xian J-7 and *Shenyang* J-8 fighters.

China made efforts to upgrade its outmoded fighters in the 1980s. However, the so-called "Peace Pearl" project undertaken with the United States in the 1980s for the improvement of the J-8II, which was a development of the J-7 (Mikjoyan MiG-21), proved to be economically costly (30–40 per cent higher than originally estimated) and technologically disappointing. China dropped the project before the Bush Administration's announcement that it would suspend the project following the Tiananmen incident of 1989. From then on, China looked to other sources to supply its J-8IIs.

Su-27 Fighters

China signed an agreement with Russia to buy Su-27s in 1992. The first 26 Su-27s were ready for combat in 1994 and were equipped with medium-range AA-10s active guidance air-to-air missiles and short-range AA-8 infra-red guided missiles (Taiwan claimed that instead of AA-10s, China's Su-27s were equipped with the more advanced R-77 medium-range missiles)[1].

The Su-27, known in the West as the "Flanker", was first deployed in 1984 in Russia and is now one of the mainstays of the Russian airforce. The 26 Su-27s deployed in Wuhu, Anhui Province at the end of 1994, could cover Taiwan with their 1,500-kilometre combat radius. However, in 1995, their threat to Taiwan was not too serious because they were small in number, their avionics were too conventional and the radar guidance system for their AA-10 intermediate-range surface-to-surface missiles was outmoded.

Later, 24 more Su-27 fighters were delivered (the deal apparently also included the AA-10 missiles), and deployed in Zhanjiang and Guangdong in the south of China. The new Su-27s were updated versions with improved avionics and a fire control radar capable of multi-target engagements (simultaneous scanning and tracking) as well as other combat support functions. However, the new batch was not delivered until 1996.

At the end of 1995, China signed a contract with Rosvooruzheniye (the main Russian dealer in arms and military hardware) to buy another 72 Su-27s as a prelude to licensing their production by Shenyang Aircraft Manufacturing Company. Moscow would also train the personnel.[2] However, the P.L.A.A.F. would not be able to upset the balance of power in the air for some time because it would take at least four or five years to get the production line operational. By that time Taiwan would have about 100 IDF [indigenously developed fighters] second-generation jet fighters,[3] 150 U.S. F-16A/B fighters and 60 French 2000-5 fighters equipped with Thomson-CSF RDY radar deal and intermediate-range missiles, which could match the Su-27s and other aeroplanes that China would have. Therefore, the Su-27s did not give the P.L.A.A.F. the air superiority over Taiwan in 1995–96 and nor would they ever.

J-10 Fighters

China was also developing its own J-10 as its next-generation fighter. Israel was reportedly covertly assisting in the development of this aircraft, especially with regard to avionics and design, drawing from technologies and expertise developed under the United States–Israel Lavi project which was shut down in 1987.

In 1987, out of fear that Israeli *"Lavi"* fighters would threaten the export market of its own F16 and F18 aircraft, the United States exerted pressure on Israel to suspend the development of this aircraft. After that, the project was reportedly taken over by China's Chengdu Aircraft Industry Company and Israeli Aircraft Industries carried on with the development of avionics equipment. Because neither China nor Israel was capable of developing the propulsion system required by the J-10, China decided in 1991 to incorporate the AI31F turbofans from Russia into the J-10s. This engine was also the propulsion system for the Su-27s.

The J-10 is a single-engine, single-seater tactical fighter, with a combat radius of 1,000 km. It is designed for point defensive warfare. Its radar and fire control system is the Israeli-made ELM-2021 system, which can simultaneously track six air targets and lock onto the four most-threatening targets for destruction.[4]

The multi-role J-10, optimized for interception, would provide an effective high-end component alongside the P.L.A.A.F.'s Su-27s and J-8II interceptors. The entire system of J-10s could match that of the *Mirage* 2000-5 fighters, which Taiwan purchased from France.[5]

The J-10s would be China's first military aircraft using widened static stability active control design and combat damage tolerance design. Compared with the J-6 and J-7 fighters now in service in the Chinese air force, the technology of the F-10s, using a large amount of advanced aerospace technology, would be almost two generations ahead.[6]

However, the development of the J-10s has not been smooth. There have been reports of several crashes during test flights. Even if China can completely resolve the problem of the J-10 fighter's engine installation, perhaps by using some of the 40 Saturn AL-31F engines imported from Russia in 1992 as spares for the Su-27, it is not likely to achieve a significant output for some years to come.[7] So, in 1995, this did not pose a threat to Taiwan.

FC-1 Fighters

The P.L.A.A.F. has designated the Su-27 and the J-10 as their new generation main fighter aircraft. However, as a supplement, China's Chengdu Aircraft Industry Company co-operated with Pakistan's Aviation Integrated Company and Russia's Mikoyan Aero-Science Production Group in the development of the FC-1 as a high-performance, low-cost, lightweight multipurpose fighter.

The FC-I was the product of a Mikoyan programme to develop an F-16-like, single-engine version of the MiG-29, known in the mid-1980s as the MiG-33. The MiG-33 design, rejected by the Soviet Air Force, became the central building block of the FC-1. This lightweight fighter makes use of the best available technology on the world market with a large part of the avionics being solicited from Europe and Israel. The FC-1 fills the gap left by the U.S. decision not to deliver F-16 fighters to Pakistan because of the latter's nuclear programme. According to Chinese sources, the aircraft is due to enter service at the turn of the century,[8] so it had not entered into the picture in 1995.

As for China's bombers, from the early 1980s, the Xi'an Aircraft Industry Company began to use home-made MK-20 engines and advanced composite materials to improve the H-7 and H-6 and equip them with terrain-tracking radar and electronic counter-measure equipment in the hope of replacing the outmoded H-5 bombers and A5 attack planes. The design was completed by Xi'an Aircraft Design and Research Institute in the late 1980s. The improved H-7, now called FBC-1 or Flying Leopard [*fei bao*], was designed as a fighter/bomber for emergencies in the South China Sea with a combat radius of 1,600 kilometres, suitable for aircraft carriers. It can carry 13 air-to-air missiles or air-to-surface missiles and it is equipped with laser-guided bombs. At the time of the Taiwan Strait Crisis of 1995–96, the P.L.A. Navy was already equipped with some FBC-1s. However, China did not publicize its FBC-1 until the Zhuhai (China) Air Show in mid-November 1998.[9]

As the J-10 will be a fighter-bomber with a maximum bomb-carrying capacity of 6.8 metric tonnes, and the Su-27 also has tremendous air-to-ground attack capabilities and a bomb-carrying capacity of nearly 6.5 metric tonnes,[10] the FBC-1 may not be the main force of fighter/bombers in China's future airforce.

By early 1996, the most advanced and operational aircraft in the P.L.A.A.F. were J-8IIs, Su-27s and a few FBC-1s. The supersonic J-8IIM, an updated version of the J-8II, made by the Shenyang Aircraft Industrial (Group) Company made its initial flight, a successful one, on 19 April 1996.[11] Other fighters, like the J-10 and the FC-1, had not yet entered service. China started negotiations for the purchase of Sukhoi-30 MKK warplanes in 1995 and reached an outline agreement for 60 of them only in 1999.[12] The Zhuhai Air Show in November 1998 showed that China's aircraft were still about 15 years, or one generation, behind the rest of the world.

Navy

The P.L.A. Navy still lags behind many other powers. China has built some new warships such as a new class of destroyer (*Luhu*, or Type 052), upgraded versions of the *Luda* class destroyers, a new class of missile frigates (*Jianwei*), and continues to purchase Russian warships. However, there has been neither a major breakthrough in China's development of warships nor in its purchase of them from foreign sources.

Destroyers

By 1996, China had 18 destroyers, among them only one 4,200-tonne *Luhu* class destroyer carrying eight *Exocet*-derivative *Eagle Strike* anti-ship missile launchers, and only two 3,250-tonne upgraded *Luda* class destroyers also with eight *Eagle Strike* launchers.

Submarines

China used to have nearly 100 conventional submarines. Over the last few years it has streamlined its submarine force and now has about 54 upgraded ones. However, most of them have to surface to fire anti-ship missiles while submarines of many other navies can fire missiles submerged.

The P.L.A. Navy's new *Song* (*Wuhan-C*) submarine programme, launched in 1994, now appears more advanced than it did at first. However, the first unit was not operational in 1995. The Navy's nuclear submarines, i.e. nuclear-powered attack submarines (SSNs) and the nuclear-powered ballistic missile submarines (SSBNs), lack the latest technology. Its sole nuclear ballistic missile-firing submarine was not operational because of design faults. There is no indication that any new nuclear submarines are being constructed. Russia is reportedly selling submarine-launched wake-homing and wire-guided torpedoes to China and may, in the future, sell submarine-launched cruise missiles.[13] This remains uncertain.

The recent Chinese purchase of four Russian *Kilo*-submarines and two Russian *Sovremenny* class destroyers may have some implications. In early 1996, China had just bought two *Kilo*-class 877EKM-type submarines from Russia, one of which served in the East China Sea Fleet and the other in the North China Fleet. It has another two *Kilo*-class 636-type submarines.[14]

The 877EKM is one of the types of *Kilo*-class submarines that are built especially for foreign sale. They are inferior to the 636 type of *Kilo*-class submarines which the Russian navy uses for its depth capabilities and speed. Since the 636-type submarine is very quiet, Taiwan's anti-submarine force, which is mainly composed of destroyers, patrol escorts and anti-submarine aircraft with a limited radius, would be stretched.[15]

The Russian *Sovremenny* class destroyer, which is described by the U.S. Department of Defence as one of the most technologically-advanced naval warships ever produced in Russia, is primarily a surface strike combatant. It is normally armed with eight launchers for the sea-skimming supersonic medium-range SS-N-22 "Sunburn" surface-to-surface missile (SSM), which has a range of 150km, two SA-N-17 "Grizzly" surface-to-air missile launchers, and two twin 130mm/70 guns. The missile has a down-link terminal seeker that can be programmed to manoeuvre and select a carrier in a naval battle group. The missile is designed specifically to get through a U.S. Navy destroyer screen and attack a carrier. This warship is much bigger, more sophisticated and much more heavily armed than China's own *Luhu* class destroyer, China's latest and largest surface combatant. The purchase of two *Sovremenny* class destroyers was proposed in 1994 and finalized only in late December 1996 during a visit to Moscow by Chinese Premier Li Peng.[16]

So, in 1996, the P.L.A. Navy did not have clear technological superiority. Its most advanced warships, the two Russian destroyers and four Russian *Kilo*-submarines had either not been delivered or were not fully combat ready.

However, although the P.L.A. air and naval forces were not up to world standards in 1995, Taiwan was also far from having control of air and sea over the Strait, at least before the delivery of the U.S. F-16s, the French *Mirage* 2000-5s and the French *La Fayette*-class frigates in 1996. Although the majority of the P.L.A.A.F. fighters were obsolete in early 1996, China has one of the largest air forces in the world with about 5,000 combat aircraft, and has the capability of penetrating and destroying Taiwan's air defence systems, and substantially neutralizing Taiwan's air force by attrition in an all-out war. In 1996 Taiwan's air force was also weak with outmoded aircraft. It only had about 350 fighter/fighter-bombers (275 Northrop F-5 *Freedom* Fighters, 50 Lockheed F-104 *Starfighters*, and 30-40 *IDFs*).

If Taiwan's airforce were substantially neutralized, the delicate naval balance across the Strait would change.

Missiles

In 1995-96, the P.L.A. missiles could neutralize Taiwan's air defence system and military harbours, and tilt the air and naval balance across the Strait. Taiwan could not effectively intercept the P.L.A. missiles.

The high accuracy of China's missiles was evident in its "exercises" in March 1996, in which none of the missiles launched missed their targets. The missiles launched were M-9s, which, although essentially Russian *Scud* missiles, had been upgraded by the Chinese so that they were much more accurate and advanced.

China used to test its missiles on land. However, over the last few years, the P.L.A. has been actively studying hydrography, topography, terrain, weather and water conditions in and near Taiwan in order to upgrade the target accuracy of its missiles firing over sea. In the March 1996 exercises, a "new device" was placed in the missiles which increases their accuracy. These military drills, according to one Chinese source, laid bare the blind spots in Taiwan's "strong net system".[17]

In early 1996, Taiwan's air defence system could not provide an effective protection against China's missiles. In 1992, the U.S. government notified Congress of its plan to sell "hardware, components and technologies to assist Taiwan in developing locally the Modified Air Defence Systems (M.A.D.S.)". Taiwan signed an NT$15 billion contract with Massachusetts-based Raytheon Corporation in 1994 to buy 100 units, based on the company's *Patriot* missile system. Raytheon was to provide M.A.D.S. firing units, missiles and related hardware as well as logistics, spare parts, installation assistance and training.[18] Following China's missile tests in 1995–96, Taiwan was worried enough to spend over US$385 million to deploy 200 fourth-generation *Patriot* missiles.[19] However, the interception rate of *Patriots* turned out to be only slightly over 20 per cent, even as low as 9 per cent according to another report,[20] instead of more than 90 per cent claimed during the Gulf War. Despite recent upgrading, its real interception rates, although they remain secret, should not be exaggerated.

Taiwan was reportedly seeking to join the U.S. Theatre Missile Defence (T.M.D.) programme. T.M.D. was a pared-down version of the Strategic Defence Initiative (S.D.I.) or "Star Wars" developed during the term of former U.S. President Ronald Reagan[21] — a future network of satellites and missile batteries to detect, track and destroy incoming ballistic missiles. However, the interception rate of T.M.D. still remained a big question, and by 1996 was still far from being completed. Taiwan was vulnerable to the P.L.A. missiles in early 1996 and would likely remain so for some time.

China's M-9 missile has a range of close to 400 miles and can carry a warhead of 1,100 lbs. Its trajectory is too flat and its flight time too short for *Patriots* to cope with. It is much more sophisticated than Iraq's *Scud* missiles. During the Gulf War, Iraq's *Scud* missiles had to fly over 600–1000 km, or about 10 minutes, to hit their targets. But it would take only a few dozen seconds for China's missiles to fly across the Taiwan Strait, making them virtually impossible for *Patriots* to intercept. Unlike the *Scud* missiles used by Iraq in the 1991 Gulf War, the warhead and body of China's M-missiles could separate when approaching the target. This makes interception difficult because the warhead is about one tenth of the whole missile.[22]

To what extent could the P.L.A.'s missiles neutralize Taiwan's air defence system built underground inside its northeast mountains of Hualien? Theoretically, China could use its tactical nuclear weapons to completely wipe out Taiwan's air defence system. In reality, this is not likely to happen. Over the past few years China has put a lot of effort into developing non-nuclear but large-scale and in-depth explosives. P.L.A. specialists believe that like the United States who used two cruise missiles (one following the other) to destroyed Iraqi underground installations in the 1991 Gulf War, China also has the same capability to destroy the hangars or Hardened Aircraft Shelters in Taiwan's Hualien mountains.[23] These hangars could probably not withstand the impact of a 250 kilogram warhead and most of China's missiles could carry a warhead of well over this weight. Another option would be to disable the runways outside these hangars and simultaneously neutralize Taiwan's ten major military airfields, by direct missile hits or thousands of electronic-magnetic mines. Even a small M-7 or M-9 missile could carry hundreds of these mines. If thousands of these mines were dropped on the runways, it would take a long time to clear them, given Taiwan's mining-sweeping capability. In the past, China produced a very large number of *Hongjian*-2 (Red Arrow-2) missiles, which could easily be upgraded to M-7 missiles for such a purpose, and at very low cost.

This action (missile attacks and mining) would be immediately followed by an overwhelming number of fighters and fighter bombers to saturate Taiwan's air defence system and prevent repair of the runways (most of Taiwan's airports are within 5 kilometres of the coast and would therefore be within easy range of the second wave of attacks by P.L.A. warships). What remained of Taiwan's aircraft would soon be grounded, putting Taiwan's airforce at a great disadvantage.

Although Taiwan is rumoured to have built some of its highways of high enough quality to use as runways for its aeroplanes in wartime, these would be ineffective without the ground service and support necessary for modern fighters. For example, one F-16 needs at least 6 tonnes of fuel for each take-off. It needs ground support while in the air and ground services for continuous missions. Moreover, any hidden aircraft, airport or runway if discovered would be destroyed or sabotaged by electronic magnetic mines dropped either by missiles or bombers. And any surviving fighters would be defenceless against a large-scale air attack by the P.L.A.A.F.

Without proper air cover and with its military harbours neutralized by China's missile attacks followed by aerial assaults, Taiwan's anti-submarine capability and naval defence would be seriously undermined. Taiwan's size does not give it enough "strategic depth" for a sustained all-out war. As a small island, its entire coastline would be a frontier and it lacks a hinterland to provide strong logistics and support for its troops and air and naval forces. If Taiwan's air defence system were to be neutralized, the whole island, especially the missile and gun batteries, would then be covered with heavy aerial and naval bombardments.

While many Western military officials dismissed China's capability of invading Taiwan in 1995–96 my impression from interviews with Chinese military specialists was that China was confident about this. The National People's Congress chairman, Qiao Shi, told a visiting professor from Georgetown University, "We know Taiwan's military very well, its quality and weaponry. If we have to go to war, unfortunately, Taiwan will be in a disadvantageous position."[24] A P.L.A. senior officer said in an internal briefing that the P.L.A. air and missile forces had the ability to knock out Taiwan's total air defence facilities in 24 hours. "Taiwan generals have exaggerated their powers manyfold, while the outside world has underestimated our ability."[25]

It is possible that the P.L.A. did not fully demonstrate their sophisticated weapons during the March 1996 military exercises as Beijing was divided about whether adopting a low profile or showing off its power was the best means of achieving China's objectives. One group, including President Jiang Zemin and top officials, urged the P.L.A. to be cautious in demonstrating its might so as not to create anxiety in the United States, Japan and other Asia-Pacific countries and nudge China's neighbours into an arms race. The other group, i.e. individual officers, felt that the P.L.A. should flex its muscles publicly to strike fear into the hearts of pro-independence elements in Taiwan as well as China's potential adversaries.[26]

It is also possible that some people chose to stress the P.L.A.'s weak points to help stabilize Taiwan's political morale and social stability in 1995–96. Only one year after the crisis, the world began to re-assess China's missile capability. For example, *Jane's Defence Weekly* says that China has a large and well-established infrastructure and technology to develop and produce short-and medium-range missiles. The significant quantities of missiles produced by China could overwhelm any T.M.D. capability planned for U.S. allies in East Asia and fundamentally alter regional calculations of the balance of power.[27] According to a U.S. Department of Defence report, China will have the industrial capacity to produce as many as 1,000 ballistic missiles over the next decade. "Coupled with improved targeting and command and control networks, it is clear the Chinese are working to develop the ability not only to saturate the air defences of Taiwan or other nations, but the fleet air defences of the U.S. Navy."[28]

What was little known in early 1996 was that China already had its own cruise missiles but chose not to "test" them in the exercises in March 1996. These cruise missiles, based on differential G.P.S. (Global Positioning System), are very accurate and difficult to intercept. According to the *Independence Post* in 1998, the updated missile is capable of turning direction three times at angles greater than 35 degrees and at pre-set points before hitting its target. This indicates that it partially out-performs the *Tomahawk* cruise missile now being used by the United States army.[29] According to Hong Kong's *Sing Tao Daily* in 1999, China's cruise missile, with a range of 2,000 km, is capable of hitting a target accurately to within 5 metres (China Academy of Science later confirmed this [30]). The Chinese military was deeply concerned when the United States began to equip its military with *Tomahawk* cruise missiles in the late 1970s. It thus set up its own cruise missile research and development institute, and developed not only cruise missiles similar to the U.S. *Tomahawk* cruise missiles but also an anti-radiation missile that was as good as the U.S. *Harm* missile, powerful enough to penetrate Taiwan's air defence system.[31]

The strength of the P.L.A. missiles was made evident during the Jiang-Clinton summit in October 1997 and U.S. Defence Secretary William Cohen's visit to China in January 1998, when Washington exerted a lot of pressure on Beijing not to sell its C-801 and C-802 cruise missiles and their production technology to Iran for shipping safety in the Hormuz Strait. U.S. officials even linked this promise to President Clinton's planned visit to Beijing for the second summit in June 1998. It is clear that Washington would not have driven such a hard bargain if Chinese missiles were not to be taken seriously.

Thus it can be concluded that in early 1996, the P.L.A. did have leverage over Taiwan, although the cost of a full and successful P.L.A. invasion would have been huge as air and sea lift capacity was limited and it lacked sophisticated co-ordination of these three services for landing.

Taiwan's Vulnerabilities

Taiwan was vulnerable at the time of China's military exercises. It had no significant means of military retaliation against China. For one thing, the United States did not sell Taiwan offensive weapons, and for another, although Taiwan had a programme to develop nuclear weapons (the Chung-shan Institute of Science and Technology was founded for that purpose) in the late 1980s, under U.S. pressure Taiwan decided to join the nuclear non-proliferation treaty and scrapped its nuclear weapons programme.[32]

Taiwan also had a programme for developing mid-range missiles called the Pegasus Project[33] which it had to give up under U.S. pressure. Instead Taiwan has concentrated on research for surface-to-air missiles.[34] Since the 1980s, Taiwan has developed the anti-ship missiles *Hsiung Feng* I and II, the air-to-air *Sky Sword* I and II and the *Sky Bow*. However, these are short range missiles, e.g. the *Hsiung Feng* anti-ship missiles have a range of 170 kilometres, and would not be able to reach the mainland.

Taiwan had about 30 *IDFs* by the end of 1995. Theoretically, an *IDF* could fly up to 600 miles or 1,100 kilometres, within reach of Wuhan City in Hubei Province. In practice it would have been difficult. China not only had fighters but also surface-to-air missiles positioned all the way from the coast facing Taiwan to its hinterland to intercept incoming *IDFs*.

According to the Chinese press in 1996, China already had its own "*Patriot*" missile called the FM-80 surface-to-air missile. It was developed by China

Changfeng Company of Science, Technology and Industry, and described as effective for the protection of airports, oil-fields and against aircraft and missiles of all kinds, as well as being all-weather with both low and super low range (below 30 metres). Its anti-air missile system had a quick reaction time (6 seconds) as well as high accuracy (80 per cent), high mobility, high automation and easy maintenance.[35] The excellent performance of the missile was also written about in other Chinese journals where its test accuracy was reported to be as high as 100 per cent.[36] The performance was enhanced following the delivery of five sets of Russian S300PMU-1 surface-to-air missiles to China.[37] Though the S300PMU-1 had not been tested on a real battlefield, it was reported to be the most advanced surface-to-air intercept missile whose capabilities were generally similar to those of the U.S. *"Patriot"* missile, as well as several more advanced functions.[38] China's anti-air missiles could have been further improved with the reported procurement of U.S. *Patriot* missile technology.[39] China also further upgraded its other anti-air missiles including *Hongqi* 61 and *Feimeng* 80 and its shoulder-launched surface-to-air missile *Hongying* 5A.

If any *IDF* fighter did reach Wuhan, it would only be able to stay there for at the most three minutes carrying four short-range missiles such as the air-to-air *Sky Sword* missiles which would cause limited damage. If it carried bombs its flight range would be much shorter.

Taiwan's navy is mainly defensive. It operates four submarines, comprising two modified *Zwaardvis*-class Dutch submarines, delivered in 1982, and two World War II-era U.S. submarines used only for training. The submarines could easily be located and destroyed.

Economic and Social Vulnerabilities

Without international support, Taiwan is economically and socially vulnerable. Taiwan's trade accounted for 85 per cent of its GNP in 1994.[40] As an island with few natural resources of its own, Taiwan relies heavily on foreign trade for its raw materials. Moreover, 99.5 per cent of imports depend on sea transportation, which is vulnerable. Coal, iron ore, oil and grain are all imported by sea. Taking 1994 as an example, Taiwan imported by sea 38.77 million tonnes of oil and natural gas, 24.48 million tonnes of coal, 8.47 million tonnes of minerals, 8.37 million tonnes of iron and steel, 6.72 million tonnes of iron ore, 2.70 million tonnes of cement, 5.45 million tonnes of corn, 2.37 million tonnes of soy beans, 1.23 million tonnes of wheat and barley, 4.08 million tonnes of timber, 0.68 million tonnes of industrial salt and 6.825 million containers.[41] Without the U.S. backing of Taiwan, the P.L.A. Navy could easily threaten Taiwan's vulnerable sea-lanes, either around the island or anywhere along its sea transportation routes. The island does not have enough "economic strategic depth". Taiwan's economy is heavily centred in a few big cities along its coast, with no supporting hinterland, making it vulnerable to P.L.A. air and sea attacks.

In early 1996, China was among Taiwan's four biggest trading partners (the others were the United States, Japan and Hong Kong) and a major source of Taiwan's trade surplus. Taiwan's trade with China accounted for 9.9 per cent of the island's total trade. It was estimated that if there was a termination of cross-strait trade and other economic links in early 1996, Taiwan's annual growth rate would be reduced by nearly 2 per cent. Taiwan's dependence on China has increased over the years, and with it, its vulnerability. By mid-1999, cross-strait trade over the previous 20 years totalled US$147.6 billion. Over the same period, the number of Taiwanese-funded companies in China had reached 42,653, involving capital commitments of US$42.8 billion and actual investment of US$22.6 billion. China had become, by 1999, Taiwan's second largest export market and third biggest trading partner. If cross-strait trade and economic links were cut off at this point in time, it would still, according to China's Minister for Foreign Trade and Economic Co-operation (Moftec), Shi Guangsheng, shave one or two percentage points off Taiwan's economic growth rate.[42] Also, in the past 20 years, Taiwan has accumulated more than US$90 billion profit in this cross-strait trade, which accounts for a large part of its foreign currency reserves.[43] Table 1 shows Taiwan's dependence on its trade with China.

Taiwan's economy could ill-afford a confidence crisis in 1995. Immediately after China launched its first missile tests near Taiwan in August 1995, Taiwan's stock markets tumbled to a two-year low. According to Taiwan's statistics bureau, due to tensions with China, the island's GDP growth was 4.86 per cent for the fourth quarter of 1995, down from an officially predicted 6.34 per cent and down from 7 per cent in 1994. Its stock market fell 27 per cent in 1995, making it the worst performing major market in Asia. By February 1996, it had fallen by another 7 per cent.[44] Taiwan's trade deficit for the first quarter of 1996 reached US$6 billion. Its economic growth in the same period was only 5.7 per cent, failing to reach the estimated lowest growth rate of 6 per cent.[45]

In 1996, after a Hong Kong newspaper reported that Beijing would announce a timetable for recovering Taiwan, investors on the Taiwan stock market sold shares in a panic. The index dropped 169.23 points or 3.48 per cent to 4,692.30, its lowest level since 25 November 1995.[46]

With China's military exercises and missile tests conducted near Taiwan, capital flow out of Taiwan surged, suggesting a confidence crisis. Taiwan's foreign deposits totalled US$100.4 billion at the end of the second quarter of 1995, but had shrunk by US$18.0 billion to US$82.4 billion by the end of the first quarter of 1996.[47] According to Taiwan's Chung Hua Institution for Economic Research, the military exercises and missile tests China held from 1995 to 1996 cost Taiwan a staggering US$23 billion. "Within half a month of

Table 1   Taiwan's Trade Surplus

Year	Total Trade Surplus (billion US dollars)	Percentage from Chinese mainland
1990	12.5	56.9
1991	13.3	78.5
1992	9.5	143.8
1993	8.0	212.5
1994	7.7	256.3
1995	8.1	299.1
1996	13.6	170.7
1997	7.6	243.9
1998*	5.5	214.3

*January to September 1998.
Sources: *Nian'an Zhongyao Jingji Tongji Shubao* [Bulletin of Important Economic Figures Across the Strait], Mainland Affairs Council, Taipei, *http://www.mac.gov.tw,* 21 November 1998.

the start of the cross-strait crisis, the stock index fell 1,000 points, the Taiwan Dollar saw a drop of NT$1.50 against the U.S. Dollar".[48]

It was obvious that fewer and fewer people were willing to enter the market with the constant threat from China and all the resultant uncertainties. Protracted tension would affect Taiwan's economy more severely than it would China's. From the second half of 1995 to early 1996 the military tension did not have a clear impact on China's economy, not even in Fujian Province opposite Taiwan where the P.L.A. had concentrated 150,000 troops to conduct military exercises.

Theoretically speaking, Taiwan could use its investments in China as leverage. However, in practice, this would be rather limited or even counterproductive. First, withdrawing all its investment would make Beijing less hesitant about going all out to use force. Second, terminating all economic relations with China could not be done overnight and would cost Taiwan more. A democracy like Taiwan could not force its 25,000 businessmen out of China. By cutting off economic ties and therefore inviting constant tension across the Strait, Taiwan's grand design to engineer itself into an Asia-Pacific operation centre would become an unobtainable dream.

Taiwan's economic vulnerability in turn affected its social vulnerability. According to Taiwan's Directorate General of Budget, Accounting and Statistics, the number of Taiwanese emigrating soared by 85 per cent in 1995. A total of 78,000 Taiwanese emigrated in 1995, compared with 42,000 people in 1994. Some 35,000 people flocked to immigration fairs held in the island's two largest cities, Taipei and Kaohsiung, in March 1996 when Beijing started the military exercises and missile tests.[49] In addition to transferring their bank deposits abroad or into foreign currencies, many Taiwanese business executives embarked on "business inspection tours" abroad. Many foreign buyers either cancelled or postponed their scheduled trips to visit suppliers in Taiwan.

The fact that Taiwan did not collapse economically and socially during the Strait Crisis of 1995–96 does not rule out its vulnerabilities. China was only sabre-rattling that time. Should China determine to go to war with Taiwan, or if a real military clash took place, or an air and naval blockade was actually attempted, its effect on Taiwan would be devastating.

Over and above any economic hardship such a situation would impose on the people of Taiwan, there are also cracks in the social fabric which could be exacerbated. There are deep-rooted conflicts potentially between various social groups, such as between the native Taiwanese and *waishengren* (those from mainland China or non-natives), or between those for Taiwan's independence and those for its reunification. Although these are not serious conflicts at the moment, they could be intensified by changes in the status quo.

Military Options

This section will discuss China's military options in 1995-96 for the purpose of explaining in the following section the rationale behind China's decision not to seek military occupation or even a small-scale military clash with Taiwan.

China's options included, first, a full-scale military invasion. As discussed above, this would have been very costly, though not impossible if China were willing to pay the price. A second option would have been missile, air force and naval attacks and bombardments without invasion. Third, a partial or full sea-air blockade supported by missiles. Fourth, an "accidental" exchange of fire which would escalate tension. Fifth, permanent or temporary seizure of some of Taiwan's offshore islands near China, such as Jinmen, Mazu, Tatan, Erhtan, Wuchiu and Tungyin, which are very vulnerable to a combined amphibious and aerial attack. Sixth, psychological warfare. This might include, for example, public threats to attack strategic locations, warning third countries away from Taiwanese waters or air space, missile tests, provocative military exercises, ship movements, harassing fishing boats and commercial vessels, increased piracy and threats to ship and aircraft movement, public threats to impose a sea-air blockade. Even if China only chose to continue to hold the kind of military exercises undertaken in 1995–96, international confidence for investment in and trade with Taiwan would continue to deteriorate and economic costs such as freight insurance would increase, severely affecting Taiwan's economy. Of course, none of these options were without some cost to China.

It was not difficult to find "excuses" to take action. The most obvious were fishing disputes and territorial disputes. There had been numerous fishing disputes since early 1995 in which the Taiwanese navy had fired on or shelled Chinese fishing vessels encroaching on its waters. In October 1995, Beijing accused Taiwan's military of killing nearly 50 mainland fishermen over the previous three years and of beating up many more who had been apprehended for "poaching" in Taiwan's waters. No incidents took place for a while after China's missile "tests" in July 1995. However, in November 1995 things began to stir again. In December 1995, China's A.R.A.T.S. sent a letter to Taiwan's S.E.F. protesting recent incidents in which Taiwanese troops fired upon and arrested mainland fishermen. The letter demanded that Taiwan immediately stop such action, return the detained fishermen and fishing vessels and confiscated property as soon as possible and compensate for losses.

On their part, Taiwan accused Chinese fishermen of over-fishing near Jinmen, Mazu and Penghu, exhausting the fish stock in the offshore islands. Local officials threatened to seize the Chinese fishing boats. Taiwan claimed that since 1994 it had instructed its navy and coastal patrol forces to step up patrols in the Penghu area to deter Chinese fishing boats from operating in the off-limit waters around Penghu.[50] Taiwan patrol boats expelled 179 Chinese fishing boats in 1992. The number surged to 1,200 in 1993, and 2,000 in 1994.[51] At the same time, Chinese fishing vessels reportedly hijacked Taiwanese fishing boats, with Taiwanese police and navy jointly launching rescue operations.

Taiwan insisted that China's fishing boats should not trespass in waters demarcated by Taiwan as "forbidden" or "restricted" areas, or they would be expelled. However, Chinese fishermen considered these waters Chinese waters, especially the waters around the off-shore islands within 12 nautical miles of China's territorial waters, which were occupied by Taiwanese troops. In fact, China reaffirmed on 15 May 1996 that four of Taiwan's island fortresses fall within its waters. Before the announcement, the two sides of the Taiwan Strait had a tacit understanding that the four islands belonged to Taipei despite the fact that they were in China's waters. The two sides had an imaginary central line dividing the Taiwan Strait. Although the narrowest gap between Jinmen and the mainland is only 2.3 km, the two sides kept to their own sides of the imaginary central dividing line. Obviously, this announcement was intended to put pressure on Taiwan by highlighting that this issue could be used by Beijing to justify its actions.

In early 1996, this problem of overlapping boundaries had not been resolved. Taiwan had not yet made clear its boundary line through the waters between the two sides of the Taiwan Strait and had not yet passed its 12-nautical-mile territorial waters law. If China had flooded these waters with hundreds of sampans and motorboats carrying out fishing operations, driving out these fishermen without clashes and bloodshed would have created a big problem for Taiwan if it had wanted to avoid provoking China.

Other excuses China could have used in the 1995–96 Strait Crisis and may use in future include Taiwan's attitude to chemical weapons, nuclear weapons, and mid-and-long range missiles. For example, although it claimed to abide by the Chemical Weapons Convention rules, Taiwan was not a signatory to the U.N. Chemical Weapons Convention (C.W.C.) and had refused to allow any international chemical weapons inspections. Its Defence Ministry stated: "We will by no means manufacture, nor will we own, chemical weapons."[52] However, this does not rule out the possibility of Taiwan "renting", "leasing" or storing chemical weapons. C.W.C. officials have reportedly voiced concern about Taiwan in the area of chemical weapons.[53]

Taiwan's policy on chemical weapons could be used by China to justify military action. China could insist on an arms inspection, like the United States did to Iraq after the Gulf War of 1991, on the grounds that Taiwan may be challenging the C.W.C. For the same reason, Taiwan's position on nuclear weapons and mid-and long-range missiles could also be used by China to justify forced arms inspections and military action, with the claim that Taiwan is challenging international conventions and United States–China agreements. This point will be dealt with in detail in Chapters 7 & 9.

Why Not Attack?

However, none of the above-mentioned scenarios took place, not even an "accidental" exchange of fire to escalate tension and make use of it. Why? This had much to do China's overall strategy.

China was faced with a dilemma: it believed that if it did not react strongly, Taiwan would drift faster beyond its control. However, if it over-reacted, this would make more of the Taiwan issue than China was prepared for at the time, and jeopardize its overall agenda which prioritized modernization.

China's overall development strategy is to concentrate on its modernization to build itself into a stronger power in the twenty-first century. Not wanting to be distracted from this endeavour, China has been keeping a low profile to avoid international and regional confrontation. The flare-up of the Taiwan issue was something China had hoped to avoid, at least at that moment. Lee Teng-hui's United States visit forced China into making a response. However, China's strong response was intended to stop or slow down what it saw as a dangerous development of the Taiwan issue. It hoped that a particularly forceful response would quieten the Taiwan issue for some time so that it could concentrate on modernization. From the very beginning of the crisis, it had no intention of using force to bring about immediate reunification.

Militarily, China had an edge over Taiwan in early 1996. But because its military edge was not that great, it served China only as a means of flexing its muscles. The cost of military occupation would be very high, even if it was successful. It has long been China's objective to turn Taiwan into its asset, and military action would be more likely to turn Taiwan into a liability. Even small-scale military clashes, short of a full military occupation, would prolong the tension and make the situation more unpredictable and difficult to control. This was also something Beijing wanted to avoid.

Military confrontation would also affect a smooth take-over of Hong Kong in July 1997. During the cross-strait tensions of 1995–96, President Jiang Zemin reportedly kept reminding the P.L.A. that Hong Kong and Macao's reunification with China would be threatened if the P.L.A. moved on Taiwan before the end of the century.[54] He even publicly stated in 1996 that the Taiwan issue should not be tackled until Beijing resumed sovereignty over Hong Kong and Macao.[55]

In my interviews, many Chinese strategists noted that Lee's United States visit and his presidential election was not worth a "complete military showdown". There were still several steps before Taiwan could declare formal independence, such as revising its constitution which was still a legal obstacle to Taiwan's formal independence. Beijing was therefore not aiming at military occupation, but raising the hurdle for Taiwan's independence. Chinese strategists in general believed that so long as China could slow down Taiwan's drift towards independence, it would have much more leverage over Taiwan and achieve reunification at a much lower cost in the next century.

Actually, at the height of the crisis, the P.L.A. only assembled in 150,000 troops along the coast facing Taiwan and mobilized only a small portion of them in the military exercises. Taiwan had a garrison of four divisions, or 50,000 troops, on Jinmen and one division, or 12,000–15,000 troops, on Mazu. This was not sufficient for an invasion of even Jinmen and Mazu, let alone Taiwan.

China was also aware that if Taiwan had not formally declared independence, excessive military action on its part would be firmly opposed by the international community. The potential U.S. involvement was another factor. A surprise overnight military solution of the Taiwan issue by the P.L.A. might provoke a less severe U.S. response than anticipated and the situation would perhaps be accepted sooner or later. However, the P.L.A. would not be able to take such quick action with only limited and acceptable casualties, especially involving civilians in Taiwan. And political resistance by local residents in Taiwan to Chinese military occupation would also be strong. Under this situation, Washington would probably have to interfere forcefully due to pressure from the American public and Congress. Given Americans' memory of the Tiananmen incident of 1989, Beijing's image as an "authoritarian" government and Taiwan's image as a "democracy", the reactions and pressure from the American people would be tremendous.

As for an air and sea blockade, theoretically, the P.L.A. could undertake one, but in reality it would be difficult because it would affect international sea transportation and provoke a reaction not only from the United States, but also from Japan and other countries.

It was obvious that China meant to bark without biting to achieve the following objectives: (1) to draw a clear line for the United States and other countries not to cross in their relations with Taiwan; (2) to scale back Taiwan's further drift away; (3) to influence Taiwan's internal politics, especially the direct presidential election in March 1996; (4) to keep the initiative in its hand and to enhance its leverage over Taiwan; (5) to satisfy domestic pressure following Lee's United States visit.

Notes

1. *Lianhe Zaobao*, 17 August 1999, p. 22.
2. Interfax News Agency (Moscow), "Russia Sells China License to Make Su-27 Fighter-Interceptors", Reuters, 5 February 1996.
3. Some sources in 1996 predicted that there would be 130 IDFs by that time. However, given its access to U.S. F-16s and French 2000-5s as well other U.S. weapons (easier than originally expected), Taiwan would likely cut down on its own IDF production.
4. "China's New Fighter Jet Not Yet a Threat to Taiwan", *Ping Kuo Jih Pao* (Hong Kong), 10 July 1997, p. 16, quoted from Reuters, 11 July 1997.
5. Ibid.
6. "China's Fighter Development with Russia, Israel Reported", *Kuang Chiao Ching* [Wide Angle] (Hong Kong), 16 November 1995, pp. 70–72, quoted from Reuters, 30 January 1996.
7. Bates Gill, "Russia, Israel Help Force Modernisation", *Jane's Defence Weekly*, from Reuters, 31 January 1996.
8. Nick Cook, "Lifting the Veil On China's Fighters", *Jane's Defence Weekly*, from Reuters, 31 January 1996.
9. *Lianhe Zaobao*, 17 November 1998, p. 18. "China's Fighter Development with Russia, Israel Reported", *Kuang Chiao Ching*, 16 November 1995, pp. 70 72, from Reuters, 30 January 1996.
10. Ibid.
11. Xinhua, "Advanced J8IIm Fighter Makes Initial Flight in Shenyang", Reuters, 2 May 1996.
12. "Warplanes Deal Struck", *SCMP*, 7 August 1999. The Sukhoi-30 is a twin-seater multi-purpose warplane designed to compete directly with the U.S. F-15 and is equipped with in-flight refuelling and ground attack capabilities. It is designed both for fighter aircraft and for delivering precision-guided weapon systems in a ground-attack role.
13. "Pointers: Plans for the Predictable Future — China", *Jane's Intelligence Review*, B.I.P. Aerospace/Defence, no. 5 (1996), p. 6, from Reuters, 1 May 1996.
14. "Taiwan: Taiwanese Paper on China's Submarine Program, Taiwan's Response", *Lien Ho Pao*, from Reuters, 12 January 1996.

15. Ibid.

16. "China Expands Reach with Russian Destroyers", *Jane's Defence Weekly*, 15 January 1997, p. 5.

17. "Taiwan: Taiwan's Air Command Keeping an Eye on China's Military", Reuters, 1 December 1995.

18. *ST*, 18 August 1995, p. 15.

19. *Janes Intelligence Review*, November 1995, p. 502.

20. Zheng, *Gudao Chanmeng* [Lingering Dreams over the Isolated Island], p. 527.

21. *ST*, 24 October 1995, p. 13.

22. *Lianhe Zaobao*, 24 December 1998, p. 16.

23. Zheng, *Gudao Chanmeng* [Lingering Dreams over the Isolated Island], p. 550.

24. "Taiwan: China Fires 3 Missiles over Taiwan, Says Report", Reuters, 25 December 1995.

25. "Army Chiefs Split on Tactics", *SCMP*, 27 August 1996.

26. Ibid.

27. Barbara Starr, "China Could 'Overwhelm' Regional Missile Shield", *Jane's Defence Weekly*, 23 April 1997, p. 16.

28. Ibid.

29. *ST*, 2 October 1998.

30. See *The Science Times*, published by China Academy of Science, quoted in Christopher Bodeen, "Taiwan Blames China for Instability", AP, 20 August 1999.

31. "China Studies War Options, Including Latest Space Arms", *ST*, 15 August 1999.

32. For Taiwan's nuclear capability and its development, see Chapter 7 for details.

33. *ST*, 11 August 1995, p. 14. For Taiwan's mid-range missile development, see Chapter 7 for details.

34. *Lianhe Zaobao*, 2 August, p. 16.

35. Pang Yan, "*Zhongguo De 'Aiguozhe'* — FM-80 *Dikong Daodan*" [China's Patriot-FM-80 Surface-To-Air Missile] *Zhishi Jiushi Liliang* [Knowledge is Strength], no. 5 (1993), pp. 6–7. Emphasis added.

36. Zhao Xianfeng. "*Hanwei Heping*" [Safeguarding Peace], *Zhongguo Qingnian* [China Youth], no. 2 (1993), p. 15.

37. "China: Russia Delivers 'Advanced Surface-to-Air' Intercept Missiles to China", *Lien Ho Pao*, 20 October 1993, p. 10, from Reuters, 25 October 1993.

38. Ibid.

39. Zheng, *Gudao Chanmeng* [Lingering Dreams over the Isolated Island].

40. *ST*, 24 July 1995, p. 36.

41. Li Jian, "*Lian'an Tonghang Dui Lian'an Guanxi Fazhan Zhi Yingxiang*", [The Impact of Direct Shipping on the Cross-Strait Relations]. A paper for the Symposium on Cross-Strait Relations, Beijing, July 1996, p. 1.

42. Mary Kwang, "China Warns Taiwan of Trade Loss", *ST*, 7 August 1999.

43. Xinhua, "*Jianchi 'Lianguolun' Jiushi Beipan Taiwan Renmin*" [The "Two States" Theory is a Betrayal of the People of Taiwan], *Renmin Ribao*, 3 August 1999, p. 4.

44. James Kynge, "Taiwan Counts Cost of China's Pressure", Reuters, 15 February 1996. And also see Cooper Karen, "Government Tries to Calm Fears over Chinese Stance", Reuters, 19 February 1996.

45. CCTV (overseas) News Program, 30 April 1996.

46. James Kynge, "Taiwan Shaken over China Reunification Report", Reuters, 29 January 1996.
47. CCTV (overseas) News Program, 30 April 1996.
48. Danny Lee, "Taiwan Strait Crisis Cost Island $37b", *ST*, 16 April 1998.
49. "Taiwan: Taiwan Emigrants Soar as Relations with China Sour", Reuters, 30 May 1996.
50. Central News Agency, "Taiwan: China Urged to Hold Fishery Talks 'Soon'", Reuters, 13 December 1995.
51. Central News Agency. "Taiwan: Taiwan Police 'Tired of Chasing Away' 'Trespassing' Mainland Fishing Boats", Reuters, 29 August 1996.
52. "China 'May Wage Information War against Taiwan'", AFP, 14 May 1999.
53. Ibid.
54. Eric Ellis, "China's Troops Ready for Drills Off Taiwan - War Games", *The Australian Financial Review*, from Reuters, 8 February 1996.
55. Staff Reporters, "Taiwan Move `Would Put HK at Risk", *SCMP*, from Reuters, 7 February 1996.

7

Taiwan after the Face-Off

After the face-off between Beijing and Taipei in 1995, Lee took a tit-for-tat stance in defiance of China's mounting pressure, which, together with the changes in Taiwan's mainland policy, will be presented in this chapter. The rationale behind this stance will be discussed in Chapter 9.

"Go Nuclear"?

Lee's initial tit-for-tat reactions included the threat to "go nuclear". Following China's harsh actions, the phrase "go nuclear" was spread around Taiwan. At one National Assembly session in late July 1995, the question was raised for Lee to clarify. Lee did not give a clear denial. He answered: "We should re-study the question (of acquiring nuclear weapons) from a long-term point of view".[1] This answer received a sharp response. The Taiwan government then quickly denied that it had any plan for developing nuclear weapons. Its explanation was that "What Mr. Lee meant by 'long-term point of view' was actually to give the matter further thought and discuss it later. In other words, it was an implicit way of saying 'no'".[2]

This explanation was weak given the fact that Taiwan did have such a programme up until the late 1980s. Suspicions were aroused again following Lien Chan's secret visit to Ukraine in August 1996 when it was reported, although denied by Taiwan, that Lien discussed the nuclear issue with officials in Ukraine. The United States once forced Taiwan to drop the Pegasus Project for mid-range missiles out of the concern that Taiwan would initiate an offensive against China, as the U.S. deal with China was not to sell Taiwan offensive weapons that could hit the mainland. However, it was reported that Taiwan was on the verge of testing its mid-range surface-to-surface missiles. According to Taiwan's *China Times*, the range of the missile was 300 kilometres (186 miles), which would enable it to hit several coastal cities in China.[3] According to Reuters, in late 1995, Taiwan was revising its domestically-made anti-aircraft *Sky Bow II* missile to a surface-to-surface missile with a target range of between 480 and 960 kilometres, enabling it to hit more of China's coastal cities and airports.[4]

It does not make military sense to spend huge financial resources to develop mid-range missiles if these missiles are not nuclear or chemical capable and thus a strategic deterrence. Is Taiwan secretly developing nuclear or chemical weapons? Through an "appropriate channel", China once sealed an agreement with the United States that Taiwan put its nuclear facilities under the supervision of international atomic agencies.[5] This was one of the conditions under which China agreed to join the International Atomic Energy Agency (I.A.E.A.). The I.A.E.A. supervision of Taiwan's nuclear development was done through an "agreed channel", commonly understood as the United States. How conscientious the Americans are is another question. Even if the United States sabotaged Taiwan's nuclear weapons project in 1988 by taking away their nuclear weapon blue prints and dismantling the equipment, it could not take away the nuclear weapon technology that the Taiwanese have in their heads. The Chinese suspect that Taiwan may secretly start the project again.[6]

Gerald Segal of London's International Institute for Strategic Studies (I.I.S.S.) made the assessment that Taiwan has the capability to develop nuclear weapons in a matter of 3–4 months.[7] If Taiwan really does have the capability at the moment or in the future, even without possessing nuclear weapons, there are varifications for China's strategic thinking and behaviour, which will in turn affect stability in East Asia. In other words, once Taiwan feels simultaneously threatened by China and abandoned by the United States, it may quickly and secretly develop nuclear weapons to protect itself, with or without a declaration of independence. Then, China either has to make concessions or take dramatic and swift military action to destroy Taiwan's nuclear capability and its means of delivery such as the mid-range missiles it is currently developing.

Calling for International Support

Taiwan's initial reactions also included naming China as the major threat not only to Taiwan's own security but also to the United States and other Asia-Pacific countries in order to win internal and external sympathy and support.

Taiwan depicted China as "the biggest potential threat" and asked Washington to make it clear to Beijing that the United States would do everything within its power to safeguard security in the area. It urged Washington to maintain its military presence in Asia, asked Japan to protest against China's missile tests and urged Asia-Pacific countries to co-operate more closely on security against China's military threat. Lee Teng-hui called on the countries in the region to "study the feasibility of forming a joint security system" because China was posing a threat to other Asia-Pacific countries as well as Taiwan.[8]

Taiwan also tried to convince the United States that it was in its best interests to stand with Taiwan against China. Lee Teng-hui said: "We deeply believe that promotion of R.O.C.–United States relations not only helps Taiwan's economic liberalization, political democratization and pluralization of society, it affords *even greater safeguards for U.S. interests in the Asia-Pacific region.*"[9] Taiwan's foreign ministry said: "We believe it is in the interest of both Taiwan and the United States if Washington decides to send naval vessels to waters near Taiwan to help maintain peace and security in the region", adding that under such circumstances, the U.S. move to dispatch warships to waters surrounding Taiwan should not be interpreted as "interference of foreign forces" in Taiwan affairs.[10]

Taiwan's then foreign minister, Chang Hsiao-yen, advised Washington to withdraw China's M.F.N. status by saying that economic sanctions would be very effective against China. The Beijing leadership owed its legitimacy to the economic growth brought about by opening the country to the outside world. If that were to be curtailed by withdrawing trading privileges and aid, its authority would suffer.[11] During my interviews, Chinese strategists described all this as Taiwan's effort to *"da qun jia"* [call on other countries to gang up on China], *"hun shui mo yu"* [stir up the water to catch the fish] and *"tuo meiguo xia shui"* [pull the United States into the troubled water].

To its own people, the Taiwan government depicted China's military exercises as intended to deprive the Taiwanese people of their rights to democracy, freedom, international dignity and living space and called on their unity and support of the government.

The March Presidential Election

In defiance of China's military exercises, Taiwan went ahead with its planned direct presidential election on 23 March 1996.

The election saw a 76 per cent voter turnout. Lee Teng-hui and Lien Chan, presidential and vice-presidential candidates of the Kuomintang, won the election with 54 per cent of the votes. Peng Ming-min and Hsieh Chang-ting of the D.P.P. with their strong platform of "Taiwan independence" lost the election with 21.2 per cent of the votes, far lower than their own expectations. Lin Yang-kang/Hao Po-tsun and Chen Li-an/Wang Ching-feng, two groups of candidates who opposed "Taiwan independence" received a total of 24.8 per cent of votes. This result, particularly that for Chen Li-an and Wang Ching-feng who did not have party support and totally depended on their self-image, was far higher than expected.

The D.P.P. was the biggest loser. It had been accustomed to winning over 40 per cent of the vote and it had been predicted that they would win at least that much.

The 54 per cent who voted for Lee were not necessarily indicating support for Taiwan's independence. While some favoured independence eventually but preferred to keep the status quo for the time being lest China resort to force, many others were in two minds about independence or preferred stability which was not necessarily equal to independence. And they believed that Lee was the only one who could tread the more stable middle path in-between the D.P.P.'s advocacy of independence and the other two groups of candidates' pro-unification stance. What is more, Lee's victory was also related to his repeated election promise that he would seek unification with China and would not pursue "Taiwan independence", as well as his promise to take steps to improve cross-strait relations after winning the election.

Presidential Inauguration

Before Lee's inauguration on 20 May 1996, there was wide international speculation that the reason for Lee's tit-for-tat stance against China was largely to gain domestic support, i.e. Lee wanted to use China as the bogeyman to win a clear mandate (over 50 per cent of the votes). Thereafter he was expected to take a meaningful if not dramatic initiative to improve or stabilize cross-strait relations. However, this did not happen.

In his inaugural speech, he expressed a general commitment to unification in the twenty-first century and highlighted the cultural and historical tradition shared by the two sides. He also said that there was absolutely no need and no possibility of adopting the Taiwan independence line. But he quoted the premise that the Republic of China was originally and already a sovereign state and stressed the separate rule on the two sides of the Strait. Apart from these general positions, conspicuously absent from his speech was any mention of some major issues. These included:

1. Taiwan agreeing in concrete terms to direct talks on ending hostilities across the Taiwan Strait;
2. A dialogue that would lead to eventual unification;
3. A dialogue about the three direct links;
4. Caution over Taiwan's excessively high profile campaign for more international recognition, particularly its effort to join the United Nations.

He did not mention the principle of "one China", but insisted on Beijing's recognition of the political reality of separation along the Taiwan Strait. There were no initiatives that could be feasibly and immediately applied to improve ties with China, except the offer to travel to China to talk about peace, but only with the consensus of the Taiwanese people. He said: "In the future, *at the call of my country and with the support of its people*, I would like to embark upon a journey of peace to mainland China, taking with me the consensus and will of the 21.3 million people [here]."[12] Actually, "the journey of peace" was not Lee's initiative. It was Chinese President Jiang Zemin who had first suggested it in his eight-point proposal in early 1995. Lee also defied Beijing by vowing to continue his "pragmatic diplomacy".

The Taiwan business community was disappointed. The stock market plunged 4.1 per cent as investors reacted coolly to hopes for improved ties with China. Investors feared that Lee's inauguration speech would be ill-received in Beijing, and this could unleash another round of military exercises.[13]

During the Strait Crisis of 1995–6, Lee had repeatedly vowed to hit China where it hurt most, i.e. military modernization, economic resistance and "pragmatic diplomacy". After his election as president he looked set to continue on this path.

Military Modernization

Taiwan has never stopped buying arms against China. In 1994, Taiwan spent US$480 million, compared with Beijing's US$440 million, on the acquisition of foreign military equipment, making it the eleventh largest arms buyer in the world.[14] After the face-off, Lee vowed to speed up the renewal of weapons. In 1996, Taiwan's Cabinet decided to boost its defence budget to more than NT$280 billion (US$10.21 billion) or about 22.8 per cent of the total government budget for the financial year beginning July 1996. This was a 13 per cent increase over the previous year, with an extra US$3.25 billion in imported or locally produced weapons funded through a "secret" allocation in the 1996 budget proposal,[15] mainly to buy more military hardware. According to Taiwan's *China Times*, during that financial year, Taiwan would spend some NT$15 billion on missile purchases, which would include purchases of U.S.-made *Patriot* missiles, French-made *Mistral* shoulder-fired rockets as well as the development of its own medium-range surface-to-surface missiles.[16]

Citing data it said came from the Defence Ministry's confidential budget proposal, Taiwan's *Tzu Li Wan Pao* revealed that the proposed defence budget would concentrate on the purchase of weapons and equipment, the construction of air defence facilities, intelligence work and the strengthening of the capacity for electronic warfare.

For the purchase of weapons and equipment, the Defence Ministry set aside over NT$60.565 billion, over NT$700 million more than the previous year. Planned purchases included F-16 fighter planes, *Mirage* 2000-5 fighter planes, C-130 transport planes, anti-submarine helicopters and E-2T early-warning planes. The budget also set aside money for other equipment, including over NT$590 million for ground force M60A3 armoured vehicles, over NT$11.24 billion for the *Patriot* anti-missile system, over NT$248 million for air defence missiles (*Avenger, Northwest Wind* and *Stinger*), over NT$590 million for *Trident* missiles, over NT$3.4 billion for anti-invasion equipment and NT$398.3 million for armoured landing vessels. It also set aside over NT$232.72 million for the construction of air defence and evacuation projects, including NT$164.97 million for projects to put oil and ammunitions underground and over NT$60 million for projects to put important facilities (including fire-prevention and gas-protection facilities of the Chingtien Command Post) underground. It also set aside NT$8.84 million for electronic warfare equipment, over NT$530 million for radar equipment and over NT$520 million for the second phase outlay of the automatic air defence system.

In addition to setting aside over NT$800 million for the collection and research of intelligence, including battle intelligence and coastal defence intelligence, intelligence training and strategic operations, it set aside over NT$240 million for reconnaissance equipment, over NT$48 million for updating the electronic reconnaissance system, over NT$160 million for the satellite reconnaissance system and NT$9.3 million for research of the satellite video processing system.

To strengthen the military's capacity and technology for manufacturing weapons and equipment, it set aside over NT$300 million for developing software for the *IDF* fighter planes, nearly NT$400 million for the verification of air-to-surface missile system, about NT$180 million for developing the *Sky Sword* land and sea launching system, over NT$320 million for developing the *Thunderbolt* 2000 artillery multi-launcher missiles and over NT$140 million for war preparation information equipment, including Lusheng No. 1 and No. 2 equipment and the war zone joint combat simulating training and analysis system.[17]

It also pushed various foreign and domestic sources for more advanced weapons. For example, according to the U.S. Defence Department, in 1996 Taiwan sought to purchase US$188 million worth of high-tech communications equipment. It asked for Mobile Subscriber Equipment made by GTE Corp., which was designed to use a large number of telephone voice and data channels, switching them automatically and constantly to provide secure communications by preventing interception and monitoring.[18] Taiwan also wanted to buy, among other things, 1,299 *Stinger* missiles, 74 guided missile launchers, 74 flight trainer *Stinger* missiles, 96 Humvee vehicles and 500 rounds of 50 calibre ammunition.[19] After its successful purchase of 1,299 vehicle-mounted *Stinger* missiles, according to Reuters reports, Taiwan went further and bought shoulder-fired *Stinger* missiles from the United States. The deal was made in August 1998, according to the Pentagon, for a proposed *Stinger* missile sale for 61 dual-mount launchers, 728 missile rounds and other materials and services for an estimated US$180 million. It was also interested in buying 131 Mk46 MOD 5-A torpedoes which would be used by its S-70 helicopters for anti-submarine warfare.[20] And from the French, Taiwan bought air-to-air *MICA* missiles for its 60 *Mirage* 2000-5 fighters.[21]

Taiwan planned in 1996 to build a seventh naval fleet, which would include six *Knox*-class frigates leased from the United States and 16 *Lafayette*-class frigates from France.[22] This meant that Taiwan was going to press the United States for the lease of another three *Knox*-class frigates after the United States had signed a lease for the first three frigates to Taiwan in June 1994 as well as press France for another ten *Lafayette*-class frigates after the purchase of six such frigates in 1990.

Taiwan reportedly approached the United States, Germany, Holland, Japan and two third world countries to purchase submarines.[23] After these efforts failed, it planned to build its own submarines using transferred technology. Taiwan's navy commissioned China Shipbuilding Corporation to build 10–12 diesel-powered submarines and put them into service in about 2005.[24]

In 1998, Taiwan Defence Ministry set a budget of NT$59.9 billion for the financial year beginning from July 1998 for the purchase of military equipment, including *Patriot* anti-missile weaponry. About NT$7.9 billion would be set aside for hardware to enhance air defence capability. The military shopping list also included AH-1W *Cobra* gun-ships and transportation helicopters, as well as radar and electronic warfare equipment.[25] Taiwan also planned in that year to buy more C-130H transport aircraft which would be fitted out with jamming equipment to obstruct Chinese military functions such as communications and the firing of missiles.[26] The first F-16 squadron was established in October 1997 and another one was formed in July 1998 with 18 F-16s. The United States sold Taiwan US$160 million worth of navigation and targeting equipment to upgrade the F-16s' capability of conducting night-time warfare and the formation of the second squadron was to boost its night-time warfare against China. These F-16s might also be equipped with AGM-65B *Maverick* missiles and *Harpoon* missiles.[27]

Taiwan also drafted in 1998 a 10-year development programme of major weapons that included long-range radar, long and medium-range surface-to-surface missiles and anti-tactical ballistic missiles. It planned to take three to four years to develop a 1,000 kilometre radar system. Several radar stations would therefore be deployed, each costing an estimated NT$3 billion.[28] By May 1999, Washington had agreed in principle to sell Taiwan two state-of-the-art early-warning phased array radar systems made by Ratheon Company. These two radar systems were only part of a long shopping list for weapons and armaments worth around US$1.7 billion brought by Taiwan's Vice-Chief of the General Staff, Teng Tsu-ling, when he visited the United States in late April 1999.[29]

In November 1998, Taiwan began hinting that it might join the U.S. T.M.D. in East Asia. Even before Washington had agreed to offer it the T.M.D., Taiwan had already, by May 1999, approved plans to expand the Tsoying Naval Base to pave the way for the acquisition of the American-built *Aegis* destroyers, at an estimated cost of NT$30 billion. It planned to spend NT$160 billion on the purchase of four *Aegis* destroyers.[30] It also planned to upgrade its own *Hsiung Feng* II missiles to give them power similar to cruise missiles.[31]

These examples might only be the tip of the iceberg of Taiwan's arms purchases in the light of the following figures. Taiwan's arms purchases skyrocketed from 1995. In 1997, according to the Stockholm International Peace Research Institute (S.I.P.R.I.), Taiwan spent US$4,049 million on conventional arms purchases.[32] The I.I.S.S. maintained that Taiwan's purchases of military hardware jumped to US$7.3 billion in 1997 from US$1.8 billion in 1996.[33] The payment for its U.S. F-16s, French *Mirage* 2000-5s and air-to-air missiles, totalling US$12.7 billion, could not fully explain such a big jump because the payments were spread out between 1992 and 1999 when the last jets were scheduled to be delivered.[34] It is clear that Taiwan has been spending more than ever before.

This trend of military modernization is not likely to slow with Taiwan's determination to resist Beijing's reunification pressure. Taiwan's Defence Minister, Chiang Chung-ling, vowed to continue arms purchases even if China renounced the use of force against Taiwan, in case China resorted to force.[35]

Economic Resistance

The second area in which Lee claimed he would hit China where it hurt was what he believed to be China's economic need for foreign and Taiwanese investment. Hence he resisted Beijing's call for an early establishment of the three direct links across the Strait and called on Taiwanese businessmen to "go slow" in their investment in China, and to "go further south" by investing in Southeast Asia and other areas. In late 1996, he changed the emphasis claiming that this was for Taiwan's economic security, so as to avoid the impression that he was retaliating against China.

Economic Brakes

At one time Taiwan had the ambition of becoming an "Asia-Pacific regional operation centre" and saw the mainland as its "main market" [*fu di*]. After the face-off, Lee Teng-hui expressed concern over the soundness of this policy several times before finally taking measures to halt the trend of increasing Taiwanese investment in mainland China.

At the National Assembly on 14 August 1996, Lee suggested a change in Taiwan's economic policy towards China. He said that "Taiwan would have to review the idea of using mainland China as a main market in our Asia Pacific centre project" and that Taiwan should look at ways of limiting investment in China to avoid over-dependence on China. He put forward a new policy of "go slowly and be patient [*jieji yongren*]".[36]

Two days after Lee's speech, Taiwan's government put the brakes on a proposal by Formosa Plastics Group to spend US$3.3 billion building a power plant in Fujian, China. Approval for the investment had been just days away. Formosa Plastics subsequently withdrew its proposal. This was a development of some significance, given that Formosa Plastics Group was Taiwan's largest non-state company and its proposed power station would have been the biggest ever Taiwanese investment on the mainland.

At the same time, the Council for Economic Planning and Development, Taiwan's top economic policy-making body, announced that it would be withdrawing a proposal to relax limits on mainland investment in Taiwan. Its head, Chiang Ping-kun, asked Taiwan businessmen to slow down their investments in China.[37]

In the following month, Taiwan's President Enterprises Group abandoned plans to build a US$100 million power plant in China[38] and China Petroleum Corporation stalled a plan for joint oil exploration with China.[39] In November, Taiwan's Mainland Affairs Council proposed a tightening of government controls on outflows of liquidity and high-technology investments to China.[40]

At the National Development Conference in December 1996, Lee once again called for a slowdown in Taiwanese investments on the mainland. After the conference, Taiwan took more measures to put the brakes on. In May 1997, Taiwan introduced new guidelines, which went into force on 1 July, on Taiwanese investments in China. The new rules set a ceiling of US$50 million for a single investment project in more than 5,000 manufacturing and agricultural product lines. Infrastructure projects, such as dams, bridges, power plants, airports, railways, highways, airports and harbours, were shifted from the "case-by-case" category, which included about 4,300 product lines, to the "banned" list, which numbered over 300 manufacturing, agricultural and service lines. The guidelines also introduced a formula to determine the ceiling for any company's cumulative mainland investments. The new rules carry fines of up to US$650,000 and a maximum jail term of five years.[41]

The new rules also imposed a ban on investment in 27 petrochemical and related industries, although these were previously allowed on a case-by-case basis. In addition, real estate development on the mainland was also prohibited on the grounds that housing development would involve huge amounts of capital and long-term development.[42]

With the concern that China would use the Hong Kong leverage, Taiwan's parliament passed a Hong Kong and Macao Relations Act in March 1997 to govern its trade and other activities with Hong Kong and Macao after their hand-over to China. The act placed strict limitations on investment in Taiwan by Hong Kong and Macao companies in which mainland China had 20 per cent or more of total capital.[43] Kuomintang, Taiwan's ruling party, was one of the world's richest with a vast business empire. Its assets were estimated to be between US$10 billion and US$25 billion and its overseas investments were also thought to be in the billions. It was among Taiwan's leading investors through its seven holding companies. When laying out its global investment priorities in a plan in June 1997, it deliberately avoided new projects in Hong Kong. It had also re-registered its Hong Kong businesses elsewhere in early 1997.[44]

In early October 1997, Taiwan devalued its currency by 13 per cent, putting it at a 10-year low. It described this as a "central bank plan" to allow the currency to float at market rates. This action triggered the second round of the currency crisis in the Asian financial crisis and caused more turbulence in Hong Kong's nervous stock market which had been trying desperately to maintain its stability amid the regional currency crisis. Many Chinese officials were annoyed. They noted that Taiwan, whose economy was one of those least affected in the region by the currency crisis, had no convincing economic reason to devalue its currency. They suspected Taiwan of the intention to destabilize Hong Kong and to embarrass President Jiang Zemin in his coming summit with President Clinton in Washington in late October.[45] Taiwan's Premier Siew Wan-chang explained the decision for the devaluation as Taiwan having to obey the rules of the market for the sake of its own economy after it failed to defend its currency.[46] Some people, including Chinese scholars I interviewed, accepted the explanation. However, some remained unconvinced. For example, Fred Bergsten, the director of the Institute of International Economics of the United States noted in December 1997 that there was no reason whatsoever to devalue the Taiwan dollar at that time.[47]

Go Further South

The Asian financial crisis which began in July 1997 offered opportunities for Lee Teng-hui to enhance Taiwan's relations with those whose economies were badly hit by the crisis and desperately needed financial support. Lee called on Taiwan businessmen to look to the hardest-hit countries for new commercial opportunities, and the motivation, as *International Herald Tribune* pointed out, was not entirely economic. In its ongoing battle with Beijing, Taiwan was hoping to break out of its international isolation by greatly expanding its commercial ties in Southeast Asia.[48]

It was no coincidence that Taiwan's businesses pushed into Southeast Asia and high-level Taiwanese officials embarked on a series of "private" visits to ASEAN countries eager to win new friendships with generous offers of aid. Among them were Vice-President Lien Chan, who visited Singapore in January 1998 and Malaysia two months later and Premier Siew Wan-chang, who visited Manila and Jakarta. In addition, high-powered Taiwanese business delegations made frequent trips to Thailand, Malaysia, Indonesia and the Philippines.

Southeast Asia soon became Taiwan's third largest trading partner after Hong Kong and the United States. At the end of September 1997, Taiwan had invested US$37.1 billion in ASEAN countries.[49] For years since adopting the "go south" policy, Taiwan had been trying to translate its huge economic stake in the region into political clout to counter China's growing influence with ASEAN members, but without much success. Taiwan had applied to be a sector dialogue partner with ASEAN in 1994 but was rejected by the association on the grounds that it would jeopardize the group's ties with China. Some ASEAN countries were willing to host high Taiwanese officials for "private" visits, either in transit or for holidays. Their leaders made "transit stops" in Taipei's airport like Singapore's Prime Minister Goh Chok Tong and Malaysia's Prime Minister Mahathir Mohamad in November 1997 and Singapore's Senior Minister Lee Kuan Yew in November 1998. However, they were unwilling to go too far in offending Beijing by, for example, developing their existing unofficial relations with Taiwan into official ones or by inviting President Lee Teng-hui for a visit. It is not yet clear how far Taiwan will go in exploiting the on-going financial crisis in order to "go further south". While the financial crisis offered some opportunities for the Taiwan government to go further south, many Taiwanese businessmen found it in their own economic interests to withdraw their investments from the unstable Southeast Asian region and transfer them to mainland China which was the least affected by the financial crisis in the region.

Develop Okinawa?

In 1996–97, Taiwan launched a high-profile drive to invest in Okinawa, Japan's least-developed region in the south, and the only Japanese local government that had an office in Taiwan (opened in 1990). It showed considerable interest in Okinawa as a possible replacement for Hong Kong as its entrepot for trade with mainland China. This approach reflected not only Taiwan's concern over Hong Kong's hand-over to China in July 1997 but also Lee's hope for "tangible" economic and political relations with Japan.

Since 1996 the K.M.T. has sent several investment missions to Okinawa and expressed a willingness to invest in tourism, electronics processing, aviation and other industrial sectors in the region. It was particularly interested in the island of Ishigaki, which lies west of Okinawa, just 240 kilometres east of Taiwan's northern Chilung port and only 35 minutes away by air.

Taiwan proposed turning it into a transhipment centre for restricted trade with China after Hong Kong's hand-over. It urged Tokyo to grant Okinawa free trade zone status, permit Taiwan's TransAsia Airways to fly to Ishigaki and relax visa requirements for the Taiwanese. It announced a US$200 million project on the island.

However, despite the good location along the region's busy sea-lanes and natural deep waters at Naha, the largest port on Okinawa, it would be hard to transform the island into a replacement for Hong Kong. Apart from very little industrial activity on the island, which has just over a million people, there is little infrastructure, and it is far away from major markets which made costs prohibitive.

Taiwan has not yet given up its efforts despite Hong Kong's smooth hand-over in July 1997. In late 1997, Lee Teng-hui still claimed to be eager to help Okinawa develop its economy and create jobs. He called for direct air links between Ishigaki and Taiwan and visa-free travel to Okinawa.[50]

Resisting the Three Direct Links

Since 1949, Taiwan has banned the three direct links, i.e. direct postal, air and shipping services, and direct trade with China. It is aware that the three direct links afford huge economic benefits but is concerned about political and security implications. Politically, Taiwan is concerned that the three direct links would make Taiwan appear to be a local government in the eyes of the international community instead of an independent and equal sovereign state. In terms of security, direct air and sea links would give Taiwan less early warning time for its air and sea defence and make the whole defence scenario too complicated to handle. Free investment in the island by China will give Beijing strong leverage.

In its Guidelines for National Unification of February 1991, Taiwan listed the three direct links as the second stage which has not yet been reached. However, faced with intense internal pressure, it has gradually relaxed the rigid ban. In May 1995, it proposed an "offshore transhipment centre" where incoming mainland cargo could be processed in bonded zones outside Taiwan customs for onward international shipment. This was intended to be a replacement for Hong Kong after its hand-over to China.

Under the plan, cargo could be shuttled directly across the Strait to and from certain Taiwan ports that would legally be considered "offshore", or outside the jurisdiction of Taiwan customs. Cargo originating from the mainland would not be allowed through Taiwan customs, while cargo from Taiwan would not be allowed to cross directly to China. "Feeder vessels" below a certain tonnage would be allowed to bring cargo to ocean-going ships berthed in mainland or Taiwan harbours.

However, Taiwanese shipping firms complained that the feeder plan was not cost-effective, promoting a revision which allowed direct crossings by ocean-going ships from five Taiwan ports, i.e. Kaohsiung, Keelung, Taichung, Hualien and Suao, to Chinese ports as part of onward trips to overseas destinations.

Beijing rejected the idea of an "offshore transhipment centre" which it did not consider to be direct shipping. In August 1996, it announced regulations on cross-strait shipping, designating Fuzhou and Xiamen as two "experimental ports" to be opened to ships from Taiwan, and unveiled its regulations for direct shipping, applicable to cargo and passenger shipping. It defined direct cross-strait cargo transport as domestic transportation under special management, and specified that only Taiwanese or Chinese companies, or joint ventures including one side or the other would be allowed to conduct business on the routes. Under the regulations, shipping companies must apply to the Chinese authorities. One clause implied that some categories of foreign shipping companies could apply for the cross-strait routes, but it left the criteria for permission unclear.

Taiwan could not accept these offers. Chang King-yuh, then the M.A.C. chairman, said: "We still do not permit direct shipping and we have our own rules to follow."[51] Taiwan first proposed that foreign ships rather than domestic ships should be approved for direct shipping. Then, because of opposition from both Chinese and Taiwanese shipping firms, Taiwan's Vice President Lien Chan proposed in early November 1996 that only Taiwan-owned but foreign-registered ships were to be approved. This meant that domestic shipping firms of Taiwan and the mainland would have to re-flag their ships under third-country registration before being allowed to sail.

Beijing balked at these proposals for limited direct links and counter-proposed its own detailed rules for management in mid-November 1996. The rules still emphasized, as they did in August 1996, that Beijing regarded the direct shipping as a domestic shipping matter under special management, specifying that all shipping companies would need its permission to conduct business on the routes.

Under this pressure, Taiwan unveiled in late November 1996 a three-stage plan. According to this plan, an "offshore" transhipment centre would be established first, which would be followed by establishment of a special economic and trade zone and finally direct shipping.[52]

The question was how Beijing would be convinced that this phased resumption of direct shipping links was sincere and not a trick to play for more time. In other words, how long would it take Taiwan to pass through the various stages to finally reach real direct shipping?

In February 1997, Taiwan quietly started allowing ships to make crossings from the mainland with only a brief stop-over in Hong Kong, although it drew the line at ships in which mainland Chinese firms had an interest of more than 50 per cent (this regulation was scrapped in June 1997). The Hong Kong-registered container ship *Lien Fung*, which had minority mainland ownership, was allowed to enter Taiwan's southern port of Kaohsiung on 23 February after a voyage from China's Xiamen port via Hong Kong. That passage, the first such quasi-direct sailing in 48 years, was the first, at least officially,[53] in which a mainland cargo was delivered to Taiwan directly by a ship starting from a mainland port without having to be transhipped in Hong Kong.

In June 1997, Taiwan officially announced the easing of restrictions on shipping across the Taiwan Strait. Ships wholly owned by China could now make quasi-direct passage via Hong Kong or a third country as long as they flew the flag of Hong Kong or a third country, not that of the P.R.C.[54]

As a separate development, another quasi-direct shipping service began in April 1997 between an offshore transhipment centre in Kaohsiung in Taiwan and the Xiamen and Fuzhou ports along the mainland coast, with six Chinese and six Taiwan firms approved to serve the route. However, Taiwan said that cargo on the route could only be processed for onward shipment to third countries and would not be allowed to go through Taiwan customs.

In April 1997, the *Sheng Da*, a freighter from China, became the first ship to sail directly to Taiwan from the mainland, steaming into Taiwan's Kaohsiung port (without starting from a third place like Hong Kong first). However, these were not yet true direct shipping links, as they had little economic and political impact. Because of the restrictions, only about 200,000 20-foot equivalent units (T.E.U.s) of Chinese transhipment cargo would enter Kaohsiung each year, tiny when compared to the five million T.E.U. which went through the port annually.[55] Taiwan still forbids direct cargo exchanges, and mainland cargo (such as the *Sheng Da* freighter) must be processed for onward passage to third countries at Kaohsiung's new offshore transhipment centre.

In February 1998, negotiators from China and Taiwan opened secret talks in Bangkok on ways to speed up cross-strait shipping. No dramatic breakthrough was made, but a similar quasi-direct sailing arrangement was extended to the route between Shanghai and Taiwan's Keelung port. In early March, the *Mild Sun*, a Shanghai container vessel but Panama-flagged, docked at Taiwan's northern port of Keelung after sailing via a third country (Japan) without going through Taiwan's customs. Again this was not direct shipping in its true sense.

It seemed that Taiwan was not willing to go too far in opening up the three direct links. In late 1997, Lee Teng-hui still said: "I dare say that the time is not yet right to start direct postal, transportation and commercial exchanges." He made it clear that Taiwan's ban on direct links with the mainland would stay in place despite mounting calls for a policy change.[56] By late 1999, there had not been any further meaningful relaxation in Taiwan's resistance against the three direct links and its "go slow" policy.

Pushing "Pragmatic Diplomacy" Further

Lee believed in his "pragmatic diplomacy" to counter-balance China's "one country, two systems" formula which he claimed would "dwarf Taiwan's international status" and "strangle Taiwan's international living space". In pushing through "pragmatic diplomacy", Taiwan, as its Foreign Minister said, prioritized expanding participation in international organizations, solidifying ties with its diplomatic allies, harnessing the strength of the private sector to achieve diplomatic objectives and expanding unofficial contacts with nations lacking formal ties with Taipei.[57] The following sections will focus on changes in Taiwan's mainland policy after 1995.

On Unification

As mentioned above, since the early 1990s, Taiwan's position on unification has changed from an earlier formulation of "one China", or the R.O.C. as the sole legitimate government of China, to "one China, two governments", "one China, two entities", "one China, two equal entities" and "one China two equal political entities" (at the same time, it also emphasized "one China two legal entities in the international arena and each equal entity has its own sovereignty"). After 1995, Taiwan dropped the "one China" and used the phrase "two equal political entities".

At the first Wang-Koo meeting in 1993, Taiwan still agreed to the "one China" principle. From 1994, it stopped mentioning this principle. At its National Development Conference in December 1996, it openly rejected it. The reason given by Lee was that "their hands would be bound" by the phrase "one China", which was often regarded by the international community as the "P.R.C." It turned down Beijing's "one China" principle as an unacceptable condition for the resumption of cross-strait talks.

At the same time, leaders in Taiwan were displaying a keen interest in the "New Taiwanese Doctrine" [*xin tai wan ren zhu yi*] and kept repeating that the "new Taiwanese" were "writing a history of the new Taiwan in the twenty-first century", and that the "new Taiwanese" would "abandon big China nationalism".

The concept of a "federation", or a confederation, or a "commonwealth" system under which China could be unified, was opposed by Taiwan before the early 1990s and thereafter was not mentioned. After the Strait Crisis of 1995–96, further changes took place. Taiwan's Vice President Lien Chan said in 1997 that national unification was a goal without a timetable or set form. "Therefore, we can neither affirm nor rule out the possibility of any system."[58] Later, he raised the notion of "one country, one good system (democracy)" as a formula for unification. However, since Lee redefined cross-strait relations in July 1999 as "a special relation between two states" without mentioning unification, Lien Chan and other Taiwan officials no longer mention a formula which encompasses "one country".

Ideologicalizing the Tension

Taiwan has been trying to ideologicalize the tension across the Strait, especially since the face-off, by depicting it as democracy vs. dictatorship instead of independence vs. reunification. It kept reminding the international community and its own people of the "communist threat" from the mainland and insisted that there would be no unification if communism in the mainland was not going to be replaced with democracy. It called for "democratic unification". Lee Teng-hui rejected both the "one country, two systems" formula and the "one China" principle. He said that China should be unified on the basis of freedom, democracy and equitable distribution of wealth, and insisted that "sovereignty lies in the hands of the people". He stressed that democracy was "the true way" to solve the unification issue.[59]

Noticing the different interpretations of democracy and human rights between Jiang Zemin and Bill Clinton at their summit in October 1997, Taiwan decided to bring the difference into full play and added the issues of democracy, freedom and human rights into its handling of the cross-strait relations. Lee said: "I have noticed that (at the summit) the U.S. President was clear in his insistence on democracy, freedom and human rights, which nearly caused unhappiness with Jiang Zemin. ... Taiwan will from now on declare that democracy, freedom and human rights are what we uphold." Lee therefore instructed the foreign ministry to "bring into play" that position.[60]

Obviously, Lee's instruction was less out of a concern for improving the situation of human rights and democracy in China than it was playing up the issue to win international support, especially U.S. support.

Pushing for More International Space

Meanwhile, Taiwan insisted on "marching into the international community", promoting "pragmatic diplomacy" and seeking "dual recognition" to expand its international profile.

The U.N. and I.M.F. Bid

Taiwan dismissed Beijing's claim that Taiwan, being part of China, should not be admitted as a member of the United Nations. It claimed that its bid for accession to the United Nations was meant to seek fair representation for its 21 million people in the world body. It would neither challenge the P.R.C.'s U.N. seat nor disavow its pursuit of eventual national unification.[61] This was what it called "parallel representation". It denied Beijing's accusation that this was in effect splitting China into "two Chinas" or "one China, one Taiwan".

As noted before, immediately after Lee's United States visit in June 1995, Taiwan greatly intensified its bid for U.N. membership and even proposed giving US$1 billion aid to the United Nations in exchange for membership. Despite its failure, Taiwan vowed to continue the effort. Faced with opposition from China and other U.N. members, Taiwan, for a time, considered settling initially for U.N. observer status before applying to become a full member.[62] However, this change of mind proved to be short-lived. From 1997, Lee Teng-hui again insisted on being accepted as a full U.N. member without becoming an observer first. In his visit to Panama in September 1997, Lee emphatically called on the global community to officially recognize Taiwan and give the island U.N. membership.[63]

At the same time, Taiwan also intensified its bid for membership of other international organizations, such as the International Monetary Fund (I.M.F.). In early 1998, Taiwan was reportedly considering giving the I.M.F. US$5–20 billion to set up an "Asia Stabilizing Fund" [*yazhou wending jijin*] to help countries hit by the on-going Asian financial crisis. Taiwan hoped that this would help in its bid for membership.[64]

"Private Visits"

After the face-off, Lee Teng-hui showed no sign of bowing to China's demand that Taipei scale back its drive to enhance its international status as an independent sovereign state. Lee's "pragmatic diplomacy" took various forms such as "transit diplomacy", "alumni diplomacy", "ceremony diplomacy" and "vacation diplomacy". Even at the height of the Strait Crisis in 1995–96, Vice-President Li Yuan-zu made a transit visit to the United States in early January 1996 on his way to attend the inauguration of the new Guatemala president. Barely two weeks after the U.S. transit visit, Li Yuan-zu made stops in San Francisco, Miami and Los Angeles on his way to Haiti and El Salvador for official visits.

Under strong American and Japanese pressure, Lee was persuaded to cancel some provocative moves in 1995–96 such as a military exercise and another trip to the United States to attend a conference in San Francisco in 1995. But in interviews with Western media, he insisted that he would continue to visit the United States.

Other high-ranking Taiwan officials never ceased their official or "unofficial" visits. For example, Vice President Lien Chan stopped over in New York on 14 August 1995 on his way to the Dominican Republic. In early 1998, he went to Singapore on a "vacation visit" and later he also went to Jordan and Malaysia for "private visits" with a transit stop in Thailand.

Taiwan's then foreign minister, Chang Hsiao-yen, paid a "private visit" to Indonesia and Malaysia in early September 1996 with a transit stop in Singapore. He also went to Jordan for "private visit" in December 1996.

Very often, the overseas trips of Taiwan's high officials followed a similar pattern. They would simply drop out of sight for days at a time before surprisingly reappearing in another country. For example, in August 1996, Lien Chan vanished from the scene for several days before resurfacing in Ukraine to receive an honorary degree and hold discussions with its state leaders. Chang Hsiao-yen's secret visits followed the same pattern.

Economic Diplomacy

Taiwan's "pragmatic diplomacy" to enhance its international status included economic diplomacy. This had two different branches. One was its economic policy towards China and Southeast Asian countries which encompassed its "go slow" and "go south" policies. The other was its economic policy towards other countries in order to maintain and win more diplomatic recognition, a drive disparaged by China as "chequebook diplomacy". For this purpose, it has spent tremendous economic resources.

For example, between 1992 and mid-1999, Taiwan gave more than US$180 million in economic assistance to Central America.[65] It also announced in 1996 that it would set up ten industrial zones in Central America and Asia to expand its foreign ties during the financial year beginning from July 1996. Its Economic Ministry claimed that its eventual goal was to set up 100 small-scale overseas industrial zones. It planned to set up one industrial zone each in Guatemala, Nicaragua, Costa Rica, El Salvador, Honduras, India, Indonesia and the Philippines, and two in Vietnam.[66]

In June 1997, Taiwan opened a joint office for five Central American countries (Costa Rica, El Salvador, Guatemala, Honduras and Nicaragua) to promote more trade and investment.[67] It took a decision to more than double its contribution to a fund for the five Central American countries from US$100 million to US$240 million in a bid to hold back Beijing's diplomatic progress in that region.[68] It also proposed bringing in Central American labourers to replace workers from countries that supported Beijing.

For a time in 1996–97, Taiwan intensified its economic aid to Panama. For example, it extended a US$70 million loan to Panama. In addition, it mapped out a series of investment projects there, including the Fort Davis Export Processing Zone, the chief investors of which were Taiwan's EVA Airways and a number of Taiwan manufacturers.[69]

It also planned to offer Panama a US$300 million low-interest loan to expand the Panama Canal. Its main purpose was reportedly to secure an invitation from Panama for Lee Teng-hui to attend a conference in 1997 on the Panama Canal's return from U.S. control, due in 2000. The catch was that the presidents of the United States and France would be there among other Western leaders, and this would be an excellent opportunity for Lee to enhance both his personal international image and Taiwan's international status. Lee finally got his invitation. However, it turned out to be a low-key affair, with neither the president of the United States nor the president of France attending the conference. U.N. Secretary General Kofi Annan and other important world leaders were also absent. Instead, only the heads of Honduras and El Salvador joined Panama President Perez Balladares and Lee Teng-hui. World leaders reportedly feared that their attendance at the conference could have a chilling effect on cross-strait tensions.

Taiwan also offered large amounts of economic aid to some African countries. However, despite the huge amount of money spent, there was no major diplomatic breakthrough in 1996–98. The number of countries with diplomatic relations with Taiwan remains roughly the same — mostly small African and Central American countries whose diplomatic recognition does not create big international waves. In some cases, there is the problem of these countries becoming an economic burden on Taiwan as they have sought to maintain their diplomatic recognition of Taipei for economic reasons, playing the "Beijing card" to squeeze more money out of Taipei and vice versa. Taiwan's efforts were dealt a severe blow when South Africa, the largest and most influential among its remaining allies, chose to recognize Beijing in December 1997.

Taiwan was determined to continue this "economic diplomacy". In April 1998, Taiwan's Foreign Ministry proposed that Taiwan should more than double the aid it provided to friendly foreign nations for 1999. It wanted to boost its "international technical co-operation" aid category by 220 per cent to NT$6.76 billion. Meanwhile, it sought another NT$5.85 billion for its "classified" aid budget, NT$1.32 billion more than it requested the previous year. While the nature of the "classified" budget remained unclear, the budget request specified that NT$2.43 billion was to be used for "solidifying" ties with Taipei's 28 diplomatic partners. Another NT$1.87 billion of the "classified" budget was earmarked for "expanding foreign relations", while NT$1.48 billion was to subsidize interest payments on loans to Taiwan's diplomatic allies.[70]

In his January 1999 visit to Haiti (one of the countries that officially recognizes Taiwan), Premier Siew Wan-chang offered the country US$8 million.

He also visited the Dominican Republic and pledged to give it US$2 million in economic aid.[71] These handouts are part of Taiwan's effort to counteract Beijing's attempts to isolate Taiwan diplomatically.

Apart from providing government economic assistance, Taiwan also asked private Taiwanese business to help promote its "pragmatic diplomacy". For example, in July 1998, Taiwan's Foreign Ministry once again urged Taiwanese companies to take part in foreign assistance projects to develop business opportunities as well as boost foreign ties. The ministry also offered low-cost financing and various aid to Taiwanese firms joining the overseas assistance programme.[72]

Since 1999, Taiwan has had two diplomatic achievements. In January, Macedonia switched diplomatic recognition from Beijing to Taipei. It reportedly received promises from Taiwan for direct economic aid worth US$235 million and the possibility of over US$1 billion in investments.[73] In early July 1999, Papua New Guinea shifted diplomatic ties from Beijing to Taipei. A leaked P.N.G. Cabinet document revealed that Taipei had pledged US$2.35 billion in return for the diplomatic switch (US$1.5 billion in grants and US$850 million in soft loans).[74]

Apart from targeting small and poor African and Latin American countries, from late 1998 Taiwan began to eye Europe where it had, at that stage, only one diplomatic partner, i.e. the Vatican. After Macedonia shifted its diplomatic recognition to Taipei in January 1999, Taiwan offered US$300 million assistance, more than any other country, to help rebuild war-battered Kosovo. In July, a Taiwanese trade delegation of 100 officials and businessmen, headed by Economics Minister Wang Chih-kang, visited Europe in what the island media dubbed as "trade diplomacy". The delegation visited Britain, Norway, Sweden and Hungary, which it intended to use as a gateway to Eastern Europe.[75]

The Dalai Lama's Visit

China was also irritated by the Dalai Lama's visit to Taiwan in March 1997. It was worried about co-operation between the independence forces of Taiwan and Tibet. It was not convinced that the Dalai Lama's visit was simply a religious visit. The Taiwan government, especially President Lee Teng-hui, reportedly supported the visit wholeheartedly. Even the meetings between the Dalai Lama and Lee Teng-hui, Lien Chan and other high officials as well as the D.P.P. leader Hsu Hsin-liang were politically significant enough. Taiwan also quietly gave approval for the Dalai Lama and his Tibetan government in exile to set up an office in Taipei. The Dalai Lama, while in Taiwan, gave public support to Taiwan's democracy, thus giving his religious tour a political tone.[76]

The Dalai Lama's visit was interpreted by Beijing as an encouragement to pro-Taiwan independence forces. It did not simply project Taiwan's international image but one which was as distinct as Tibet, one that was fighting for democracy and freedom just like the Tibet leader, and one that was fighting against being reunified by the Beijing government.

National Development Conference and Freezing of the Provincial Government

Between 23 and 28 December 1996, the National Development Conference was held, during which the K.M.T. and the D.P.P. reached a consensus that the development of cross-strait relations should be based on the "two equal political entities" principle. The conference also proposed freezing the Taiwan provincial government.

Beijing considered the conference as a deal between the K.M.T. and the D.P.P. to push further towards Taiwan's independence.[77] The conference at least signalled a trend — in recent years the K.M.T. and the D.P.P. had been successfully narrowing their differences with regard to their mainland policies. For example, the D.P.P. held a three-day seminar to discuss and set its China policy in February 1998. The result was that, to use the words of Taiwan's Premier Siew Wan-chang, "there is not much difference between its [D.P.P.] proposed China policy and the current policy of the K.M.T.".[78]

Beijing was irritated by the conference proposal and the subsequent decision by Lee Teng-hui to freeze the Taiwan provincial government. The conference proposed freezing elections for the provincial governor and the provincial assembly, which, in the eyes of Beijing, was to deny the fact Taiwan is a province of China. China's Foreign Minister Qian Qichen said: "The conference tried to negate the status of Taiwan being a province of China in the name of 'constitutional reform'".[79]

Beijing was also worried that after freezing the election of "National Assembly deputies", another decision taken by Lee following the conference proposal, the seats in the "National Assembly" would no longer be allotted to deputies representing various provinces and municipalities on the mainland as they used to, but by representatives of various political parties in Taiwan, thus severing Taiwan's ties with the mainland. Under this new system, the D.P.P. would get more seats, expanding pro-Taiwan independence ranks while sharing the power with the K.M.T.

Taiwan said that these various decisions were aimed at streamlining the government to improve its administrative efficiency and had nothing to do with so-called Taiwan independence as Beijing claimed. However, while these decisions would indeed help improve administrative efficiency, they also, as a matter of fact, made it easier for Taiwan to drift further towards full independence.

In October 1998, Taiwan's legislature finally voted in favour of virtually abolishing Taiwan's provincial government in all but name. It decided to shrink the provincial government over two years. The central government would appoint a new governor to succeed the incumbent governor Soong Chu-yu, who had been elected to the post by popular vote four years before. The provincial assembly would then be replaced by a 21-member advisory body appointed by the premier. The central government would take over the provincial government's debts and massive assets, including its banks, an alcohol and tobacco monopoly and various land holdings. Its more than 10,000 employees would either choose to retire or find jobs elsewhere.[80]

"Flexible Engagement"

While adopting a defiant posture, Lee also claimed to be entering into a "flexible engagement" with Beijing. Hence, Taiwan did not completely cut off its economic and cultural ties with the mainland. This was because it could not afford the high cost of severing all these ties overnight. In the first instance, this would push China to take harsher military action. Second, it would also invite opposition from people in Taiwan, especially business people. Third, Taiwan benefited tremendously from existing economic ties with the mainland. Fourth, Taiwan hoped to use economic engagement in exchange for Beijing's concessions to its political demands. Taiwan's Vice Premier Hsu Li-te made this point very clear when he said: "As long as mainland China responds in goodwill, we'll further ease restrictions on mainland-bound investments as well as on cross-strait commercial and personnel exchanges."[81]

Though Taipei did not completely cut off economic ties with China, fewer and fewer measures have been taken for a strong push towards better economic and cultural links between the two sides. Some of the earlier measures to encourage better ties had either been compromised or retracted. For example, the "go slow" policy replaced an earlier call to "use the mainland as its main market [*yi dalu wei fudi*]" to turn itself into an "Asia-Pacific regional operation centre". Across the Taiwan Strait, different political interests and perceptions, deep distrust and hurt feelings have been making it difficult for the two sides to reach a significant deal. This was best reflected in the tug-of-war between the two sides on the resumption of the second round of the Wang-Koo meeting as will be discussed in Part IV.

Notes

1. *ST*, 8 August 1995, p. 28.

2. Ibid.

3. Liu Joyce, "Taiwan Silent on Reported New Anti-China Missile", Reuters, 11 September 1996.

4. "Taiwan: Taiwan Denies Developing Medium-Range Missiles", Reuters, 27 December 1995.

5. "Top Chinese Official Rules Out Nuclear Attack on Taiwan", *ST*, 11 November 1998. Also see Daniel Kwan , "Mainland Rules Out Nuclear Attack", *SCMP*, 10 November 1998. See remarks by Sha Zukang, head of the arms-control division in China's Foreign Ministry. However, Taiwan denied such an agreement but at the same time insisted that its "official line of not developing or owning nuclear devices remained unchanged."

6. For more on Chinese suspicions, see Zheng, *Gudao Chanmeng* [Lingering Dreams over the Isolated Island], pp. 575–6.

7. Segal's assessment was reported by Taiwan's CTN TV (*Chong Tien*) on 10 November 1998. At the same time, Taiwan denied having such capabilities.

8. "Taiwan: Taiwan in Regional Security Pact Call", *SCMP*, from Reuters, 20 August 1995.

9. "Taiwan: President Lee Urges U.S. to Keep Selling Defensive Weapons", Reuters, 25 January 1996.

10. Central News Agency, "Ministry Declines Comment on Reports on U.S. Warship's Passage through Strait", Reuters, 27 January 1996.

11. Graham Hutchings and Simon Scott Plummer, "International — Taiwan Digs In as China's Missiles Fly", Reuters, 13 March 1996.

12. "Taiwan: President Stresses Economic Development, Mainland Relations", Reuters, 21 May 1996. Emphasis added.

13. Willy Wo-Lap Lam, "China Urges Lee to Act on Unity", *SCMP*, 21 May 1996.

14. *ST*, 6 October 1995, p. 19.

15. "China's Territorial Ambitions Must Be Nipped in the Bud", *Sydney Morning Herald*, from Reuters, 30 March 1995. "Taiwan: Lee Plays Down Fear of Clashes", *SCMP*, from Reuters, 29 January 1996. Similar figures were also reported. For example, another report put the Taiwan Defence budget at US$10.6 billion or 24.5 per cent of the national budget. See Alistair McIntosh, "China's Might Casts Shadow over Prosperous Asia", Reuters, 1 December 1994. Another report put it at "a record US$9.3 billion for the year ending June 1997, making it the biggest single item at 21 per cent of the budget", with a "separate special budget of US$2.1 billion for the purchase of fighters". See "Taiwan: Russian Fighter Sales to China a Threat", Reuters, 25 April 1996.

16. "Taiwan: Taiwan to Spend NT$15 Billion on Missile Purchase", Reuters, 13 March 1996.

17. "Defence Budget to Account For 21% of Government Spending in 1997", *Tzu Li Wan Pao* [Independence Evening Post] (Taipei), 31 March 1996, p. 3, quoted from Reuters, 10 April 1996. See also *Jane's Defence Weekly*, B.I.P. Aerospace/Defence, 1 May 1996, p. 12.

18. "USA: Taiwan Seeking U.S. Military Communications", Reuters, 10 May 1996.

19. "USA: Pentagon Rejects Chinese Bid to Block Taiwan Sale", Reuters, 23 August 1996.
20. "Stinger Missiles Deal Still on Track", *SCMP*, 8 August 1998. See also Vivien Pik-Kwan Chan, "Arms Sales to Taipei 'Assault on Sovereignty'", *SCMP*, 29 August 1998.
21. "Taiwan: French Mica Missiles Delivered to Taiwan", Reuters, 8 December 1996.
22. "Taiwan: Taiwan Wants to Buy Two Dutch Submarines", Reuters, 26 December 1995.
23. CTN TV News Programme, 8 July 1999.
24. The number was variously reported to be between six and ten. At present Taiwan is seeking the technology transfer from the United States and Germany. The submarine, to be based on Germany's Type 209–1200 or 209–1400, might be built in the United States and assembled and armed in Taiwan. The United States stopped building diesel-powered submarines long ago. Germany's Type 209 is still the best diesel-powered model. The Type 209-1400 can remain 250 metres under the sea for 50 days. With a top dive speed of 25 knots, it can sail for up to 400 nautical miles carrying 36 crew and 16 heavyweight torpedoes. "Taipei Seeks U.S. , German Help for 10 Submarines", *SCMP*, 19 January 1999.
25. "Taiwan Sets Aside $14b For Military", *SCMP*, 13 March 1998.
26. "New Air Force Unit for Taiwan", *ST*, 15 June 1998.
27. "Second Squadron of F-16s", *SCMP*, 24 July 1998.
28. "Taiwan Starts 10-Year Weapons Program", *SCMP*, 13 July 1998.
29. "U.S. Agrees to Sell Hi-Tech Radar Systems to Taipei", *SCMP*, 1 May 1999.
30. "Naval Base Expansion to House New Destroyers", *SCMP*, 18 May 1999. The 8,000-tonne *Aegis* destroyers serving in the U.S. Navy are armed with 90 Standard II surface-to-air missiles, eight *Harpoon* ship-to-ship missiles, MK32 torpedoes and *Tomahawk* cruise missiles. The highly computerized *Aegis* destroyers are designed to counter short and medium-range missiles, an important part of the proposed T.M.D.
31. Taiwan proposed spending NT$20 billion over the next financial year to boost its ability to detect and shoot down Chinese missiles
32. See Table 2.
33. "Taipei Boosts Arms Spending 'By Billions'", *London's Financial Times*, quoted in *SCMP*, 24 October 1998.
34. Ibid.
35. *Tzu Li Wan Pao*, 11 December 1996, p. 2, quoted from Reuters, 16 December 1996, "Taiwan: Defence Minister on Beijing Counterpart's U.S. Visit".
36. *Chung Kuo Shih Pao*, 14 August 1996.
37. "Taiwan: Taiwan Says Time to Slow Investment in China", Reuters, 13 September 1996.
38. Kevin Chen. "Taiwan Investment in China Seen Cooling — Analysts", Reuters, 1 December 1996.
39. Ibid.
40. "Taiwan: Taiwan Urged to Tighten Economic Policy on China", Reuters, 17 November 1996.
41. Dennis Engbarth. "Cross-Strait Rules Ease Curb Fears", *SCMP*, 29 May 1997. Also see Bruce Cheesman, "Taiwan Confirms New Rules on China Investments", *Business Times* (Singapore), 29 May 1997.
42. Central News Agency, "Taiwan Bans Investment In Mainland China Infrastructure", Reuters, 7 July 1997.

43. "Taiwan: Companies 20% Capitalized by Mainland Forbidden to Invest in Taiwan", Reuters, 20 March 1997.

44. "Taiwan: HK Absent from Taiwan Ruling Party Investment Plan", Reuters, 25 June 1997.

45. For example, see Tom Korski, "Villainous Taiwan Sabotaging Markets", *SCMP*, 11 March 1998.

46. *Lianhe Zaobao*, 14 March 1998, p. 30.

47. Ibid.

48. Richburg Keith, "Rich Taiwan Sees Bargains All Around", *IHT*, 22 January 1998.

49. Vivien Pik-Kwan Chan, "Opposition Attacks Taipei Plan to 'Win Friends on Back of Financial Crisis'", *SCMP*, 13 January 1998. According to Sinanet Newsline (19 February 1998), by early 1998, Taiwan's investment in Southeast Asia was US$36 billion.

50. "Direct Mainland Links Ban Will Stay, Says Lee", *SCMP*, 21 October 1997.

51. Ted Plafker, "China Opens Strait Link", *SCMP*, 21 August 1996.

52. Laura Tyson, "Taiwan Plan To Restore China Shipping Link", *Financial Times*, 28 November 1996, p. 4.

53. Unofficially, despite the ban, many Taiwanese ships, as a matter of fact, had already sailed directly across the Strait, either with a very brief stop-over in Hong Kong or even without such a stop-over. In the latter instance, commissioning agents in Hong Kong sent forged documents, by helicopter for example, to the ships before they reached a Taiwan port so that the captains of the ships could show the Taiwan authorities that the voyage did not violate the official ban because they had passed a third place.

54. "Taiwan: Taiwan Further Eases Rules on China Shipping", Reuters, 16 June 1997.

55. George Hsu, "China Ship in Taiwan Port After Historic Crossing", Reuters, 19 April 1997.

56. "Direct Mainland Links Ban Will Stay, Says Lee", *SCMP*, 21 October 1997. "Taiwan Feels Time Is Not Right for Direct Links with China", *ST*, 28 October 1997.

57. "Island's Foreign Minister Issues Alert over Further Switches in Relations", *ST.*, 1 January 1998.

58. "Taiwan: Premier Lien Chan on Cross-Strait Dialogue, Reunification, Hong Kong", Reuters, 30 June 1997.

59. "Taiwan: President Outlines Conditions for Reunification", Reuters, 18 December 1996. "Taiwan Hopes to Keep Status Quo with China for Now", *ST*, 2 July 1997.

60. Lee San Chouy, "New Ties 'Must Not Hurt Island'", *ST*, 31 October 1997.

61. "Taiwan: Foreign Ministry Dismisses Beijing's Argument Against Taiwan UN Membership", Reuters, 31 July 1996.

62. Remarks by Taiwan's foreign minister, Chang Hsiao-yen, in December 1996. See "Taiwan: Taiwan Says It May Seek UN Observer Status", Reuters, 26 December 1996.

63. "Lee Tells World to Recognise Two Entities", *SCMP*, 12 September 1997.

64. *Lianhe Zaobao*, 28 March 1998, p. 32.

65. "Central Americans Back UN Bid", *SCMP*, 12 August 1999.

66. "Taiwan: Taiwan to Expand Foreign Economic Ties", Reuters, 12 May 1996.

67. "Taiwan: Taiwan to Open Office for Five Allies", Reuters, 3 June 1997.

68. "Taipei to Double Aid to 5 Central American States", *ST*, 1 September 1997.

69. "Panama: Loan of 70m Dollars from Taiwan Linked to Ties With Beijing", Reuters, 23 June 1997.

70. Jason Blatt, "Bid to Double Aid for Allies", *SCMP*, 8 April 1998.

71. "Taipei's $62m Offer to Haiti", *SCMP*, 18 January 1999.

72. "Taiwan Sets Aside $1.5b for Allies", *SCMP*, 27 July 1998.

73. Nicole Winfield, "China Vetoes Macedonia Resolution", *The Washington Post*, 25 February 1999. Macedonia Foreign Minister Aleksandar Dimitrov said in late January 1999 that Macedonia stood to benefit from more than US$1 billion in investments from Taiwan. "Mainland Threatens Skopje over Ties", *SCMP*, 1 February 1999.

74. "No Money Promised, Says Taipei", *ST*, 8 July 1999. "Pact to Let Taiwan Fish in PNG Waters for a Year", *ST*, 10 July 1999. However 16 days later, the new Prime Minister Sir Mekere Morauta switched P.N.G.'s diplomatic recognition to Beijing on 21 July 1999, accusing the previous Prime Minister Bill Skate of establishing diplomatic ties in an "irregular way" with Taiwan. See "Papua New Guinea Plan Axed", AP., 21 July 1999.

75. "Taiwanese Trade Team on European mission", *SCMP*, 20 July 1999.

76. "Exiles To Open Taipei Office", *SCMP*, 8 September 1997.

77. "Editorial on Proposal to Abolish Province Status", *Wen Wei Po* (Hong Kong), 3 January 1996, p. A2, from Reuters, 8 January 1997.

78. *Lien Ho Pa*o, 23 August 1998, p. 13.

79. "Chinese Military Leader Warns on Taiwan Policies, U.S. Intervention", *Ping Kuo Jih Pao*, 27 January 1997, p. A12, from Reuters, 28 January 1997.

80. "Name Stays But Island's Provincial Government to Go", *SCMP*, 10 October 1998.

81. Central News Agency, "Taiwan Vice-Premier Urges Resumption of 'Constructive Dialogue' with China", 25 March 1996, from Reuters, 26 March 1996.

8

China after the Face-Off

China's sharp response to Lee's visit to the United States also reflected a major change in its Taiwan policy, which will be discussed in this chapter. The rationale for the change will be presented in Part IV.

Rising Nationalism and Domestic Politics

To the Chinese, at least the Chinese on the mainland, the Taiwan issue is a very emotional one because it touches upon the bitter memory of 150 years of humiliation by the West and 100 years by Japan. They can agree to the "one country, two systems" formula for Taiwan, accept Taiwan's status quo as such for the time being, and may even endorse the Taiwan model of democracy in future if it is proved to be successful. However, they cannot accept Taiwan's independence, which in their eyes is tantamount to Taiwan being "snatched away" by foreign powers as it once was. China has lost a lot of territory over the last 150 years. This territory was ceded to foreign powers in formal treaties, mostly following China's military defeats. No matter how the Chinese now feel about these treaties, they have to accept them as historical facts, as well as accept their consequences, such as the current China–Russian border and Mongolia's independent status. However, Taiwan is different. To the Chinese, it has been returned to China by formal international declarations and they will not accept its independence without a good fight.

With this background, no leader in China will accept the independence of Taiwan, both because of the national interest and their own political survival. The leadership in China today derives its reputation and legitimacy to rule largely from its success in terms of domestic economic reform and reunification. Mao Zedong became modern China's founding father by liberating it. Deng Xiaoping was supported by the Chinese because of his role in saving China from the political chaos of the Cultural Revolution, in opening China to the outside world for its economic modernization and in seeing to the return of Hong Kong and Macao to China. The third generation of leaders, led by Jiang Zemin, would become national heroes if they were to succeed in getting Taiwan reunified with China. On the contrary, if they fail and Taiwan becomes an independent country, their political careers would be in great jeopardy and they would not be viewed favourably in history. Even if the status quo is maintained, they risk being seen as incompetent leaders. Jiang Zemin once said at an internal meeting, "I shall have failed in my job as party chief if significant progress on Taiwan cannot be made during my term in office."[1]

This popular strong sentiment gives Chinese leaders few choices on the Taiwan issue, and since the early 1990s, it has intensified as a result of rising nationalism against what was popularly regarded in China as the U.S. policy to contain China's rise. Consequently, there has been increasing bitterness against the United States. Unfortunately, Lee's United States visit and his speech at Cornell University came just at this time and were therefore easily interpreted by many Chinese on the mainland as "Chinese in Taiwan helping foreigners to contain their fellow Chinese on the mainland". Behind this lurks the memory of "Chinese traitors" who helped the Japanese against their own fellow Chinese in the Resistance War against the Japanese Invasion in the 1930s and 1940s. During the 1995–96 Strait Crisis some Chinese even cursed Lee Teng-hui, likening him to Wang Jingwei (the most notorious "Chinese traitor" in the Resistance War against the Japanese Invasion in the 1930s and 1940s). This is why there was such emotional and popular support for a harsh reaction to Lee's United States visit and his Cornell speech.

Despite the U.S. visa decision, Tang Shubei went ahead with his scheduled visit to Taiwan from 26 to 30 May 1995. While in Taiwan, he signed an eight-point agenda to reaffirm China's invitation to Koo for the second round of the Wang-Koo meeting. I gathered from my interviews that Tang got Jiang Zemin's personal approval for this.[2]

Why didn't Jiang cancel the trip? There were at least three reasons. First, as mentioned above, Beijing suspected the U.S. visa decision was a U.S. scheme to sabotage the upcoming second round of the Wang-Koo meeting. At that time, Beijing was not aware of Lee's efforts behind the U.S. visa decision. Second, Jiang wanted to wait and see how Lee would behave before making such a major policy reversal. Third, Beijing did not anticipate Washington's sudden change of mind after its repeated high-level assurances that it would not issue the visa. Taken by surprise, Jiang could not reverse a major policy himself, as such a move required the consensus of the Political Bureau of the C.C.P. Given the inefficiency of China's policy making at that time, it took some time to co-ordinate a consensus. During this time, popular anger against Lee and pressure on Jiang began to mount as more and more information about Lee's secret push for the visa came to light in the Western press. Lee's embarkation on his U.S. trip and his Cornell speech finally convinced Chinese leaders of his true intentions and whipped up popular anger and political pressure to such a degree that no leader in China could afford to appear soft.

Actually, while Jiang sent Tang to visit Taiwan, he also prepared himself for the worst. He arranged for articles criticizing Lee to be prepared, although he did not allow them to be published until after Lee's Cornell speech. Jiang's motivation for doing this could be subject to various interpretations. However, one thing is clear and that is that the consensus among Chinese leaders on Lee's true position on reunification and on a major reversal in the Taiwan policy took place only at that time, i.e. *after* Lee's Cornell speech. At the same time, domestic political pressure also reached new heights.

During that period, the P.L.A. took an uncompromising stance with regard to Lee. Believing that the United States had taken a tougher line with China since the end of the Cold War, the P.L.A. viewed Beijing's United States policy as being too soft. They contended that this soft policy would exacerbate the tendencies in Taiwan (and Tibet) to split away from the mainland. Before Lee's United States visit in 1995, the P.L.A. had argued that the United States should not be counted on to keep its promise and would likely allow Lee's visit. However, the Ministry of Foreign Affairs (M.F.A.) insisted that Lee's United States visit was not likely since Washington had given China a very high-level and clear promise that they would not give Lee the visa. As the P.L.A.'s assessment turned out to be correct, its voice became louder and it was consequently given more attention.

However, differences still existed. At an enlarged Central working meeting at Beidaihe in July 1995, the Taiwan issue was discussed at length. Some M.F.A. officials once again stressed the need for diplomacy. They described Lee's United States visit as a minor ripple and not worthy of aggressive retaliation. They were particularly concerned that China–United States relations could be undermined by a vociferous Chinese attack on Lee's visit. Military representatives at the meeting, however, argued for a strong response.[3]

It should be noted that it was not only the P.L.A. but also many civilians who took a very strong position, including some people in the M.F.A. The difference lay only in the stress on diplomacy or military action. Different views and assessments did exist in the P.L.A. and civilian think-tanks. It would be a misconception to view the P.L.A. as hijacking foreign policy making given that within the P.L.A. there were also voices warning against taking too harsh a tack with Taiwan.

A common interpretation of China's harsh reaction is that it was the result of a power struggle of one faction trying to replace another. Lee's United States visit and his Cornell speech stirred up strong emotions in all the factions. They began to doubt the soundness of the Taiwan policy and demanded an explanation of the situation and even a revision of the policy. Though people responded differently, this obviously could not be called a power struggle. Their responses were largely based on emotions rather than on factional ideology.

Indeed, the loss of face from being taken for a fool by Washington and Lee played a much bigger role than it normally did. Personal political consideration also played a role because no one wanted to be accused of being unpatriotic, especially when the power transition (from Deng politics to Jiang politics) had not been completed. We should not exaggerate these elements, however. They influenced to various degrees, but did not hijack China's foreign policy-making. This point can be proved by China's subsequent actions towards the United States and Taiwan as will be examined below.

Counter-Measures

The Central meeting at Beidaihe in July 1995 adopted a policy, described as "verbal attacks and armed threats". China decided to respond sharply and keep the pressure up on Lee for a certain period of time. Meanwhile, it would *"ting qi yan, guan qi xing"* [listen to his words while watching his acts] before deciding to ease the pressure. Thus, Lee's response as well as the political effects would be guaged while military exercises were conducted. Thereafter it would be decided whether or not to continue with the next round. Beijing did decide to hold another round of military exercises and missile tests in March 1996 for two reasons. In the first instance, Lee was still considered to be holding an uncompromising stance. Secondly, Beijing was encouraged by what it saw as the positive effects of its previous military exercises on Taiwan politics, i.e. the big drop in votes for the D.P.P. in the local election in late 1995. However, when the March 1996 presidential election in Taiwan produced what Beijing saw as an undesirable outcome, it made a swift policy adjustment.

In a three-day enlarged meeting of the Political Bureau of the C.C.P., only four days after Taiwan's presidential election, the leadership decided that, in view of the current situation in Taiwan, "verbal attacks and armed threats" were no longer appropriate tactics. It decided that Jiang's eight-point proposal would still be the main theme of the Taiwan policy. It would strictly observe the principle of "one China", oppose Lee's "pragmatic diplomacy" and urge Lee to live up to his promise made before the election to alleviate tension across the Strait and promote the establishment of the three direct links as quickly as possible.

Meanwhile, under the principle of "one China", the two sides should first hold talks on ending the state of hostility between them. The most desirable outcome would be an agreement to maintain relatively stable relations between the two sides. If Taiwan made "goodwill gestures", dialogue between the two sides could be resumed within the year. However, this dialogue would include a "political dialogue". If cross-strait relations could be gradually improved, the "Regulations Governing Navigation between the Two Sides of the Strait", which were adopted earlier by Beijing, would also be formally promulgated.

Beijing did not have great expectations of Lee. The relations between the two sides of the Strait would likely advance in a tortuous manner of *"da da tan tan"* [fight and talk].[4] China's Taiwan policy should be *"gang zhong dai rou, rou zhong dai gang, gang rou bin yong, shi ke er zhi"* [hard but soft, soft but hard, apply soft and hard means at the same time, but avoid overdoing it].

This policy has been largely followed to date.

Diplomatic Blockade

A brief look at the measures taken by Beijing will show that although it may make concessions on political and economic aspects of *bilateral* relations, it always holds a firm position on the matter of international sovereignty. In other words, Beijing may continue to give economic sweeteners to Taiwanese businessmen and tolerate political differences, but it will not let Taipei expand its international space.

This is not only because Beijing still cherishes a strong sense of national sovereignty but also because it is suspicious of "international interference", especially by the United States and Japan. With regard to the United States, China's strong response during the Strait Crisis has been discussed above. With regard to Japan, the Chinese believe in their heart of hearts that Japan is the country that is to blame for all the problems of the Taiwan issue. It was Japan that snatched Taiwan from the defeated China at the end of the last century and from then on Taiwan became an issue. During the Strait Crisis, Japan did not openly support Taiwan, invite Lee to visit his alma mater in Japan, or endorse the U.S. presence near the Taiwan Strait. If it had, China's protest to Japan would have been much stronger. However, China never trusts Japan entirely, describing it as "a swimming duck" which looks quiet on the surface of the water but whose feet keep paddling unseen under the water. Despite Japan's official "one China policy", some Japanese politicians contemplated a "flexible management" of Japan's Taiwan policy by supporting its membership in international organizations such as the World Health Organization.[5] Some called for Japan's support for Taiwan's eventual independence.[6]

China was upset by the Clinton-Hashimoto declaration in April 1996 which proposed the revision of the 1978 Guidelines for the United States–Japan Security Co-operation. Washington requested that Japan increase its contribution to regional security. In the revised guidelines, released in September 1997, Japan agreed to provide logistical and rear-area support for U.S. military operations in some 40 areas, including support for humanitarian relief such as transportation of refugees, rescue operations, inspection of foreign ships, evacuation of non-combatants, granting the use of military and civilian facilities to U.S. aircraft, vessels and military personnel, and rear-area support such as the supply of oil and spare parts to U.S. aircraft and vessels, medical supplies and medical treatment. Operational support such as intelligent information sharing and mine-sweeping were also included.

What China was most concerned about was the geographical scope of the new guidelines. According to the guidelines, Japanese rear area support would cover military emergencies in "areas surrounding Japan". Despite China's request for clarification, both Washington and Tokyo refused to state explicitly that the geographical scope does not cover Taiwan. They only noted that "areas surrounding Japan" is not a geographical concept, but a "situational concept" and could not be defined on a map.

In August 1997, Chief Cabinet Secretary Seiroku Kajiyama and other Japanese officials caused a row by stating that the guidelines would cover the Taiwan Strait.[7] Despite China's pressure, Tokyo did not come up with the explicit clarification that Beijing demanded. It kept reassuring Beijing that this guideline was not targeted at China. During his visit to Beijing in July 1999, Japanese Prime Minister Keizo Obuchi said Japan would not support Taiwan's independence and it would not interfere in the issue. He noted: "It is impossible for our country to support or take any action for Taiwanese independence." He also assured Beijing that "the Japan–United States security arrangements are solely for our self-defence and do not target any countries or regions".[8]

However, this Japanese assurance rests on a condition, hinted at by Obuchi when he said, "The Strait dispute should be resolved peacefully by Chinese people".[9] Obuchi reaffirmed the "one China" policy, but only in accordance with the 1972 China–Japan Communiqué. In this communiqué Japan recognized that the P.R.C. is the only legitimate government of China. But it only "understands and respects", without committing itself to, Beijing's assertion that Taiwan is an inalienable part of China.

During President Jiang Zemin's visit to Japan in November 1998, Japan reaffirmed the same "one China" policy, but rejected the Chinese insistence that Tokyo take a firmer and clearer stand on Taiwan by reiterating the "three no's" as U.S. President Bill Clinton had done in Shanghai five months before. It agreed to reiterate verbally the first two of the "three no's", namely "No to Taiwan's independence" and "No to two Chinas, or one China, one Taiwan". But it would not budge on the third, i.e. "No to Taiwan's membership in international organizations based on statehood".

China is also on guard against Taiwan's making use of the Asian financial crisis to advance its political ties with ASEAN countries and its international profile as an independent state. It reminded those affected of Taiwan's political motivation behind its proposed economic aid and required them to keep their relations with Taiwan on a non-governmental, economic and cultural footing as well as to avoid "any form of official contact" with Taiwan. It also made it clear that China did not devalue its currency partly for their sake. The hint was clear — ASEAN should not hurt China's interests by accommodating Taiwan's political wishes.

For the same reason, China rejected Taiwan's proposals for Beijing and Taipei to co-host regional meetings to discuss co-operation during the Asian financial crisis. It also rejected suggestions that Taiwan could provide financial aid as a member of the Asia Pacific Economic Co-operation (A.P.E.C.) forum.[10]

On Arms Sales

China is especially sensitive to foreign arms sales to Taiwan. As discussed in Part II, Beijing has exerted a lot of pressure on Washington to terminate its arms sales to Taiwan. One case in point was Beijing's hard bargaining with John Holum, the U.S. Acting Under Secretary of State for Arms Control and International Security Affairs, when he was in Beijing in March 1998 to prepare for the Jiang-Clinton summit in June 1998. The United States side, according to China, made some concessions in closed-door talks. John Holum promised that the United States would faithfully carry out the 17 August 1982 communiqué and was ready to reduce its arms sales to Taiwan leading to the final solution of the issue in time.[11] However, at and after the summit, the United States did not go very far in placating the Chinese on the issue and instead pushed for the T.M.D. sale to Taiwan.

Subsequently the United States has not given up or even reduced its arms sales to Taiwan and remains ambiguous, for example, about the 17 August 1982 Communiqué on the ceiling and gradual reduction of arms sales to Taiwan and how to interpret and carry out the Taiwan Relations Act (A.C.T.). China likewise has adopted an ambiguous position on its missile export policy as a corresponding bargaining chip. It even made a de facto link between its missile export policy and U.S. arms sales to Taiwan. On 21 February 1992, China promised to observe the then guidelines and parameters of the Missile Technology Control Regime (M.T.C.R.), but it only agreed to sign it after negotiation on certain terms. When the United States announced its sale of F-16 fighters to Taiwan in September 1992, China immediately terminated negotiations on the M.T.C.R. On 7 January 1993, the United States revised the M.T.C.R. On 4 October 1994, China agreed to resume negotiations on the M.T.C.R., not on the basis of the revised M.T.C.R. but on its previous draft, i.e. the one that China had agreed to observe in 1992. After the United States issued the visa to Lee Teng-hui in May 1995, China again terminated negotiations on the M.T.C.R.

China also played the Iran card by giving Washington the impression that there was a de facto linkage between U.S. arms sales to Taiwan and China's alleged missile and nuclear technology export to Iran. During the Jiang-Clinton summit in June 1998, Clinton announced publicly that Jiang Zemin had agreed not to sell Chinese missiles and technology to Iran. However, China (Jiang) chose not to confirm or deny it on the same public occasion, and no mention was made of it in subsequent agreements and written statements of the summit, or in its second white paper on defence released in July, shortly after the summit. In this white paper, China was just as ambiguous about the M.T.C.R. which was consistant with the position it took during the Jiang-Clinton summit when Jiang only agreed to consider joining the M.T.C.R.[12] After the summit, China reportedly continued to export to Iran and Pakistan the missile technology listed in the annex of the M.T.C.R., of which the United States was trying to persuade China to be a member.[13] Such Chinese ambiguity was employed as a bargaining chip to match the U.S. ambiguity in its arms sales to Taiwan.

China also used the M.T.C.R. issue to pressure the United States not to develop its planned T.M.D. in East Asia, particularly if Taiwan was to be included. In February 1999, a senior Chinese official described it as a violation of the M.T.C.R. "Since the U.S. can lead the way in breaking this regime [M.T.C.R.], other countries have an absolute right not to follow the rules of this regime and undertake co-operation on missiles and missile technology with third countries."[14] It attacked the T.M.D. as a means by which the United States aimed to "project the establishment of a minor N.A.T.O. in Asia" and saw it as "a major potential threat to the security of Asia, especially China". "If our Taiwan were to be included in the system, that would be an even more serious matter, which would mean an enormous threat toward China's state security and its military strength."[15]

Chinese leaders repeatedly warned the United States about the T.M.D. In March 1999, Foreign Minister Tang Jiaxuan reacted strongly: "If some people intend to include Taiwan under the T.M.D., that would amount to an encroachment on China's sovereignty and territorial integrity and would also be an obstruction to the great cause of peaceful reunification of the motherland."[16] Senior Chinese officials repeatedly warned that the provision of the T.M.D. to Taiwan would be the "last straw" in China–United States relations.[17]

Another potential arms seller is France. In the early 1990s, France sold 60 *Mirage* fighters and some other military equipment to Taiwan. China retaliated by turning down the French bid for the underground train project in Guangzhou and closing the French consulate there. France eventually promised not to sell any more arms to Taiwan.

Following the secret visit to France by Taiwan's Air Force commander-in-chief Huang Hsien-jung and an unannounced visit to Belgium by Taiwan's Foreign Minister in late 1996, and amid reported potential arms sales to Taiwan by these two countries, China once again exerted pressure on France and Belgium over arms sales.[18]

In 1997, China greatly improved its relations with France with both sides declaring that they had built a global partnership. The new Chinese Premier Zhu Rongji's successful visit to France in April 1998 further reduced Chinese concerns about future French arms sales to Taiwan.

In the early 1990s, the Israel Aircraft Industries (I.A.I.) signed a memorandum of understanding to supply know-how for a US$160 million maintenance centre operated by the Taiwanese Air Force. In March 1995, China successfully exerted pressure on Israel to freeze further talks on the centre. China is still keeping a watch out for potential Israeli arms sales to Taiwan although such sales do not appear likely in the near future. It is also keeping an eye on the Netherlands and other potential submarine sellers that Taiwan has approached.

On "Pragmatic Diplomacy"

Beijing tried hard to push back Taiwan's every effort at enhancing its international profile. It insisted that Taiwan renounce "pragmatic diplomacy" and take "concrete actions", including an end to its efforts to join the United Nations and to establish official relations with other nations, as well as an end to international visits by Taiwanese leaders.

It tried to sabotage Taiwan's effort to become a U.N. member and prevent it from joining major international organizations that require statehood as a precondition for membership, such as the I.M.F. and the World Bank. It demanded that Taiwan accede to certain conditions when joining international tripartite organizations (government, private and academic), such as the Pacific Economic Co-operation Council (P.E.C.C.), or other international organizations, where statehood is not strictly required, such as the Asian Development Bank (A.D.B.), Asia Pacific Economic Co-operation (A.P.E.C.) and the W.T.O. It tried to make sure that its agreeing to Taiwan's joining such organizations would not give the world the impression that China would finally make concessions on its "one China" policy. On the W.T.O. issue for example, China insisted that Taiwan could only enter as a separate customs territory and being a part of China it should not enter it before China does.

China was particularly sensitive about Taiwan's participation in international forums to discuss security issues and overseas visits by its defence officials. It maintained the security issue between mainland China and Taiwan was China's domestic affair which brooked no intervention by foreign countries and should not be internationalized. China was adamant that the issue of Taiwan's security should not be discussed between Taiwan and other countries because only sovereign states had the lawful status and qualifications to discuss such issues. Therefore, China opposed Lee's proposal of the Asia-Pacific security system and Taiwan's effort to join C.S.C.A.P. It finally agreed to Taiwan's participation in C.S.C.A.P., but only as an observer on the condition that it was in a private capacity and that the Taiwanese participant was holding U.S. citizenship, as Kau Ying-mao was.

China also worked to strengthen relations with those countries that might be tempted to shift diplomatic recognition as a result of Taiwan's economic diplomacy. In 1996, President Jiang Zemin visited six African countries with promised and actual political and economic assistance. Foreign Minister Qian Qichen also visited Africa for the same purpose. Hu Jintao, then a member of the Standing Committee of the Political Bureau of the C.C.P., embarked on a "party diplomacy" tour to Central America, seeking to set up trade or representative offices in regional countries that had no diplomatic ties with Beijing. Li Peng also visited Central and South America in an attempt to blockade Taiwan's influence in the region.

Beijing tried to persuade Taiwan's remaining diplomatic allies (26 countries by late 1998) to drop formal recognition of Taipei. In August 1996, the West African state of Niger shifted its diplomatic relations to Beijing, followed by South Africa in December 1997, the Central African Republic in January 1998, Guinea-Bissau in April 1998 and Tonga in October 1998. Papua New Guinea switched its diplomatic recognition to Beijing on 21 July 1999, only 16 days after it had set up diplomatic ties with Taipei.

China made use of its diplomatic weight, especially its right to veto, in the U.N. Security Council to exert pressure on the staunch diplomatic allies of Taiwan who played a very prominent role in helping Taiwan diplomatically, especially in the United Nations where every year since 1993 they had tabled a motion calling for the restoration of Taiwan's seat. China, for example, warned Guatemala in late December 1996 against supporting Taiwan's bid for U.N. membership and its invitation of Taiwan's foreign minister to attend the signing of the peace settlement in that country on 29 December, where he would meet many leaders and high officials from countries that have no diplomatic relations with Taiwan. The Chinese warning was made at a time when Guatemala was expecting a U.N. plan to send a peacekeeping mission for which China had the veto power to block.

Though China did not say clearly it would exercise its veto, its warning was a veiled threat. "It (Guatemala's support of Taiwan's U.N. bid) will seriously destroy the political foundation for co-operation between China and Guatemala in the United Nations". Though it did not elaborate on what was meant by this, the message was clear. Several days before the statement, China had balked at the U.N. plan to send military observers to Guatemala to implement a new peace agreement.[19]

In early January 1997, China vetoed a resolution to send 155 military observers to Guatemala to monitor the demobilization of military forces and the disarming of the guerrillas according to the peace agreement. It was the first time Beijing had used its veto power in nearly 24 years.

On 20 January, China and Guatemala reached an agreement regarding their differences. Guatemala agreed not to support a resolution in the U.N. General Assembly promoting Taiwan's admission into the organization as an independent country. It also reportedly "conveyed" to Beijing its "understanding" about the sensitivity stirred up in China over the invitation made to the Taiwanese foreign minister one month before. China finally allowed the U.N. Security Council to authorize the dispatch of officials to monitor the peace process in Guatemala.[20]

When Macedonia shifted its diplomatic recognition to Taipei, China severed ties with it in late February 1999 and vetoed a U.N. Security Council resolution to extend the stay of peacekeepers in Macedonia for six months.

China was also closely watching and taking steps to minimize the impact of any transit visits or private visits made by high Taiwanese officials to countries with no diplomatic relations with Taiwan. It was particularly sensitive to any such visit by Lee Teng-hui. It was successful in blocking Lee's effort to attend A.P.E.C. forums overseas and his effort to visit his alma mater in Japan, i.e. Kyoto University. In early 1998, China postponed its Defence Minister Chi Haotian's visit to Singapore in protest to Taiwanese Vice President Lien Chan's "holiday" to that country.

Military Pressure

In April 1996, President Jiang Zemin reiterated China's position on the use of force for reunification. He said: "If Taiwan pursues independence and if foreign forces intervene in the Taiwan issue and hinder China's peaceful reunification, then the mainland will have to use force to safeguard national sovereignty and territorial integrity. This is not to be doubted. If China renounces the use of force, foreign countries will become wildly ambitious, the Taiwan independence force will become more arrogant, and they will more rampantly carry out their plot to disintegrate China's territory. If some people in Taiwan pursue Taiwan independence, split China's territory and refuse to be Chinese, then the issue will not be one within Chinese people, and the issue 'Chinese people should not fight Chinese people' will not exist."[21]

China has for a long time insisted that it would use force in two instances, namely "foreign intervention" in the Taiwan issue and the "independence of Taiwan". However, the term "foreign intervention" is open to a wide range of interpretations because it does not specify that only a physical foreign military presence in Taiwan is considered an intervention. For example, are foreign arms sales or "renting" advanced weapons an "intervention"? And what about foreign political intervention? The condition of the "independence of Taiwan" instead of a clear and formal declaration of independence also allows for a wide range of interpretations. Sometimes, Beijing makes it even more ambiguous by using the expression "Taiwan's pursuit of independence" as Jiang did in the above quotation.

Apart from these two instances, Chinese officials occasionally add a third, i.e. "if there is an uncontrollable incident in Taiwan". The third precondition is sometimes interpreted as a civil war, widespread social turmoil, or a large-scale persecution of Chinese from the mainland by local people.

China believes that its clear determination to use force under these conditions has successfully deterred Taiwan's further drift towards independence. Eventual reunification with Taiwan depends less on "sweeteners" at the present stage than on the future success of China's modernization drive, including military modernization.

The P.L.A. believes that it enjoyed military advantage over Taiwan before the delivery of the U.S. F-16s and the French *Mirage* 2000-5s. To maintain and enhance the military advantage, President Jiang Zemin agreed to the P.L.A. request, for example at a military product exhibition in early 1996, to put more funds into high military technology research, acquisition and production of more advanced military weaponry.[22]

It was reported that China originally planned to build aircraft carriers during the "10th Five-Year Plan" period of 2001–2005. However, in light of cross-strait relations, and especially the dispatch of two U.S. aircraft carriers during the Taiwan Strait Crisis in March 1996, there was pressure to obtain aircraft carriers earlier. Jiang Zemin reportedly approved the implementation of the plan ahead of schedule.[23] Though there is no hard evidence yet that Jiang has set a definite date for acquiring the aircraft carriers, there is no doubt that the Chinese are making preparations. For example, the P.L.A. began training its pilots to land and take off using a model of an aircraft carrier runway as early as in the 1980s. At the same time China purchased a de-commissioned aircraft carrier from Australia for "scrap" (actually for research). In mid-1998, China again bought a de-commissioned Russian aircraft carrier for research.[24] In late December 1996, the P.L.A. finalized its purchase of two Russian-built *Sovremenny* destroyers.

Since 1996, China has made a greater effort to improve its surface-to-surface short and medium range missiles such as the M-9 and M-11 and especially land-attack cruise missiles for theatre warfare and strategic attack. According to a U.S. Department of Defence report in 1997, the first land-attack Chinese cruise missile would be ready to be air-launched from Chinese bombers after 2000.[25] However, I gathered from my interviews that China already had cruise missiles in the early 1990s, which were further improved through the study of unexploded U.S. *Tomahawk* cruises missiles (from the Gulf War of 1991) which Iraq sold to China. By 1996, the Chinese cruise missiles were already very accurate but China chose not to show them off in the March 1996 military exercises in the Taiwan Strait.

China also paid a lot of attention to the development of information warfare and electronic warfare capabilities, such as computer hackers (e.g. planting misleading information, altering data, shutting down vital operations in an opponent's computerized control and command systems, or planting computer viruses), electronic weapons (e.g. procuring state-of-the-art intercept, direction finding and jamming equipment), directed-energy weapons (e.g. laser guns to paralyse satellites, micro-wave beams, particle beams, high energy radio frequency [H.E.R.F.], acoustic cannon, plasma guns, high energy ultrasonic weapons, subsonic wave weapons) and non-directed energy weapons (e.g. Electro-Magnetic Pulse [E.M.P.]. China has actually acquired the technology to make E.M.P. miniature warheads which have the power to shut down all electronic systems in a limited area before an invasion, without casualties and without affecting neighbouring regions.[26] Major units of the P.L.A. have developed more advanced electronic surveillance and interference capabilities. More P.L.A. navy vessels have been equipped for electronic warfare, and the P.L.A. air force now possesses more than ten specially equipped electronic warfare planes.[27] The P.L.A. also simulated more computer-virus offensives in exercises, for example in Shenyang, Beijing and Nanjing in 1997–99.

In 2000, the P.L.A. will put another six military satellites into orbit to provide enhanced high-definition pictures of military establishments and movements on Taiwan.[28]

The P.L.A. troops, especially the infantries in Nanjing and Guangzhou Military Regions and even the P.L.A. armoured troops in Shenyang Military Region, have been focusing more attention on their forced cross-strait landing and occupation capabilities, especially rapid and large-scale landing of heavy armoured vehicles, anti-tank capability and the co-ordination of the three services.[29] A military airport has been built in the north-western Gansu Province, next to the Dingxin airbase, which is identical to Chingchuankang Airport in central Taiwan, so it can practise bombing the island.[30]

During cross-strait tensions following Lee's announcement of the "two states" theory in July 1999, China for the first time officially announced it had its own neutron bomb. It was known to have exploded a neutron bomb in 1988, but in keeping with its secret military traditions, it had never announced the achievement before. Though the announcement was made in the process of rejecting U.S. allegations that China stole its nuclear technology, it has implications for Taiwan.

After the announcement, Chinese specialists claimed that the neutron bomb would deter those advocating independence in Taiwan. A Chinese military journal, *China's Defence News*, issued a disguised warning by saying that the neutron bomb would prove effective in an armed assault on Taiwan.[31] Meanwhile, Chinese Foreign Ministry spokeswoman Zhang Qiyue, when asked at a news conference, would not comment clearly on whether China would use the neutron bomb against Taiwan. She said: "China's nuclear policy is clear and therefore it is up to you to ponder." Zhang warned Taiwan never to "underestimate the firm resolve" of the Chinese government to enforce its territorial integrity.[32] Her answer was different from that given by Sha Zukang, director general of the Foreign Ministry's arms control and disarmament division, in 1996. He had first broached the idea that Taiwan was not a foreign territory and therefore theoretically China's nuclear policy of constraint would not apply. Later, under media pressure, he explained that China would not use nuclear weapons against its fellow Chinese on Taiwan.[33]

Given a situation where China feels that it has no other choice but to use force immediately, it may have to take effective action and achieve the swift occupation of Taiwan out of a concern of foreign invention if it drags on too long. If China can achieve this with conventional military means, it may not use neutron bombs. If not, the possibility of China using it in the second wave, when its conventional military offensive is defeated by Taiwan, cannot be excluded. Another factor in favour of using neutron bombs is that China developed them and miniaturized nuclear warheads in the 1970s and 1980s. Its tactical nuclear warhead can be as small as a 500-tonne T.N.T. In other words, the damage, caused by neutron bombs (if they are also thus miniaturized) can be limited to a very small area, paralysing, for example, a military airport, naval base, or underground military base without killing residents in the nearby cities. And the radiation dissipates fast. Thus, it may avoid the massive civilian casualties and city destruction often associated with using heavy conventional military weapons.[34] However, due to the huge political cost, neutron bombs have been considered more as deterrence than their actual use.

Political Pressure

Beijing's pressure on Taiwan reached a peak immediately after Lee's Cornell speech. China vowed to throw Lee into the "historic dustbin". It blamed cross-strait tension on the "divisive activities" carried out by the Taiwan authorities in the international arena. It claimed that cross-strait relations would develop normally only when the Taiwan authorities had given up their pursuit of "Taiwan independence" and their moves to create "two Chinas" or "one China, one Taiwan" in word as well as in deed. Taiwan, as a regional economy, could only take part in non-governmental economic and trade activities in the international arena. Taiwan's relations with other countries should therefore be non-official and non-governmental.

Regarding the direct presidential election, China said: "No matter how the way of electing Taiwan's leaders changes, the stark reality that Taiwan is a part of China's territory and its leaders are only leaders of one region of China cannot change."[35]

As for the form of government for a future reunified China, Beijing refused to accept the form of a federation or confederation, or two central governments. It insisted that the future China would be only one nation, one state and one central government.[36]

It warned: "So long as the Taiwan authorities continue activities aimed at splitting the motherland, our struggle against separatism and 'Taiwan independence' will not cease for a single day."[37] This reflected its new policy, adopted at the Beidaihe meeting in July 1995, that every move by Lee towards Taiwan's independence should be resolutely pushed back, without hesitation or tolerance. It called on Taiwan to respond to Jiang's eight-point proposal and take concrete action for political talks, including a way to end the hostility between the two sides. It insisted that political talks had to begin first, because negotiations on practical matters between the two sides (there had been 17 such negotiations between A.R.A.T.S. and S.E.F. before Lee's United States visit in 1995) had often stalled over political obstacles.[38] It emphasised the "one China" principle.

As for Lee's offer to make the peaceful journey to China, it said that it had already made its own offer in Jiang's eight-point proposal to welcome Taiwan leaders to the mainland. It insisted that Lee should come in "an appropriate capacity", i.e. not as state president.

What should be pointed out is that Chinese pressure during 1995–99 had been declining until Lee put forward his "two states" theory in early July 1999. By 1998, China was already showing considerable flexibility, best exemplified in its position regarding the resumption of cross-strait talks as discussed below.

Resumption of Cross-Strait Talks

Following Lee's Cornell speech, China announced that it was postponing indefinitely the second round of the Wang-Koo meeting. Taiwan condemned China for such unilateral action. It called on China to "pick up where it left off" and resume the meeting. It sent Koo Chen-fu, instead of an economic minister, as Taiwan's special envoy to the A.P.E.C. meeting in Osaka, Japan in late 1995 with the purpose of speaking to the Chinese president Jiang Zemin there. Jiang, however, only shook hands with Koo at an A.P.E.C. reception, avoiding any formal or informal meeting to discuss cross-strait relations.[39]

China refused to accept Taiwan's condemnation. It said that it was Taiwan who should be responsible for the failure of holding the second round of the Wang-Koo meeting because Lee's United States visit and Taiwan's subsequent actions had poisoned the atmosphere that was needed for such a meeting. Unless Taiwan did something to improve the atmosphere, it would refuse to resume the meeting.

To Beijing, an early resumption would have left Taiwan and other countries with at least three "undesirable" impressions. First, it would appear that China did not take very seriously visits by Lee and other high-ranking Taiwanese officials to countries that have no diplomatic relations with Taiwan. Second, it would have to tolerate Taiwan's diplomatic push without being able to stop it. Third, it needed the resumption of talks more than Taiwan.

Later on, with the improvement in China–United States relations, China perceived the bargaining environment to be better and adjusted its position. It then called for the resumption of talks but stressed that political as well as practical matters should be discussed under the "one China" principle. At the 15th National Congress of the C.C.P. in September 1997 and the third anniversary of the eight-point proposal in January 1998, President Jiang Zemin called for an end to the state of enmity across the Strait, early peaceful reunification and early resumption of cross-strait talks. He insisted on the "one China" principle and discussion of political issues. He also called on all parties (not only the K.M.T.) in Taiwan to conduct talks with Beijing on reunification.

Faced with this change in Beijing's posture, Taipei retreated from its early eagerness for the resumption of talks. It refused to resume talks under such demands from Beijing. It insisted that the second round of the Wang-Koo meeting should only be limited to discussion on practical and technical issues and should not touch on political matters as Beijing had demanded. It also insisted that the "one China" principle should not be a precondition for the resumption of talks and that the two sides should be regarded as equal entities in the talks (in July 1999, Lee changed from using the phrase "two equal entities" to "two states".

In response to Jiang's call, Lee said that the state of enmity between China and Taiwan would end only if Taiwan was treated as an equal entity. He said the mainland must recognize the existence of the R.O.C. and that China and Taiwan had been under separate governments since 1949. Recognizing this fact was the first step towards cross-strait negotiations by both sides.[40] It rejected Beijing's call for all the parties in Taiwan to attend talks on reunification, insisting that "negotiations are conducted between states, not between parties".[41] It also called on Beijing to renounce the use of force in reunification before holding peace talks.

With Taiwan's strong opposition to political negotiations and insistence on discussing practical issues, Beijing readjusted its position again. It asked Taiwan to engage in talks not on political issues alone but on practical issues as well, or meetings to discuss the process and technical issues leading to political talks before eventually holding such political talks.

As for Taiwan's insistence on not using the "one China" principle as a precondition for the resumption of the Wang-Koo meeting, it said that "one

China" was a principle but not a precondition. At the same time, it made a concession on the "one China" principle. In November 1997, in a fresh interpretation of the "one China" principle, Wang Daohan noted that "'one China' refers to a China that has yet to be reunified, the one that both sides should together move towards" and that "one China does not equal the People's Republic of China, nor does it equal the Republic of China, but a reunified China jointly built by people on both sides of the Taiwan Strait".[42]

From early 1998, further changes took place. In January 1998, Wang Daohan again called for the resumption of cross-strait talks. He suggested that "as the first step, the two sides of the Taiwan Strait should start negotiations on ending cross-strait hostility under the 'one China' principle" and that "on this basis, both sides can together assume the responsibility in safeguarding China's sovereignty and national unity, and jointly plan future cross-strait development".[43] He also came forward with three proposals in an article published in January 1998, namely holding negotiations to end hostilities, boosting cross-strait economic co-operation despite political differences and enhancing cultural exchanges and co-operation.[44]

In the same month, while calling on Taiwan to enter into political negotiations, Beijing promised to treat Taipei as an equal, saying "such talks will not be conducted as central-to-region talks". While insisting that political negotiations preceded all other discussions, Beijing reaffirmed that those talks were to be "procedural" in nature, paving the way for the resumption of cross-strait dialogue.[45]

Beijing explained that it had to say "one China" to the international community because it could not afford not to. But once engaged in bilateral talks with Taiwan, it would not say "one China" because this talk would be about domestic affairs not international affairs.

It further softened its conditions by saying that Taiwan did not have to recognize Beijing as the central government before starting political negotiations. Tang Shubei said in late January 1998, "We do not think cross-strait negotiations require the precondition that Taiwan first recognizes the People's Republic of China Government as the central government. As long as it promises to accept 'one China', and 'Taiwan is a part of China', our negotiations on 'one China' are solved".[46]

On 26 January, Vice Premier Qian Qichen gave an official endorsement of this shift in position on the "one China" principle, which he also reaffirmed in April 1998. He said: "Standing firm on the 'one China' principle is to stand firm that there is only one China in this world and Taiwan is a part of China, that China's national sovereignty and territorial integrity cannot be divided".[47] This reinterpretation of the "one China" policy was strikingly different from before. He now chose not to mention that the P.R.C. was the sole legitimate government of China. And he did not liken the government on the island to a provincial government by mentioning Taiwan as a part of China instead of a "province" of China as Beijing had done in the past.

In 1998, Wang Daohan also presented an "86-character definition" of the "one China" principle. It reads: " There is only one China in the world. Taiwan is a part of China, not yet unified. Both sides should work together, under the one China principle, to discuss reunification in consultations based on equality. The sovereignty and territorial integrity of a country are inseparable. Taiwan's political status should be discussed under the one China prerequisite.[48]

Subsequently Wang Daohan on several occasions suggested to Taiwan that, firstly, the sovereignty of China could be shared (between Beijing and Taipei) but not divided and, secondly, if Taiwan accepted the "one China" principle, Beijing would be willing to change the national title (i.e. the People's Republic of China), national flag and national anthem. These proposals and offers by Wang, Qian, Tang and other Chinese officials were publicly reaffirmed at the highest level, i.e. by Chinese President Jiang Zemin, on 11 November 1998. Jiang especially emphasized China's willingness to discuss the change of national title, national flag and national anthem for reunification, and made the offer of high positions in the central government for people from Taiwan without a corresponding requirement that officials from the mainland take up positions in Taiwan after reunification.[49]

Despite these initiatives from Beijing, Taiwan still insisted on separate rule. It pointed out: "Our Government is clear about the 'one China' stance. That is, China is currently ruled separately by two entities".[50] It urged Beijing to display more flexibility by acknowledging Taiwan as an equal political entity. It continued to call for a resumption of the Wang-Koo meeting but only wanted to discuss practical issues not political issues. However, its tune and manner were slightly different. In March 1998, Chang King-yuh, then M.A.C. chairman, said that Taipei was willing to have full-blown political negotiations, but only "in due course". According to him, ending the state of bilateral hostility and the "one China" principle were issues that could be discussed after step-by-step contacts and negotiations. He chose to emphasize that semi-official talks on technical issues must come first.[51] He did not say how long this would take, or how many steps there would be before political talks could be held, or who was going to decide and according to what standard. At the same time, Taiwan's other leaders emphasized "democratic unification" as the goal of any talks with the mainland.[52]

In February, China's A.R.A.T.S. sent a fax to Taiwan's S.E.F. agreeing to Taiwan's suggestion to resume cross-strait talks. The letter appeared to accept Taiwan's preference for resuming technical dialogue before the two sides moved on to political negotiations. It read: "We are willing to discuss procedural matters regarding opening political talks across the Taiwan Strait. ... And we are prepared to resume discussions of economic and technical issues".[53] However, it wanted the "discussions" to lead to "political talks".

The first talk between China and Taiwan since May 1995 finally took place in late July 1998 between Li Yafei, a deputy secretary-general of China's A.R.A.T.S. and Jan Jyh-horng, a deputy secretary-general of Taiwan's S.E.F. It was described as an "exchange of opinions", instead of a formal talk, on a future "visit" to China (not a formal meeting) by S.E.F.'s chairman Koo Chen-fu. It focused on procedural and economic issues. It was agreed that Koo Chen-fu would "visit" the mainland in the same year to meet his mainland counterpart Wang Daohan.

This was not considered to be a resumption of the Wang-Koo meeting. Koo's visit to the mainland would just be to see Wang Daohan and other friends there. Li proposed that Wang and Koo meet each other at a "research seminar" to be jointly organized by A.R.A.T.S. and S.E.F., with each side responsible for inviting its own delegates. However, Jan preferred a "gradual" approach, i.e. S.E.F. Secretary General Shi Hwei-yow should first hold preparatory talks with his counterpart, A.R.A.T.S.' Secretary-General Tang Shubei, before Koo travelled to the mainland to "visit" and meet Wang, and not at a seminar jointly hosted by the two sides as A.R.A.T.S. proposed.[54]

Beijing hesitated for some time about Taiwan's insistence on the trip by Shi Hwei-yow for preparatory talks to arrange for Koo's visit. One reason was that the arrangement of Koo's visit could be made during Li Yafei's visit to Taiwan and through correspondence between S.E.F. and A.R.A.T.S. Shi's visit was not necessary. Second, since Shi had been appointed as the Secretary General of S.E.F. to replace of Chiao Jen-ho in February 1998, Beijing had tried to avoid meeting him. Shi Hwei-yow was known in Beijing as a "*ding men gang*" [recalcitrant], a hawkish figure with a strong Taiwan ideology and "the man of the king" (Taiwan President Lee Teng-hui). When he was a deputy of S.E.F., he had often blocked preliminary agreements in past cross-strait talks.[55]

Nevertheless, Beijing finally agreed to Shi's trip to the mainland and he came in late September 1998. Koo's visit to China was then scheduled for 14–19 October and A.R.A.T.S. agreed to arrange a meeting between Koo and President Jiang Zemin on 18 October.

Beijing wanted Koo's visit to be aimed at starting a series of political negotiations for reunification. But Taipei wanted to keep the visit on a more general level and start with small-scale practical talks to build up confidence.

Koo finally made his trip to China as scheduled. However, as will be discussed in Chapter 9, this trip illustrated clearly the huge gap between the two sides, difficulties in achieving an early reunification and uncertainty over the future development of cross-strait relations.

Economic Engagement

Since China changed its Taiwan policy in the late 1970s, it has been consistent in pushing for economic and cultural exchanges across the Taiwan Strait in the hope of establishing sooner the three direct links for earlier economic integration and political reunification. China took measures to encourage Taiwanese investment such as enacting the Law for the Protection of Investment of Taiwan Compatriots by the National People's Congress in 1993 and the 22 provisions formulated by the State Council, as well as adopting special preferential policies and regulations by the central and local governments for Taiwanese investment and trade.

Taiwan benefited tremendously from this open policy with a huge trade surplus in its favour. Cross-strait trade has jumped from US$77 million in 1979 to over US$20 billion in 1998, which is an average annual increase of more than 40 per cent.[56] In the five months from January to May 1999, trade volume was as huge as US$9.84 billion. Taiwan had accumulated more than US$90 billion profit in this cross-strait trade over the period 1979–99.[57] This is partly due to the strong Taiwanese business competitiveness and also, to a significant degree, to the preferential policy given by Beijing *only* to Taiwanese businessmen for political reasons.

However, after the face-off in 1995, quite a number of Chinese took the view that without the special preferential policy, Taiwanese businessmen would not have been as competitive as other foreign and local businessmen. They saw the Taiwanese as being ungrateful for the preferential treatment which had enabled them to make huge profits. They were even seen, whether intentionally or unintentionally, as helping other powers to contain the rising China by challenging earlier reunification. On the other hand, Taiwan felt that, to use Lee Teng-hui's words, "Communist China is trying to use our people to coerce our government and use commerce to achieve political coercion in order to pressure our government".[58]

Yet, Beijing still continued to push for closer economic ties with Taiwan. Despite conducting the military exercises, it quickly moved to reassure Taiwanese businessmen that their interests would not be penalized because of Lee's behaviour. It continued its preferential policy towards them and encouraged them to keep their commercial activities and investment in China.

It asked local governments to take steps to attract more Taiwanese investment. For example, in Beijing, the municipal government unveiled a plan in August 1996 to build an industrial park and a science park housing Taiwan-funded companies, with preferential treatment given to Taiwanese investors in the parks. It also set up a service centre to provide consultation and legal services to Taiwanese investors. It promised Taiwan businessmen "lucrative" profits.[59] In early 1997, in another bid to boost investment from Taiwan, the municipal government called on its various departments to reduce bureaucratic hurdles for

Taiwanese investment.[60] It took measures to enforce the implementation of the Law for the Protection of Investment of Taiwan Compatriots and promulgated its own "Several Stipulations of Beijing Municipality on Encouraging Investments by Taiwan Compatriots".

The municipal government introduced a system of reception days for Taiwan businessmen. Under the system, the mayor and relevant department heads would meet Taiwan investors regularly for their views (once every six months for the mayor and once every three months for the department heads). Meanwhile, all subordinate districts and counties established Taiwan affairs offices or relevant co-ordination bodies to provide services for Taiwan-invested enterprises in their localities or in their industries. Many law offices were set up, aimed at providing better legal service for Taiwanese investment.[61] In October 1996, the municipality granted approval for the establishment of 1,604 enterprises with Taiwan investments, involving a contractual amount of investment totalling US$2.469 billion.[62]

Other municipalities and provinces took similar measures to encourage more Taiwanese investment. Officials of the State Council's Taiwan Affairs Office and leaders at different levels often held forums with Taiwanese businessmen for problem shooting.

Meanwhile, commercial and cultural officials and well-known figures continued to visit Taiwan. For example, several months after China's March 1996 military exercises, there was an unusually large number of such visits. Among the visitors were senior officials from Fujian Province, the head of the Shanghai Stock Exchange, bankers and financial officials, the president of Air China and senior officials from China's Telecommunications Ministry. In July 1996, a 22-member Chinese delegation of harbour bureau chiefs and shipping executives visited Taiwan to study direct shipping services across the Taiwan Strait. The delegation included top executives of nine major harbour bureaus: Dalian, Qinhuangdao, Tianjin, Qingdao, Shanghai, Ningpo, Yantai, Xiamen and Guangzhou.[63] Other visitors included Zhang Xuwu, vice-chairman of the All-China Federation of Industry and Commerce, Jing Shuping, chairman of the All-China Federation of Industry and Commerce and Guo Dongpo, head of the China Council for the Promotion of International Trade. Chinese academics, specialists and officials in their private capacities also went to Taiwan for seminars on cross-strait relations.

China's policy to "separate politics from economy" worked well, at least before Lee adopted the "go slow" policy on 14 August 1996. While the two sides had been engaged in a political "cold war" since June 1995, economic relations strode forward with once-unthinkable deals. For example, China worked out a deal with Taiwan on 13 June 1996 guaranteeing Taiwan Airlines' right to fly to Hong Kong long after it was to be handed over to China on 1 July 1997. In return, a Hong Kong airline owned by a Chinese state company was allowed to fly Taiwan routes. China also lured Taiwan's petrochemical giant, Formosa Group, to invest US$3.3 billion for a power station in Fujian with a high profit return rate (if not for Lee's 14 August decision to "go slow", the deal would have gone through). In July, oil giants from both sides, Taiwan's China Petroleum Corporation and China's National Offshore Oil Corporation, signed a historic oil-exploration pact, the first direct co-operative agreement linking state firms from Taiwan and China in any sector.

Despite the on-going military exercises from 1995 to 1996, cross-strait investment and trade continued. According to statistics from China's Ministry of Foreign Trade and Economic Co-operation (M.O.F.T.E.C.), Taiwanese businessmen signed investment contracts for 4,778 projects in China in 1995, although this was down by 23.5 per cent compared with 1994. However, contracted investment rose by 7.1 per cent to US$5.77 billion.[64]

As for trade, China imported US$14.78 billion worth of goods from Taiwan in 1995, up 4.9 per cent from 1994. Its exports to Taiwan totalled US$3.1 billion in 1995, up 38.1 per cent from 1994.[65] According to Taiwan's Board of Foreign Trade (B.O.F.T.), in 1995 Taiwan's indirect trade with China rose 27.1 per cent (compared with 1994) to US$20.99 billion, with exports rising 22.1 per cent to US$17.89 billion, while imports surged 66.3 per cent to US$3.09 billion.[66] The fact that the figures given by both sides are only slightly different (due to different ways of calculating) reflects this surging flow.

According to B.O.F.T., in 1996, exports to China accounted for 16 per cent of Taiwan's overall exports.[67] This reflected the importance of China as a big market. It is likely that these figures may have understated real exports to the mainland by as much as 20 per cent. Much of Taiwan's trade with China was done via Hong Kong and Hong Kong customs figures were incomplete. There is evidence that a considerable amount of trade was conducted directly in defiance of the official ban without being properly recorded. If this is taken into account, China was perhaps Taiwan's second most important export market after the United States. As Taiwan's Vice Premier Hsu Li-teh noted after China took over Hong Kong in July 1997, it undoubtedly would become Taiwan' biggest trading partner.[68]

Among Taiwan's four biggest trading partners in 1996, i.e. the United States, Japan, Hong Kong and China, the sources of Taiwan's trade surplus were Hong Kong and China. For example, in 1995, there was US$16 billion deficit in its trade with Japan. This deficit was balanced by the surplus in its trade with the United States, which was US$5.8 billion and with Hong Kong (including China), which was US$18 billion.[69] In other words, its trade with China and Hong Kong was its main source of foreign currency surplus, especially after Hong Kong's hand-over to China in July 1997.

In 1995, about 1.5 million people from Taiwan visited China, over 100,000 more than the year before. More than 4,800 mainland people visited Taiwan in comparison with 3,900 people in the previous year.[70]

Despite China's March 1996 military exercises, this trend continued to surge well into 1996 before Lee Teng-hui's "go slow" policy, announced on 14 August 1996, began to present some difficulties. Before then, approvals for investment projects in China in July 1996 amounted to US$230 million, a 99.16 per cent jump from June. In the first seven months of the year, investment projects totalled US$786 million, up 17 per cent from the same period in 1995. Between January and July, investment in electronic and electric manufacturing rose 43 per cent from a year earlier to US$187.6 million, followed by investment in transport equipment which rose 42 per cent to US$88.36 million. Investment in the chemical industry rose 9 per cent to US$81 million and that in food manufacturing gained 18 per cent to US$77 million.[71]

According to Taiwan's B.O.F.T., in the first six months of 1996, the indirect trade between Taiwan and China rose 1.5 per cent over the same period the year before to US$10.44 billion.[72] Statistics released by the Directorate General of Budget, Accounting and Statistics (D.G.B.A.S.) under Taiwan's Executive Yuan showed that a total of US$520 million in outward remittances were channelled from Taiwan to China in the first ten months of this year, up 18.4 per cent year-on-year. Inward remittances to the island from China grew 4.7 per cent during the period to total US$60 million.[73]

Lee Teng-hui was worried about the political implications of this persistent trend and put a sudden brake on this trend on 14 August 1996 with the announcement of the "go slow" policy. Yet, China still made the effort to encourage further economic engagement. Jiang Zemin chose to make a prominent appearance by meeting a Taiwanese business delegation headed by Kao Ching-yen, chairman of Taiwan's Chinese National Federation of Industries and head of the President Enterprises Group in late August 1996. Jiang told Kao that China would not allow political differences with Taiwan to interfere with trade and investment and vowed to "protect all the legitimate rights of Taiwanese investors no matter what the circumstances".[74] It has since worked out and published detailed application rules for the Law on the Protection of Investment of the Taiwan Compatriots. As for Taiwanese investment and other business in China, Beijing adopted the policy of "*tong deng qing xing, tai zi you xian*" [give preference to Taiwanese investors if under the same situation].[75]

China emphasized that it was not in Taiwan's interest to prevent its entrepreneurs from investing in the mainland. It repeatedly claimed "we will not affect or interrupt cross-strait economic co-operation with political differences, but rather will promote such relationships by encouraging Taiwan business people's investment and follow the law of protecting Taiwan compatriots' investment and expand trade as well".[76]

It was not easy for Taiwan to reverse the trend. Although Lee Teng-hui repeatedly appealed for restraint in the flow of capital to the mainland, the pace and concentration have not slowed down significantly. By early 1997, investment was showing signs of a new surge despite the government's call for restraint and tighter screening of applications. Larger conglomerates like President Enterprises Group and Wei Chuan Foods continued increasing investments on the mainland market but used different ways and means so as not to violate the government ban.[77] Other Taiwan producers of foods and petrochemical intermediates followed suit, and information product suppliers were the most active in branching out to the mainland.

The Hong Kong Card

Hong Kong's hand-over to China in July 1997 was China's strong leverage over Taiwan. Taiwan has huge investments and wide-ranging business, social, political and cultural interests in Hong Kong, servicing them through state-funded but technically unofficial agencies. Because of the official ban on direct links with China, at least 70 per cent of Taiwan's annual trade with mainland China was routed through Hong Kong.[78] Its investment in China, estimated at US$30 billion and accounting for at least 43 per cent of its combined overseas investment in 1998, was mostly channelled through Hong Kong.[79]

In 1996, Taiwan's exports to Hong Kong stood at US$26.80 billion (most of them were destined for China) while imports (from Hong Kong) were just US$1.70 billion.[80] About 38 per cent of Taiwan businesses received orders in Hong Kong, 50 per cent used the territory as a transhipment base and 20 per cent sought funding there.[81] Taiwan's three main ports, Kaohsiung, Keelung and Taichung, depended upon Hong Kong for 38 per cent, 32 per cent and 61 per cent of their container traffic, respectively.[82]

The huge commercial interest of other countries in Hong Kong could also be used to China's diplomatic advantage. Those countries that refused to switch their official diplomatic relations from Taipei to Beijing had their consulates general in Hong Kong closed or downgraded to a non-governmental status. South Africa's decision to switch its official diplomatic recognition from Taiwan to China, for example, was partly to protect its interests in Hong Kong after the hand-over.

However, Beijing did not use Hong Kong to press Taiwan as hard as many had expected before the hand-over. It appeared more interested in making Hong Kong's hand-over a self-evident model for Taiwan's reunification than in exploiting it in a rash and crude manner. It intended to use the model to allay Taiwanese and international doubts about the possibility of "peaceful reunification" and the success of the "one country, two systems" formula and to enhance its international image.

The Hong Kong card was also a two-edged sword. Its failure could also be profoundly damaging to China in both the long and the short term. If pressed too hard, Taiwan could also do much damage to Hong Kong at a time when the latter badly needed stability and international confidence during the Asian financial crisis. It was in China's interest to play the Hong Kong card in a cautious, subtle and patient manner. Therefore, China showed a lot more tolerance towards Taiwan's presence in Hong Kong than many had expected. It set general policies to define a broad framework in which to confine Taiwan's activities in Hong Kong after July 1997. On 21 June 1995, Chinese Foreign Minister Qian Qichen announced seven principles as the basis for handling post-1997 Hong Kong–Taiwan relations. They include the following major points:

1. Existing non-official interactions between Hong Kong and Taiwan can continue, including economic and cultural exchanges and Taiwan's business operations in Hong Kong.
2. The rights of Taiwanese residents are protected by law.
3. On the basis of the "one China" principle, air and shipping routes between Hong Kong and Taiwan will be considered special routes between regions and proceed on the basis of mutual benefits.
4. Official contact between Hong Kong and Taiwan is subject to Beijing's authorization and approval of the Hong Kong Special Administration Area (S.A.R.) chief executive.
5. Taiwan's offices and personnel can stay in Hong Kong, provided they follow Hong Kong's Basic Law and do not act against the "one China" principle, or harm Hong Kong's stability and prosperity, and refrain from activities inconsistent with their registered operations.
6. The "one China" principle stipulates that there is only one China, and Taiwan is a part of it.
7. Beijing represents the only official Chinese government.[83]

Under this general framework of seven principles, China encouraged Taiwanese businessmen to continue their investment and business in Hong Kong. Taiwanese organizations in Hong Kong were allowed to stay so long as they were registered as non-governmental so as not to violate the "one China" policy. Political activities by Taiwanese residents in Hong Kong, such as public protests and even celebrations of the R.O.C. anniversary on 10 October were surprisingly tolerated so long as they were of individual character and acceptable size.

Beijing also showed a surprising spirit of compromise in reaching a memorandum on 24 May 1997 with Taipei agreeing to Taiwan's demand that no flags (in place of the P.R.C. flag) need be hoisted when its ships visited Hong Kong after July 1997. Under the May pact, Hong Kong-registered ships would fly the flag of the post-colonial Hong Kong Special Administrative Region on their stern flagpoles and no flags on their masts during the time between entering and leaving Taiwan ports. Between entering and leaving Hong Kong's ports,

Taiwan-registered commercial vessels would not fly a flag on either mast or flagpole. Vessels registered in either the mainland or Taiwan could fly their company flags and signal flags.[84] This compromise solved the shipping issue to the satisfaction of all three sides.

Push for the Three Direct Links

China has been pressing for the three direct links since the late 1970s and has intensified this effort in recent years. Jiang Zemin called for the three direct links in his eight-point proposal in early 1995 and reiterated the call on many subsequent occasions.

At present, like the trade between the two sides, all letters, parcels, phone calls and faxes are principally diverted via Hong Kong. China is keen for direct post and telecommunications. It suggested that a direct mail route be set up by sea and air, and that "conditions" be created for a direct cross-strait undersea fibre optic cable, as well as co-operation on direct telecommunications by cable and satellite.[85]

After losing the civil war in 1949, the K.M.T. retreated to Taiwan and Taiwan adopted an official Three-No's policy, i.e. no negotiation, no concession and no contact. Limited relaxation of this policy began to take place from the mid-1980s. By 1998, it had agreed to cross-strait transhipment sailing (though it is not direct sailing in a strict sense because of its limitations as discussed in previous chapters). Recently it modified this rigid position on the three direct links. It now stipulates that China should take concrete actions to show its goodwill before the two sides hold talks on the three direct links.

Taiwan has not elaborated on what these "concrete actions" and "goodwill" should be. They seem to include its insistence that China must first of all acknowledge Taiwan as an equal political entity and renounce the use of force. It is clear that there are no technical difficulties as far as setting up the three direct links is concerned. The only obstacle is political will. Taiwan's reluctance to agree to the three links is easy to understand. It is first of all concerned about its security and stability, and second, it intends to use the three direct links as a bargaining chip.

The K.M.T. government in Taiwan is facing mounting pressure to open the three direct links, not only from Beijing but also from its own businessmen and even the D.P.P. Among them are prominent and influential businessmen who used to enjoy good relations with Lee. For example, Y.F. Chang, chairman of Taiwan shipping giant Evergreen Marine who used to be a closed friend of Lee, publicly branded Lee's "go slow" policy as "naive".[86] Many other businessmen joined him. Among them was Formosa Plastics Group chairman Wang Yung-ching, whose planned power plant in the mainland was forced to close down with Lee's "go slow" policy. This resentment is being exploited by the D.P.P., whose leaders challenged the K.M.T. by calling for an earlier lifting of the ban on the three direct links.

With the Asian financial crisis, Lee's "go south" and "go slow" policy has come under increasing pressure. In March 1998, Taiwan's China External Trade Development Council started cautioning Taiwanese businessmen to "go anywhere but south" because investors were sustaining great losses as a result of instability there. In mid-1998, Taiwan had to put a stop to its "go south" policy. Chiang Ping-kun, chairman of Taiwan's Council for Economic Planning and Development noted that the government was "no longer encouraging Taiwanese enterprises" to invest in Southeast Asia. In September, the Taiwan government urged Taiwanese manufacturers to refrain from making new investments in Southeast Asia. A study by the Central Bank of China (C.B.O.C.) revealed that the banking sector as a whole lost about US$4.8 billion from their Southeast Asian exposure. It therefore advised other banks to put a temporary halt to fresh loans for Southeast Asian projects. Without backing from banks, the "go south" policy was thwarted.[87]

The setback in Lee's "go south" policy added pressure to Lee's "go slow" policy. According to Taiwan's Ministry of Economic Affairs, investments in China increased by 42 per cent to US$695 million in the first six months of 1998. By contrast, investment flow into Southeast Asia had declined, particularly investments in Indonesia and Thailand.[88]

The Economic Importance of the Three Direct Links

The two sides could have saved millions of dollars each year by having direct telephone lines using undersea cables or satellites, instead of routing calls through third countries/places, like Hong Kong, Singapore or even the United States. This indirectly cost each side, taking 1995 for example, about US$18 million. Taiwan already makes more telephone calls to China than to anywhere else in the world. The most effective approach would be to lay a fibre-optic cable between China's Xiamen and Taiwan's outlying island of Jinmen, just a few miles from the mainland.[89]

Direct shipping will bring immediate and direct economic benefits to Taiwanese businessmen by cutting costs and thereby make them more competitive. In 1984, there was only one ship from Taiwan which passed the mainland via Hong Kong to load and unload 5,000 tonnes of goods. In 1989, however, there were as many as 139 with 790,000 tonnes of goods. In 1990, 232 ships called in with 1.47 million tonnes of goods. In 1991, 497 ships called in with 3.87 million tonnes of goods. Since 1991, there have been more than

400 ships docking from Taiwan every year.[90] With this huge volume of shipping, the economic benefits of direct shipping are obvious.

Direct shipping can also save Taiwan's shipping industry from its current difficulties. Although Taiwan has many shipping companies, most of them are small in size. For example, in 1993, out of 116 shipping companies, 84 of them (72.5 per cent) had only 1–2 ships and 80 of them (68.8 per cent) had the dead-weight tonnage of below 10,000–20,000 tons. Eighty of them had registered funds of below NT$100 million.[91] They were faced with difficulties arising from increasing costs and competition from foreign counterparts. In 1993, for example, of a total of 52,211 ships visiting Taiwan, 38,674 were foreign, comprising 74.1 per cent and 13,537 were Taiwanese, comprising 25.9 per cent.[92] With direct shipping, Taiwan's shipping industry would find it much easier to overcome their difficulties.

Taiwan's harbours would also benefit from direct shipping. For example, in 1986, Taiwan's (mainly Kaohsiung Harbour) container handling capacity was 4.1 million teu and that of Hong Kong was only 2.27 million teu. In 1995, Hong Kong handled 12.6 million teu, making it the centre of sea transportation in East Asia, whereas Kaohsiung handled only 5.2 million teu as it was hit by the lack of direct cross-strait shipping. China's harbours at that time and at present still do not have the capability to become container handling centres like Kaohsiung harbour.[93]

A direct link is also expected to help lower costs considerably and increase the competitiveness of Taiwan's textile industry, which is heavily reliant on transhipment of goods through Hong Kong at present. Following the opening of the Taiwan market for textiles made in mainland China by Taiwan-invested manufacturers, the establishment of direct links will serve to facilitate co-operation between raw material suppliers in Taiwan and Taiwan-invested garment makers in the mainland. This will promote an effective cross-strait division of labour and will raise the overall competitiveness of Taiwan's textile industry.

Textile transhipment trade between the mainland and Taiwan has been vibrant for years. Statistics from the Taiwan Textile Federation show that, at present, 40 per cent of Taiwan's textile exports are shipped through Hong Kong and this figure is increasing each year. Yet transhipment through Hong Kong is both slow and expensive. Goods that are shipped through Hong Kong often face delays of up to two weeks. In addition, when Taiwan-invested garment makers in China ship fabric from Taiwan for processing, and then send the semi-finished products back through Hong Kong to Taiwan, they are subject to an import tax (12.5 per cent in 1996). As a result, many companies ship the finished goods back to Hong Kong and then on to other countries. This is inconvenient and it also prevents Taiwan from taking advantage of China's processing operations.[94]

In these circumstances, Lee's "go slow" policy is faced with mounting pressure from Taiwan businessmen. Most Taiwanese investments in China are small in size and lack the advanced management and high-technology of Western multinationals. They have made profits in past years partly because of a lack of strong international competition. Now, with more and more big multinationals from the West entering the Chinese market, they are finding it difficult to compete with them without the three direct links and because medium and large-sized Taiwanese companies (including banks) continue to be banned from setting up establishments in China to provide them with cheaper materials as well as better financial and technical services. The lack of clarity and stability in cross-strait relations has made Taiwanese businessmen less inclined to plan for the longer term and more likely to work towards quick and short-term profit. This has greatly diminished their chance of profitability. With increasingly fierce competition from more multinationals in the mainland, this once-successful hit-and-run business practice without long-term planning and commitment no longer works.

Many Taiwanese businessmen have already aired their complaints about Lee's "go slow" policy and his refusal to establish the three direct links. This is a card that China has been playing to its advantage, prompting Lee to accuse China of "using commerce and our people to pressure our government".

The W.T.O. Card

Both Taipei and Beijing are now in the process of applying for World Trade Organization (W.T.O.) membership. The question is whether Taiwan will be able to exercise the right of exclusion to declare Beijing excluded from privileges accorded to other W.T.O. members under provisions contained in the charter once the two are admitted as full members. If the right of exclusion is waived, Beijing could force Taiwan to further relax its ban on the three direct links which Taiwan has up till now refused to do on grounds of security. Otherwise, Taiwan has to treat China in the same way it treats other full W.T.O. members, which will mean it cannot continue to refuse to set up the three direct links. Taipei will feel at a great disadvantage if Beijing becomes a full member while Taiwan is kept outside the W.T.O. However, Taiwan would feel the same way if it is not able to have the right of exclusion after becoming a full W.T.O. member.

As early as 1992, the W.T.O. board committee had agreed to the Chinese insistence that China be granted W.T.O. membership ahead of Taiwan. The W.T.O. card should not be over-exaggerated. Even if the two joined it at the same time, and Taiwan fails to get the exclusion right, it may also continue to constrain *its own* investment in and trade with China because the W.T.O. does not deprive its members of the right of self-constraint. However, the W.T.O. forbids its members to discriminate against other members when they come to trade. Taiwan may be able to somehow compromise (though not completely break) this rule by citing its national survival as a reason. This is also a reason why China insisted that Taiwan should not be admitted into the W.T.O. ahead of China. As a W.T.O. member, Taiwan may be able to exert its influence on rule-making.

The Shanghai Card

China is also using the Shanghai card to engage Taiwan economically. It is building Shanghai into a world-class economic, financial, technological, transportation and cultural centre in East Asia. The strategic implications are tremendous, both for its future position in East Asia and its reunification with Taiwan.

One of China's strategic errors was being slow in opening up Shanghai to economic development. From the late 1970s, it began opening up Shenzhen, Zhuhai, Shekou, Shantou and other cities, whereas Shanghai was only opened up in the early 1990s. The main reason was that Beijing was very cautious and tended to conduct economic reform in certain areas as an experiment before promoting the experience nation-wide.

As Shanghai's economy comprised a significant portion of the national total in the early 1980s, Chinese leaders were very reluctant to experiment with Shanghai when the country first opened up. In other words, should China's economic reform fail, it would only lose the economies of a few special economic zones. This would not seriously damage its whole economy like a breakdown of Shanghai's economy would. Only in the late 1980s, when China felt confident enough, did it begin to open up Shanghai. Shanghai's economic reform did not really make big strides until the early 1990s.

If Shanghai had been developed earlier into a major economic, financial, technological, transportation and cultural centre for East China and East Asia, China would have been in a much better position in dealing with Taiwan now. China was reluctant to come down harder on Taiwan during the strait crisis of 1995–96 or to use the Hong Kong card to exert more pressure on Taiwan. One major reason was the concern over its economies in both East China and South China (including Hong Kong).

From this perspective, Beijing would view with suspicion Taiwan's effort to build itself into an Asia-Pacific operational centre. Should Taiwan's efforts be successful, international opposition to Chinese pressure on Taiwan for reunification would be much wider and stronger than during the 1995–96 Strait Crisis. Tang Shubei said in 1996 that Lee Teng-hui's plan for setting up the "Asia-Pacific regional operational centre" had the motive to seek independence. He disclosed that the C.C.P. had already formulated the strategic principle, "stabilize Hong Kong, develop Shanghai". On the one hand, the stable transition of Hong Kong around 1997 as well as Hong Kong's status as a navigation centre must be guaranteed. On the other, the building of Shanghai as an international navigation centre would be accelerated to defeat Taiwan's plot of building the "Asia-Pacific operation centre".[95]

China is now fast building Shanghai into a major economic centre. One purpose is to compete with Taiwan as an economic centre in East Asia. While its efforts cannot be confidently said to be a success in the future, Taiwan's efforts to build itself into an Asia-Pacific operational centre are unlikely to succeed. The reason is simple. Many international investments would flow to Taiwan or set up their regional headquarters in Taiwan mainly with the purpose of tapping the potential huge markets in mainland China as well. If Hong Kong and Shanghai can become and remain strong economic centres with easy access to the Chinese market, there will be little need for international investors to go to Taiwan in order to reach China. Even if, for a period, international investors do not feel comfortable with and confident in Shanghai, they will hardly have confidence in Taiwan if the tension across the Taiwan Strait remains. Without China's co-operation, Taiwan's plan to become such a centre will not go far. A repeat of the military tensions in 1995–96 will deprive Taiwan of much of the international confidence it needs for such an effort.

The High Technology Card

China would like to see economic integration with Taiwan. But the question is, who depends on whom? China's current policy is to keep itself in the driver's seat [*yi wo wei zhu*], making Taiwan's economy dependent on the mainland so as to deprive Taiwan of the economic resources and political will for independence. In this light, Taiwan's effort to upgrade its industry through high technology and to become a regional technology centre will be seen by Beijing as resistance to such a strategy. For the same reason, Taiwan is also suspicious of China's bid to become the world's No. 2 technological power by 2020 through massive investment in high technology. China is already strong in basic science research but weak in applied science and technology. Should China become the No. 2 technological power and devote its scientific and technological resources along with its cheap labour to areas Taiwan is currently developing, Taiwan will find it has less economic leverage in its future bargaining with China.

The economies of both sides supplement each other strongly and the two have much more to gain if they co-operate closely in the field of technological and economic developments. Unfortunately, different political pursuits have made this co-operation difficult.

China can play the card in two ways. One is to pool its resources to develop high technology in competition with Taiwan in order to edge out Taiwan with its cheap labour and better basic science research. The other is to incorporate Taiwan's development of high technology industry into its own. In her visit to Taipei in July 1998, China's Science and Technology Minister Zhu Lilan called on Taiwan's industries to jointly develop technology industries of mutual interest. China now mainly targets those Taiwanese companies with high technologies and invites them to build science parks in China. For example, over the period 1997–99, despite Lee's "go slow" policy, Taiwanese electronics companies, a crucial source of the island's economic growth, still moved 29 per cent of their computer-related manufacturing to China.[96]

Notes

1. Willy Wo-Lap Lam. "Jiang Vows to Pin Clinton to Taiwan Pledges", *SCMP*, 4 June 1998.
2. The interviews were conducted in China in October 1996.
3. "China: China's Policy towards Taiwan, Jane's Intelligence Review", Reuters, 1 December 1995.
4. "Taiwan: China Reportedly Intends to Isolate Taiwan Internationally", *Lien Ho Pao*, 8 April 1996, p. 1, from Reuters, 10 April 1996.
5. See remarks by Hiroshi Yamada, a Diet member from the defunct Shinshinto, *The Japan Times*, 3 January 1996, p. 1.
6. For example, Professor Kosaka Masataka of Kyoto University believed that Taiwan is entitled to be independent from China based on the principle of national self-determination. See Kosaka Masataka. "Diplomacy and Security in the Twenty-First Century", *Japan Echo*, Winter 1996, p. 68.
7. Mary Kwang. "Hashimoto Admits He Failed to Win China Over on U.S.–Japan Pact", *ST*, 7 September 1997.
8. Mary Kwang, "China, Japan Agree on WTO Entry", *ST*, 10 July 1999. "Japan PM Assures Beijing Tokyo–U.S. Pact No Threat", *SCMP*, 9 July 1999.
9. He said: "It is impossible for our country to support or take any action for Taiwanese independence. The Strait dispute should be resolved peacefully by Chinese people." See "Defence Pact Worries Zhu", *SCMP*, 10 July 1999.
10. Mary Kwang, "Crisis Talks: China Rebuffs Taiwan", *ST*, 8 April 1998. Also see "Taiwan Group in U.S. to Push Forum Idea", *SCMP*, 13 April 1998.
11. *Lianhe Zaobao*, 1 April and 3 April 1998.
12. "U.S. Officials Say China Still Sells Missile Data", *IHT*, 13 November 1998.
13. Ibid.
14. "'Veiled Threat' on Missiles", *SCMP*, 27 February 1999.
15. These quotations are from *Banyuetan* [Half-Month Forum] (Beijing), quoted from Oliver Chou, "Beijing Targets U.S.–Japan Pact", *SCMP*, 9 February 1999.

16. John Pomfret, "Beijing Hardens On Missile Shield", *IHT*, 8 March 1999.

17. Ibid.

18. "China Launches Offensive against Taiwan by Warning France and Belgium", *SCMP*, 11 December 1996.

19. "China: China Warns Guatemala against Backing Taiwan", Reuters, 26 December 1996.

20. "United Nations: Guatemala Resolves Differences with China over Taiwan", Reuters, 23 January 1997.

21. "China: Chinese President Reportedly Meets Taiwan Presidential Aide", *Wen Wei Po*, 27 April 1996, p. A2, from Reuters, 30 April 1996.

22. From my interview with a Chinese strategist in Beijing in 1996.

23. "China: China to Produce First Aircraft Carrier by the Year 2000", *Ping Kuo Jih Pao*, 4 January 1997, p. A14, from Reuters, 6 January 1997.

24. Qing Wen, *"Zhongguoren Yuan Le Hangmu Meng?"* [Have the Chinese Realized Their Dream of Having Aircraft Carriers?], *Lianhe Zaobao*, 18 September 1998, p. 25.

25. Barbara Starr, "China Could 'Overwhelm' Regional Missile Shield", *Jane's Defence Weekly*, 23 April 1997, p. 16.

26. "Beijing Explores Use of High-Tech Weapons", *ST*, 5 November 1998. Anne Gruettner, "Taipei 'Ready to Buy U.S. Missile Defence'", *SCMP*, 22 April 1999.

27. "Warning on PLA Electronic Ability", *SCMP*, 18 May 1998.

28. It was reported by *United Daily News* and *Chung Kuo Shih Pao*, quoted in *ST*, 15 March 1999.

29. See, for example, Liu Xiaojun, *"Zhongguo Jundui Jiaqiang Kuahai Jingong Nengli"* [Chinese Troops Enhance Their Capability of Cross-Sea Offensive], *Lianhe Zaobao*, 28 July 1997, p. 13.

30. "China Builds Airport Copy", *China Times Express* [Taiwan], 28 April 1999.

31. "Beijing's Neutron Bomb Option", *ST*, 8 August 1999.

32. Joe Mcdonald, "China: We Have Our Own Neutron Bomb", AP, 15 July 1999.

33. China's nuclear policy reads: "never use nuclear weapons first and never use them against non-nuclear countries".

34. Zhao Yunshan, *Xiaoshi zhong de lian'an* [Bi-Coast Disappearing] (Taiwan: Xinxinwen (New News) Publishing Company, 1996), Chapter 3.

35. "China: Chinese Spokesman Says Taiwan Must Abandon 'Splittist Activities'", *Wen Wei Po*, 14 February 1996, p. A1, from Reuters, 15 February 1996. Also see "Taiwan: Taiwan Radio Cites Chinese Spokesman on Presidential Elections, U.S. Relations", Reuters, 26 March 1996. Xinhua, "Beijing Meeting Marks First Anniversary of President Jiang's Statement on Taiwan", Reuters, 1 February 1996.

36. *Lianhe Zaobao*, 3 August 1996, p. 24.

37. Zhongguo Xinwen She, [China News Agency] (Beijing), "Chinese Work Conference on Taiwan Ends", 29 April 1996, from Reuters, 1 May 1996.

38. Mary Kwang, "Taiwan Fanned the Flames of Asian Turmoil, Says China", *ST*, 13 March 1998. Also from a presentation given by A.R.A.T.S. Councillor Zhang Mingqin at the East Asia Institute of the National University of Singapore on 18 January 1999.

39. *ST*, 21 November 1995, p. 10.

40. "Only One Way to End China Enmity", *ST*, 15 September 1997.

41. Jason Blatt, "The KMT Rejects Talks Plea", *SCMP*, 17 October 1997. According to *China Times Express* of 16 October 1997, more than 400 of the 2,000-plus delegates to the K.M.T.'s 15th National Congress, which convened in August, signed a petition for the K.M.T.'s central headquarters to resume negotiations with Beijing.
42. Lee San Chouy, "Beijing Redefines 'One-China Principle'", *ST*, 18 November 1997. Mr Wang was quoted as saying so to a visiting group from Taiwan's Alliance for Democratic Reform.
43. Jason Blatt and Daniel Kwan, "Taipei Hesitant in Responding to Olive Branch", *SCMP*, 1 January 1998.
44. "ARATS Chief Urges Restart of Unity Negotiations", *SCMP*, 3 January 1998.
45. Daniel Kwan, "Beijing Promises to Treat Taipei as Equal in New Negotiations", *SCMP*, 5 January 1998.
46. "Beijing Softens Taiwan Stance", *SCMP*, 27 January 1998.
47. Daniel Kwan and Jason Blatt, "Qian in Appeal to Taiwan over Talks", *SCMP*, 20 April 1998.
48. The Association for Relations across the Taiwan Strait, 1998 *Nian Zhongyao Wenjian Xuanbian* [Selected Important Documents of 1998] (Beijing: The Association for Relations across the Taiwan Strait, 1999), p. 150. Wang also repeated it to Koo Chen-fu on 14 October 1998 when Koo visited China.
49. *Lianhe Zaobao*, 14 November 1998, p. 32.
50. "Beijing Softens Taiwan Stance", *SCMP*, 27 January 1998.
51. "Taipei Implores Beijing to Resume Negotiations", *SCMP*, 26 March 1998.
52. For example, see Taiwan Premier Siew Wan-chang's remarks in "Taiwan Urges 'Democratic Reunification'", *SCMP*, 21 February 1998.
53. "Beijing Softens Line on Taiwan", *SCMP*, 25 February 1998.
54. Daniel Kwan, "Split over Pace of Dialogue as Talks Reopen", *SCMP*, 24 April 1998.
55. Vivien Pik-Kwan Chan, "Beijing Tries New Reunification Strategy", *SCMP*, 9 April 1998.
56. *Hong Kong Economic Journal*, quoted in "Too Much for China to Lose", *ST*, 22 July 1999.
57. Xinhua, "*Jianchi 'Lianguolun' Jiushi Beipan Taiwan Renmin*" [The "Two States" Theory is betrayal of People of Taiwan], *Renmin Ribao*, 3 August 1999, p. 4.
58. Kevin Chen, "Taiwan's Lee Accuses China of Political Coercion", Reuters, 14 September 1996.
59. "China: Beijing to Build Parks to Lure Taiwan Investors", Reuters, 29 August 1996.
60. "China: China Capital Calls for More Taiwan Investment", Reuters, 5 January 1997.
61. "Beijing Municipality Promotes Economic Ties with Taiwan", *Renmin Ribao* (overseas edition), 27 January 1997, p. 5, from Reuters, 12 February 1997.
62. Ibid.
63. Central News Agency, "Mainland Harbour Administrators Arrive for Visit", from Reuters, 24 July 1996.
64. Jane Macartney, "China to Separate Taiwan Politics from Economics", Reuters, 17 March 1996.
65. Ibid.
66. "Taiwan: Taiwan–China Trade Rises 27.1 Percent in 1995", Reuters, 1 March 1996.
67. "Cross-Strait Trade Exceeds US$20 Billion in 1995", *Taiwan Business News*, from Reuters, 4 March 1996.

68. "Taiwan: Vice Premier Wants Economic Focus in Cross-Strait Relations", Reuters, 7 May 1996.

69. From my interviews with Wang Daohan in October 1996.

70. "Taiwan: China–Taiwan 1995 Relations Reviewed", China Radio International (Beijing), from Reuters, 3 January 1996.

71. "Taiwan: Taiwan July Investment in China Up 99 Pct", Reuters, 10 August 1996.

72. "Trade with China Rises", *SCMP*, 28 August 1996.

73. "Outward Remittances to Mainland China in First 10 Months Up 18.4 Percent", *Taiwan Business News*, from Reuters, 11 December 1996.

74. "China: China Says Politics Won't Hurt Trade with Taiwan", Reuters, 29 August 1996.

75. From presentation given by A.R.A.T.S. Councillor Zhang Mingqin at East Asia Institute of the National University of Singapore on 18 January 1999.

76. Xinhua, "Chinese Foreign Minister Urges Industrialists Not to Prevent Investment in Mainland", 7 April 1997, from Reuters, 9 April 1997.

77. "Taiwan: Mainland Investments", Reuters, 18 February 1997.

78. Bruce Cheesman, "Taiwan Plans a Wake for the Old Hong Kong", *The Australian Financial Review*, 16 April 1997, p. 9.

79. Christopher Bodeen, "Taiwan Keeps China Investment Limit", AP, 2 April 1999.

80. Kevin Chen, "Hong Kong Hand-Over Leaves Taiwan Exposed", Reuters, 23 March 1997.

81. Cheesman, op. cit.

82. Bruce Cheesman. "HK–Taipei Shipping Links Preserved", *The Australian Financial Review*, 28 May 1997, p. 16.

83. *Renmin Ribao*, 22 June 1995.

84. "China: China and Taiwan Confirm Hong Kong Shipping Pact", Reuters, 16 June 1997.

85. "Taiwan: Mainland Demands Taiwan Allow Direct Postal, Telecom Links", Reuters, 6 February 1996.

86. CNN, News Program, 16 October 1997.

87. Ching Cheong, "Taiwan Shelves Go South Policy on Investments", *ST,* 26 September 1998.

88. Ibid.

89. Alice Hung, "Taiwan, China 'Unofficially' Mull Direct Telecoms", Reuters, 24 July 1996.

90. Li Jian, *"Lian'an Tonghang Dui Lian'an Guanxi Fazhan Zhi Yingxiang"*, [The Impact of Direct Shipping on the Cross-Strait Relations], p. 2.

91. Ibid., p. 3.

92. Ibid.

93. Ibid., p. 5.

94. "Direct Links Expected to Benefit Taiwan's Textile Industry", *Taiwan Business News*, from Reuters, 27 January 1997.

95. "Cross-Strait Relations Official — New Guiding Principle towards Taiwan Proved Correct", *Ming Pao* (Hong Kong), 20 January 1996, p. A2, Reuters, 7 February 1996.

96. Christopher Bodeen, "Taiwan Keeps China Investment Limit", AP, 2 April 1999.

Part IV

Conclusion

9

Stalemate and Dilemma

In previous chapters, the policies and positions taken by Beijing, Taipei and Washington have been discussed in detail. In this chapter, the rationale behind those "given facts" is examined to illustrate the stalemate and dilemma Beijing is faced with in cross-strait relations.

Strategy and Rationale

The key to understanding China's Taiwan policy and its future direction lies in the understanding of its perception of (1) the international situation, (2) United States/Japan intentions with regard to Taiwan, (3) the intention of Taiwan leaders (as a whole) with regard to reunification and (4) the domestic situation.

China's persistent suspicion of U.S. intentions with regard to the Taiwan issue has long been a major factor in its Taiwan policy. Even Mao Zedong, aware that Chiang Kai-shek resisted what he saw as U.S. intentions to keep Taiwan permanently from the mainland, lent him political support. Mao said in a speech to the C.C.P. leaders in 1959: "At this point, our choice in Taiwan is between Hu Shi/Chen Cheng and Chiang Kai-shek. Who is better? Faced with this choice, I think that Chiang Kai-shek is better. Chen Cheng and Hu Shi *have more connections with the United States* and therefore Chiang Kai-shek is better."[1]

Mao was more concerned about U.S. intentions than his arch political rival Chiang and backed Chiang against Chen Cheng and Hu Shi. In 1988, Deng Xiaoping expressed the same concern. He said: "So long as Taiwan has not been reunified with the mainland, the status of Taiwan, the status as part of the territory of China, remains uncertain. Nobody knows when it will be snatched away from us once again in the future".[2]

China has always been suspicious that the United States and Japan are against Taiwan's reunification for both geo-political and ideological reasons. This explains China's strong opposition to the "internationalization" of the Taiwan issue.

In 1979, its slogan was "placing the hope (of reunification) on the government of Taiwan". In 1981, it added one more sentence: "placing the hope on the government of Taiwan and placing the hope on the people in Taiwan *too*". Later, it deleted the word "too". From 1991, it changed the wording to "placing the hope on the government of Taiwan but placing more hope on the people in Taiwan". After Lee Teng-hui's U.S. trip in 1995 and during the subsequent Taiwan Strait Crisis of 1995–96, it deleted the first sentence, i.e. "placing the hope on the government of Taiwan". It only chose to say "placing the hope on the people in Taiwan". After the March 1996 presidential election in Taiwan, it even stopped for a while talking about "placing the hope on the people in Taiwan". In the statement by President Jiang Zemin at the Fifteenth C.C.P. National Congress in September 1997, he only chose to say "placing the hope on those people in Taiwan who have a glorious patriotic tradition".

This change of wording reflects the evolution of China's assessment of Taiwan politics and its increasing disillusionment with the leaders in Taiwan and even the people of Taiwan over reunification. We all know that there are now very few people in Taiwan who can meet China's standard of *"having a glorious patriotic tradition"*. This is the dilemma China is faced with now. After 1998, China almost stopped mentioning "placing the hope on those people in Taiwan who have a glorious patriotic tradition."

Beijing was convinced that unlike Chiang Kai-shek and Chiang Ching-kuo, Lee firmly believed in pursuing Taiwan's independence, either in the name of the Republic of Taiwan or the Republic of China. Hence, it changed its strategy towards Taiwan. In a reversal of its previous strategy of keeping the United States away, China has, since 1996, concentrated its efforts on the United States. This is because, firstly, it believed that nothing, neither hard nor soft tactics, would have any effect on Taiwan, at least so long as Lee Teng-hui was in power. Secondly, without strong U.S. support, Taiwan's effort to seek independence would be futile. Thirdly, although Washington would not support an early reunification, it would not support a dramatic change in the status quo in near future either. It would gradually and eventually come to see the strategic rationale of working out a co-operative relationship with China for its long-term global and regional strategic interests. So U.S. co-operation, however limited, was not only needed, tactically if not strategically, but also possible.

Working on the United States

Jiang Zemin said in 1996:

> The Taiwan independence movement's gaining force is not an isolated phenomenon. Without the fostering and support of foreign forces, the Taiwan independence

movement would not be so rampant. Taiwan independence elements put up a show on the front stage while foreign forces hide behind the screen. Some Taiwan leaders have tried to strengthen their hands with foreign backing, involve foreign forces in Taiwan affairs and beg foreign countries to support Taiwan in creating two Chinas or "one China, one Taiwan" in the international community.[3]

Whether China liked U.S. "interference" or not, it could not resolve the Taiwan issue without U.S. "involvement" in one way or another. In other words, China had to work on the United States. Such work was not aimed at soliciting U.S. support for reunification but at isolating the independence movement in Taiwan from international support and confining Taiwan's international efforts to a space that was to be negotiated between China and the United States.

After much effort, relations between Beijing and Washington improved. In October 1997, President Jiang Zemin embarked on a formal state visit to the United States. The last such visit had been undertaken 11 years before by former Chinese President Yang Shangkun. One year later, in June-July 1998, a second summit took place between President Jiang Zemin and President Bill Clinton.

Washington often chose to send messages to Taiwan through former high officials. In January 1998, a high-powered delegation, headed by former Secretary of Defence William Perry, visited Taiwan after its visit to Beijing and Hong Kong. Its members included former National Security Adviser Brent Scowcroft, former Chairman of the Joint Chiefs of Staff John Shalikashvili and former Commander-in-Chief of the Pacific Command Ronald Hays. Perry reportedly carried a message from Beijing that it was ready to open talks with the island with no preconditions. Perry obviously exerted some pressure on Taiwan to return to the negotiating table with Beijing to stabilize cross-strait relations. He publicly expressed his "optimism" that cross-strait talks would resume in the same year.

In March 1998, former chairman of the America in Taiwan Association Natale Bellocchi warned Taiwan not to hold out too much "unrealistic hope" of American support in the event of a cross-strait conflict with China. He told Taiwan there was a growing preference among U.S. strategists for the two squabbling parties to come to some form of commitment to overcome the current stand-off.[4]

Former U.S. Under Secretary of Defence Joseph Nye warned: "The U.S. does not want to be involved in a Chinese civil war. How Americans will respond will depend on the circumstances. If it is viewed as arising out of a provocation by Taiwan, it will be a mistake to assume there will always be two carriers". He proposed that Taiwan could say it would not declare independence and China could agree to allow the Taiwanese more "international space" such as more acceptance at some international forums and making less fuss over the overseas visits of Taiwanese leaders.[5]

On another occasion, Joseph Nye also proposed replacing the existing U.S. policy of strategic ambiguity with clear commitments from Washington, Beijing and Taipei. The United States, besides not supporting Taiwanese independence should the island declare it, would also ask other countries to refrain from extending official recognition to Taiwan. On the flip side, Washington would oppose Beijing should the latter resort to military force. Meanwhile, China should accommodate Taiwan's desire for more international space. In exchange, the island should accept the "one China" principle, pledge not to declare independence and open itself up to more cross-strait exchanges.[6] Such proposals, particularly the United States persuading others not to recognize Taiwanese independence, were very striking.

Like Joseph Nye, Harvard University Professor Ezra Vogel also saw the emergence of not just "one country, two systems" but "one country, three systems", a formula rejected by Taiwan as inapplicable.[7] He noted: "The long-run power situation, the realpolitik, is such that China itself will grow increasingly relative to Taiwan, both in economic and military power." This would make it "very hard" for Taiwan to declare independence. In the end, the two sides would find some formula under which "the mainland has some kind of sovereignty" while Taiwan would have foreign relations and its own military.[8]

Taipei noticed the unfavourable shifts in the attitude of some U.S. policy-makers towards Taiwan. In May 1998, Tien Hung-mao, a top mainland and foreign policy adviser to Lee Teng-hui, warned that U.S. officials increasingly felt Taiwan should accept Beijing's claims over the island. Taiwan was alert to any agreements, open or secret, resulting from the top-level exchanges of visits between Beijing and Washington. Some officials in the U.S. policy-making establishment advocated chipping away at America's defence commitments to Taiwan and freezing weapons sales to the island. Visits from former high-ranking U.S. officials and top scholars in early 1998 were widely viewed as a strategy to gently nudge Taiwan into reopening talks with Beijing.[9] The most telling blow to Taiwan was the public affirmation of the "three nos" by President Clinton during his visit in China in June 1998.[10]

In 1999, U.S. Deputy Assistant Secretary of State, Stanley Roth, proposed that Taipei and Beijing sign "interim agreements" on certain difficult topics to pave the way for the eventual settlement of the Taiwan issue. Washington officials also urged Taiwan and China to set up a hotline and establish a direct link between their military forces so as to avoid a confrontation resulting from a misjudgement by either side.[11]

However, the main purpose behind U.S. efforts is to have stability across the Strait. Unless there is a significant change in the international strategic balance of power producing a situation in which the United States badly needs China's strategic support, Washington will not go very far in meeting China's reunification request. This was why after the public presidential announcement of the "three no's", Washington, defying Beijing's protest, sent its energy minister, Bill Richardson, to visit Taiwan in November 1998 to assure Taiwan publicly that there was no change in Washington's Taiwan policy. It continued to sell advanced weapons to Taiwan, including two power phased array radar and two E-2T *Hawkeye* 2000E aircraft and other early-warning radar systems to enhance its air defence. It was considering covering Taiwan within the T.M.D. system and selling it *Aegis* destroyers to counter Chinese short and medium-range missiles. In the U.S. Congress, there has been strong support for Taiwan's security against China's pressure. Aware of all this, Beijing was not expecting much more from Washington than efforts to constrain Taiwan from pushing too hard at further independence, which would be in U.S. interests too.

Working on Taiwan

In this section, China's policy towards the K.M.T. and the D.P.P. in the changed situation since the 1995–96 Strait Crisis is discussed.

Working on the K.M.T.

Disillusioned with Lee, Beijing did not trust his K.M.T. government's commitment to reunification. Any "friendly" gestures from the K.M.T. government had either been limited and conditional, or were more for international and domestic political consumption than aimed at a real breakthrough for reunification. Many of the gestures came from officials from ministries and departments other than the presidential office and the president himself. In Taiwanese politics, the president still carries a lot of weight. The final mainland policy choice rested with Lee Teng-hui himself. He often vetoed these initiatives and gestures by his subordinates and even denied remarks he had previously made. For example, in July 1996, Premier Lien Chan and other officials were still pushing for "taking mainland China as the main market" [*yi dalu wei fudi*] for Taiwan to become an "Asia-Pacific regional operation centre". However, at the National Assembly on 14 August 1996, Lee suddenly reversed this policy by proposing (and later adopting) the policy of "go slow and be patient" [*jieji yongren*]. In another example, in 1997, several months of highly publicized new initiatives by Taiwanese officials to improve relations with Beijing were sabotaged by Lee's publicly calling Beijing "stupid" during his visit to Paraguay in September 1997. He said: "Don't be scared by the size of Communist China. Regardless of how big it is, it is no bigger than my pa. ... And what's the use of being big. (China) is just stupid".[12] Two months later, in two separate interviews with *The Washington Post* and *The Times* of London, Lee even declared that

Taiwan is "an independent, sovereign country, just like Britain or France".[13] He repeated the statement several times in both Mandarin and English and therefore a misreading of his words by journalists was very unlikely. However, he later denied this by saying that he had been misquoted by journalists.

In his book *The Future of Asia,* which is a collection of his speeches during the years up to 1996, Lee categorically refused to accept the "one China" principle, claiming "at the moment, on the one side of the Taiwan Strait is water, on the other side is oil. The two just do not mix well".[14]

In May 1999, Lee mapped out his vision for Taiwan in his new book *Taiwan de Zhuzhang* [Taiwan's Viewpoint]. (The title of the English version of the book is *With the People Always in My Heart.*) In the book, he urged Beijing to give up its concept of a "Great China" and divide China into seven autonomous regions, Taiwan, Tibet, Xinjiang, Mongolia, north-eastern China, southern China and northern China.

To Beijing, these remarks reflected Lee's true voice. Chinese strategists told me that Lee was arrogant and hostile to China, slippery at making deals and skilful at deceiving. They complained that as far as China's diplomacy in the 1990s was concerned, it suffered much more at the hands of this slippery Lee than with any other country.

Some K.M.T. officials I interviewed told me that when Taiwan put forward the six-point proposal in April 1995 in response to Jiang's eight-point proposal, they really wanted to seek some co-operation across the Strait. They said that although Beijing was not satisfied with the six-point response, there were some common points of co-operation between the two sides. They told me that they were actually preparing the details for mutual co-operation, especially agricultural co-operation.

However, even if these K.M.T. officials were sincere enough, Beijing was doubtful about their president. While these K.M.T. officials were sincerely drafting details for cross-strait co-operation, Lee Teng-hui was going in the opposite direction by actively and secretly working for a diplomatic coup against Beijing, i.e. his United States visit. The K.M.T. officials I interviewed said with much regret that history had been unfair to the Chinese on both sides of the Strait because it had not given Taiwan enough time (there was only about one month between Taiwan's six-point proposal in April and the U.S. announcement that Lee had been granted a visa) to prove its sincerity by substantiating and realizing these co-operation proposals. Chinese officials I interviewed blamed Washington for starting the troubles across the Strait. But they also insisted that Lee himself was to blame too. He was at least not as sincere as some of the other K.M.T. officials when it came to reunification. While making the six-point response, his right-hand man Liu Tai-ying was secretly lobbying the United States for Lee's United States visit. Liu did not even hint at this when he came to Shanghai to talk to Wang Daohan in early 1995.

Through my interviews and through reading the official Chinese press, it became clear that the Lee Teng-hui factor loomed very large in Beijing's configuration of cross-strait relations. Many Chinese officials placed their hopes on the K.M.T. after 2000 when Lee would leave office. They were interested in some K.M.T. officials who they said "still have some patriotic feelings towards their motherland". Though the current democratic politics in Taiwan do not allow any new leaders to pursue immediate reunification, other leaders would at least behave differently from the "die-hard" Lee. At the same time, some Chinese officials I interviewed also expressed their concern over the younger generation (*zhong sheng dai*) of K.M.T. leaders who might accept Lee's "pragmatic diplomacy". They hoped to see some co-ordination between the pro-reunification New Party and pro-reunification members of the younger generation of the K.M.T. They also hoped that the younger generation of K.M.T. members would improve the party's relations with China after Lee Teng-hui.

Working on the D.P.P.

At one time Beijing had a deep distrust of the D.P.P. and refused to have anything to do with it as it openly advocated Taiwan's independence, even to the point of writing it into its Party Charter. However, the increasing influence of the D.P.P. in Taiwan politics has forced Beijing to realize that it can no longer avoid it and has to deal with it in one way or another.

Beijing's policy with regard to the D.P.P. began to change slightly in the early 1990s. It maintained contact with members of the D.P.P. who visited the mainland on sightseeing tours as individuals, or invested in enterprises in the mainland. The C.C.P. United Front Work Department noted:

> As long as these people are not acting on behalf of the D.P.P., they are welcome to start investment projects in the mainland or to conduct fact-finding tours. But they will not be entertained if they come here to discuss the issue of Taiwan independence. Mainland China is maintaining some contact with the Democratic Progressive Party, but it cannot be considered a contact between two parties. China is maintaining personal contact with individual members of the D.P.P. but not with the party as a whole.[15]

However, the contact started. For example, in March 1993, a D.P.P. leader, Chang Chun-hong, met Chen Andong, deputy director of the Third Division of Department on United Front of the Central Committee of the C.C.P. in Shenzhen, China. China's A.R.A.T.S. chairman, Wang Daohan, also met Chang Chun-hong, Chen Zhongxin (in Chinese *pinyin*) and other leaders of the D.P.P. on several occasions.[16]

The policy continued to change after 1995. In a reversal of an earlier policy of negotiating with the K.M.T. only, President Jiang Zemin, in his eight-point proposal in early 1995, encouraged not only the K.M.T. but also "all the parties and people from all walks of life" to come up with "constructive suggestions" on reunification. In May 1996, Jiang noted that as long as the D.P.P. gave up its Taiwan independence stand, the mainland could have a dialogue with them.[17] He repeated this stand with some modification at the Fifteenth Party Congress of the C.C.P. in September 1997. He said that China "welcomes all the parties in Taiwan and people of all circles, *except those who stubbornly stick to Taiwan's independence*, to visit the mainland to exchange views on cross-strait relations and reunification matters."[18]

After the D.P.P.'s shock victory in local polls in December 1997,[19] Beijing, while warning the D.P.P. against "Taiwan independence", expressed its hope that "*various parties* in Taiwan will go along with the trend of the times and do something practical to develop cross-strait relations".[20]

Although the D.P.P. has a pro-independence reputation, some of its leaders have made adjustments to the party's mainland policy. It has played down its independence profile in order to become Taiwan's ruling party. Individual D.P.P. leaders have expressed their willingness to open a dialogue with the C.C.P. aimed at restoring the three direct links. They have set aside the sensitive issue of Taiwan's sovereignty and the pro-independence clause in the Party Charter as being of historical value. They have supported cross-strait dialogue and claimed that the D.P.P. "is pragmatic and responsible" and "does not seek to provoke China by making unnecessary declarations (of independence)."[21]

One of China's top Taiwan specialists, Li Jiaquan, noticed that the D.P.P. has "displayed more flexibility on cross-strait policy than the K.M.T.".[22] Tang Shubei expressed hope for a working relationship with the D.P.P. should it take power.[23]

Some Chinese strategists argued in internal discussions that the prospect of the D.P.P.'s victory as a ruling party might not be a bad thing. For one thing, the K.M.T. might feel forced to liberalize its mainland policy as this would help maintain its mandate. Second, this would intensify conflict between the K.M.T. and D.P.P., especially as many D.P.P. leaders were prosecuted by the K.M.T. before the mid-1980s. Third, to be a ruling party, the D.P.P. would have to compromise its pro-independence stance to have stable relations with China in order to win the confidence of nervous voters and international investment. This would intensify internal divisions within the D.P.P. (there were four main factions and two small ones within the Party). Fourth, this would also intensify its conflict with both the New Party and the Taiwan Independence Party. Fifth, it would enhance the apprehension of the United States and other countries about a premature and uncontrolled conflict between China and Taiwan that could destabilize East Asia. And these countries would exert pressure on the D.P.P.

government. Thus, the D.P.P. would not go too far or be too radical even if it was voted into power.

These scenarios, they argued, pointed to the fact that a potential D.P.P. government was likely to be a weak one, especially as the D.P.P. lacked (and could not effectively control as the K.M.T. did) financial and personnel resources to rule effectively. This would put Beijing in a better position to influence Taiwan politics.[24]

Despite the different voices amongst Chinese strategists, Beijing was still taking the K.M.T. as its favoured negotiation partner. It was mainly using the D.P.P. as leverage to push the K.M.T. government into negotiation with China.

Taiwan Pushes Ahead

The 1995–96 Taiwan Strait Crisis resulted from a combination of policy errors and miscalculations on the part of the three parties: the United States, China and Taiwan. In Taiwan's case, its reading of Chinese politics and the international situation led to over-confidence which resulted in its being too pushy at a delicate time. In other words, had Lee been more cautious some of the tension could have been avoided.

Initially, Lee's style was extremely cautious. Only after the end of 1993, once he had ensured his control of the K.M.T., did he begin publicly ridiculing the Chinese leaders on a regular basis. It seemed to be more than just "over-confidence" or "a slip of the tongue". Lee's words seemed calculated to put Taiwan in the international limelight so that it would not be forgotten. Taiwan banks on international media coverage. For example, its efforts to win over one small country from China as a new diplomatic ally do not carry much political importance, given that Taiwan has fewer than 30 such diplomatic allies. The importance lies in the high international media coverage that Taiwan wants, and this explains why Taiwan has spent so much effort and money on these countries. This also shows why, after the Taiwan issue had calmed down, Lee chose prominent occasions to make other "big splashes". One such occasion was in late 1997 when Lee declared Taiwan to be "an independent, sovereign country, just like Britain or France" and another was when he depicted cross-strait relations as "special state-to-state relations" in an interview with the German radio station Deutsche Welle in 1999. On those two occasions, cross-strait tensions had subsided and China had done nothing to prompt Taiwan or Lee to make such a surprising move. Taiwan seems convinced that its survival needs international attention and that silence only works against it. In this sense, out of the three parties (China, Taiwan and the United States), Taiwan has been the leading party, with the other two parties often having their agendas hijacked. This point is discussed further in Chapter 10.

Taiwan's Reading of China's Internal Politics

Taiwan's "over-confidence" was related to its reading of China's internal politics. Like many countries, Taiwan predicted that the Beijing government would collapse soon after the Tiananmen incident of 1989. When it did not, it believed that Jiang Zemin was only a transitional weak leader, and that post-Deng China would likely be plunged into chaos.[25] As late as 1996, Lee was still saying things like: "Jiang Zemin can promote dozens of generals but can he control them? Deng Xiaoping can control the generals but can he think properly now?" That Jiang's leadership was beyond challenge was clearly shown at the Fifteenth C.C.P. National Congress in October 1997. But Lee still believed that China would eventually disintegrate into turmoil. This spurred his appeal to Taiwan businessmen not to shift their investment from Indonesia to China due to the chaos he predicted would descend there. On many occasions since 1996, Lee has made similar predictions to justify his "go slow" policy.[26]

Lee obviously underestimated Beijing. Taiwan mistakenly believed that after making a few protests against Lee Teng-hui's United States visit, Beijing would quieten down. Thus, only a few days after Lee's United States visit and without waiting to see China's response, Lee sent Premier Lien Chan to visit three European countries which had no diplomatic relations with Taiwan, asked Vice Premier Hsu Li-teh to visit Canada, claimed Tiawan would give US$1 billion to the United Nations in exchange for membership and called on Taiwan to "make full use of the excellent situation" following his United States visit to "go all out" to "challenge the impossible".

Lee should have handled all this more prudently. His Cornell speech could have been more diplomatically worded, instead of which it was excessively provocative. He did not seem concerned about doing anything to pre-empt or cushion China's reaction. He did not make any effort, whether sincerely or not, to pass any message to or seek a tacit understanding with China before he made his provocative United States trip and Cornell speech. This he could have done through China's Tang Shubei who was visiting Taipei from 26 to 30 May (Washington announced the visa decision on 22 May). He did not even meet him, let alone seek, through him, Beijing's understanding. He did not ask him to pass any message on to Beijing. If he had tried, China's response would have been less violent, partly because the very fact he had made the effort would have indicated to Beijing that Lee still cared about cross-strait relations enough to give Beijing some face, even though he did not necessarily intend to set his agenda according to Beijing's wishes.

Taiwan's Reading of International Support

At the same time, Taiwan was over-confident of international support. In early 1996, the Taiwan government asked its cabinet-level Council for Economic

Planning and Development (C.E.P.D.) to commission local scholars and experts to prepare a comprehensive report on U.S. interests in Taiwan as a basis to evaluate the possible U.S. response to cross-strait conflict in March 1996. Their report pointed out that Taiwan was far more important to the United States politically and militarily than economically. Politically, the report said, if Taiwan continued to exist, the United States could use Taiwan to check mainland China's activities in the international community. If cross-strait relations retained a certain degree of tension, it would be easier for the United States to sell arms to Taiwan, mainland China and Southeast Asian nations. As the United States regarded mainland China as the biggest threat in the Asia-Pacific region, it had actively developed a strong defence line in the west Pacific, from Japan to South Korea, Taiwan and the Philippines, to contain Beijing's expansionism. The report said Taiwan was an important point in Washington's west Pacific defence line and that "Taiwan can serve as an immovable aircraft carrier".[27]

This "confidence" in U.S. support stiffened Taiwan's resolve in its tit-for-tat confrontation with Beijing. It also confirmed Beijing's perception that while claiming "Chinese should help Chinese", Taiwan had actually long been ready to offer itself to Washington as "an immovable aircraft carrier" to contain China's rise in exchange for their support of its separation from China.

However, international support should not be overestimated. During China's military exercises in March 1996, Australia was the only country in the Asia-Pacific region that officially supported the United States dispatching two aircraft carriers to the waters off Taiwan. And it was not long before Canberra began to make initiatives to improve its relations with Beijing through, for example, Prime Minister John Howard's visit to Beijing in March-April 1997, its more flexible position on the issue of China's human rights situation and a substantially lowered profile in its relations with Taiwan, such as a ban by Canberra in April 1997 on ministerial visits to Taiwan.

Unlike Australia, Japan's support of the U.S. aircraft carriers was not public. While Washington criticized China's missile tests as provocative and demanded their suspension, Japanese Chief Cabinet Secretary Seiroku Kajiyama confined himself to saying Tokyo would continue to seek China's self-restraint on such tests. Foreign Minister Yukihiko Ikeda even said the Chinese military exercises taking place in high seas could not be rebuked under international law.[28]

Japanese Prime Minister Ryutaro Hashimoto did instruct his government to study how to support the United States during the March 1996 military exercises. However, Japan did not make any waves at that time. Later, Tokyo enhanced its defence alliance with Washington through a joint declaration in April 1996 and a review of guidelines for security co-operation with the United States in 1997. Future Japanese support is likely, but only in a cautious and qualified way.

Without Washington taking the lead, Tokyo will feel uncomfortable going too far in supporting Taiwan's confrontation with Beijing.

During China's March 1996 military exercises, most Asian countries asked *both* China and Taiwan to restrain themselves to avoid an outbreak of armed conflict. Indonesia's Foreign Minister Ali Alatas said: "Indonesia will not interfere in this problem because this country is of the view that the problem of reunification is an internal matter for the Chinese people and Indonesia will uphold the one China policy which we have been adhering to so far". He told a parliamentary committee hearing that Indonesia was watching developments in the Taiwan Strait closely but added that Jakarta had no intention of becoming involved.[29]

Thailand gave clear support to Beijing. Foreign Minister Kasem Kasemsri said that Beijing had a legitimate right to undertake exercises to deter a breakaway by what it regarded as its territory.

Others, such as South Korea, Chris Patten (Hong Kong's then governor) and the Philippines only stressed the need for dialogue and peaceful solutions to the rising tensions between China and Taiwan, short of outright support for Taiwan.

Asian countries did not answer Taiwan's call on the international community to take action against China's missile tests in March 1996. And the European Union only said it deeply regretted the missile tests.

Taiwan did not expect the United States to improve its relations with China so quickly after the Strait Crisis and to go so far as to have the president publicly declare U.S. support of the "three-no's" policy regarding Taiwan in 1998.

Koo's China Visit in 1998

Three years after suspending the Wang-Koo meeting, Koo Chen-fu finally made his trip to China on 14–19 October 1998. This trip, however, illustrated the huge gap between the two sides, the difficulties in achieving an early reunification and the uncertainty over the future development of cross-strait relations.

He landed in Shanghai and met with his Chinese counterpart, Wang Daohan. The two reached a four-point consensus, namely to hold dialogues on various topics, including political and economic issues; to increase cross-strait exchanges at all levels; to give greater attention to functional issues such as providing help in cases involving the personal safety and loss of property of each other's residents in each other's territory; and to set up a return visit to Taiwan the next year by Wang Daohan.

Koo then went to Beijing and met with Jiang Zemin in his capacity as general secretary of the C.C.P. instead of P.R.C. state president. He also met other Chinese officials including Vice-Premier Qian Qichen in his capacity as standing member of the C.C.P. Political Bureau, State Council Taiwan Affairs Office

Director Chen Yunlin and A.R.A.T.S. Vice Chairman and Secretary General Tang Shubei.

For the trip to come about, both sides had to make some concessions. Beijing no longer insisted on having political talks and Taiwan softened its stance by saying that it would not exclude the possibility of a political dialogue, but that the two sides needed to work out practical issues first, such as agreements on settling fishing disputes and hijacking cases which were negotiated in the past but never signed.

Though they were the highest-level meetings on Chinese soil between Taipei and Beijing representatives since 1949, there was no breakthrough. In terms of substance there was not much achievement. They fell short of formal negotiations or talks and were categorized as a "simple visit". As Taiwan's Premier Siew Wan-chang stressed: "It's a meeting, not negotiations; it's a visit, not talks." Koo was authorized only to have "exploratory conversations" with his hosts.[30]

Differences

At the time of Koo's visit in China, Lee Teng-hui publicly refused to accept the "one China" principle and China's "one country, two systems" proposal. He asked China to "face the reality of 'one divided China' and each has its own right to secure a place in the international arena".[31] With Lee watching from behind, Koo couldn't break new ground in his visit. Koo told his hosts that the R.O.C. was a sovereign state and would accept no lesser status. He did not mention whether the P.R.C. and the R.O.C. could be merged into one central government. To the shock of his hosts, Koo told them for the first time that the Potsdam Proclamation of 26 July 1945 returned Taiwan to the R.O.C. not the P.R.C. And, as Lee Teng-hui often repeated, the R.O.C. has remained a reality up to this day since its founding in 1912.

Koo told his hosts that China's democratization was one condition for Taiwan's agreeing to reunification. He told Jiang Zemin: "Only when the Chinese mainland has achieved democracy can the two sides of the Taiwan Strait talk about unification".[32] In response, Jiang said democracy was not the only workable political system in the world.[33] On a later occasion, China dismissed Koo's insistence on democracy as impractical: "The reunification that we are talking about concerns issues relating to the territorial integrity of the country, not which system is better".[34]

At talks with Qian Qichen, Koo sharply criticized Beijing's efforts to internationally isolate Taiwan. He said that Beijing's failure to recognize the existence of a separate government on Taiwan was the main obstacle to improving relations.

China does recognize the existence of Taiwan. However, the point is whether this government should be another central government of China. China urged Taiwan to stop this "ostrich mentality". Qian Qichen told Koo that "fewer and fewer" countries maintained relations with the island and the trend of its isolation would continue.[35] Two weeks after Koo left, on 2 November, Tonga officially switched diplomatic recognition from Taiwan to China. On 20 November, Taiwan won a diplomatic victory by establishing formal ties with the Marshall Islands in the Pacific. This diplomatic tug-of-war between Taiwan and China has been going on despite the Koo visit.

How to Interpret This?

Koo's visit did not achieve much substantial progress in cross-strait relations. Beijing wanted political negotiation or, if this was difficult for Taiwan, a preparatory talk on procedural matters leading to political negotiation. Qian Qichen told Koo during his visit that "should Taiwan still find it difficult now to enter into preparatory talks on procedural matters leading to full-fledged political negotiation, we could start with an academic forum first to exchange views".[36] Koo only agreed to listing the political issue as one of the issues in future talks, but stressed that greater attention should be given to functional talks, i.e. discussing technical and practical issues as Taiwan had insisted. Such an agreement is evasive and lacks long-term commitment. In the first instance, there was no definite binding agreement on what the political issues for discussion should be, which issue should be discussed first, and whether political issues should be discussed from the first round, and at every round, of the coming negotiations. Second, the discussion of the political issue could be finessed among the discussion of a big bunch of technical and practical issues. Third, Taiwan at the same time also insisted that it would agree to reunification talks only after democratization in the mainland. This could mean that substantive political talks would not start until this democratization took place.

The crux of the issue is that Beijing wanted to see a link between the improved cross-strait relations and reunification, while Taiwan wanted their separation. In other words, Beijing wanted to improve its relations with Taiwan in order to get closer to reunification while Taiwan wanted to have economic and political benefits without moving closer to reunification.

Koo's visit was a success not so much as a step towards reunification, but as a means of highlighting, or in the words of Taiwan's M.A.C. Vice-Chairman Lin Chong-pin, managing to "shout aloud" the existence of the R.O.C.[37] Koo successfully used the stage set up by China, i.e. high international media coverage, to publicize once again Taiwan's position to the world. He made known two key conditions for Taiwan's agreeing to reunification: (1) recognition of the R.O.C. as equal; and (2) democratization in the mainland. His statement that the Potsdam Proclamation returned Taiwan to the R.O.C. not the P.R.C. was also made with the purpose of attracting international attention.

This claim, however, does not stand on firm legal ground. When the Potsdam Proclamation returned Taiwan to China, the P.R.C. was not yet founded and the R.O.C. was then the sole legal representative of China. So, the Potsdam Proclamation returned Taiwan to the R.O.C. (as was written on the document) as the sole legal central government of China, and not as a choice of one of two central governments of China. It is more accurate to say the Potsdam Proclamation returned Taiwan to China, not necessarily the R.O.C. or the P.R.C.

The situation has changed since the C.C.P., in a civil war, drove the K.M.T. government off the mainland to Taiwan and established the P.R.C. in 1949. The R.O.C. today is different from the R.O.C. in the past. Today's R.O.C. is, to use Lee Teng-hui's expression, "R.O.C. in Taiwan" whereas the R.O.C. previously was the "R.O.C. in China". The latter suggests the central government of China or the legal representative of China while the former implies a government of the Taiwan area alone. Legal evidence is that the United Nations Charter of 1945 used the term "R.O.C." whenever it referred to China. After the P.R.C. was accepted in place of the R.O.C. seat in the United Nations in 1971, the U.N. did not see the need to change the term "R.O.C." in its 1945 Charter to the P.R.C. And the P.R.C. automatically inherited the rights and obligations in the 1945 Charter where the term "R.O.C." was used. This shows that to the United Nations, the term "R.O.C." or "P.R.C." only means the representative of China. The representative may change from time to time while China remains the same. So, to be technically accurate, the Potsdam Proclamation returned Taiwan to China, whether this China has the national title of the R.O.C., the P.R.C. or another title in future.

Notes

1. Chen Dunde, *Mao Zedong yu Jiang Jieshi* [Mao Zedong and Chiang Kai-shek] (Beijing: Ba Yi Publishing House, 1993), pp. 302–06, quoted from John W. Garver, *Face Off: China, the United States, and Taiwan's Democratization* (Seattle: University of Washington Press, 1997), p. 157. Emphasis added. Also see Zheng, *Gudao Chanmeng* [Lingering Dreams over the Isolated Island], p. 367.
2. *Guangming Ribao* (Beijing), 7 January 1988, p. 3
3. "Chinese President Reportedly Meets Taiwan Presidential Aide", *Wen Wei Po*, 27 April 1996, p. A2, from Reuters, 30 April 1996.
4. Ching Cheong, "Don't Bank on U.S. Military Aid, Taipei Told", *ST*, 23 March 1998.

5. Kwan Weng Kin, "Taiwan Must Give Up All Bids for Independence to Boost China Ties", *ST*, 20 November 1996.

6. Lu Ning, "China May Have Got Big One from U.S.", *Business Times*, 22 January 1998.

7. "U.S. Officials 'Softening Taiwan Stand'", *SCMP*, 7 May 1998.

8. Lu Ning, *op. cit.*

9. "U.S. Officials 'Softening Taiwan Stand'", *SCMP*, 7 May 1998.

10. President Bill Clinton said: "I had a chance to reiterate our Taiwan policy, which is that we don't support independence for Taiwan or 'two Chinas' or 'one Taiwan, one China' and we don't believe that Taiwan should be a member in any organization for which statehood is a requirement". See "U.S. Lawmakers Affirm Support for Taiwan", *ST*, 22 July 1998.

11. "Taiwan Isolation 'Delays Unity'", *SCMP*, 31 December 1998.

12. "Taiwan's Lee Steps Up War of Words against China", CNN News Program, 18 September 1997.

13. *ST*, 9 November 1997, p. 23.

14. Yap Gee Poh, "Teng-Hui's Book of Speeches Upsets China," *ST*, 12 December 1996. The book is published in Japanese, accompanied by interpretation and comments by Japanese foreign affairs commentator Hideaki Kase.

15. "China: Chinese Party Official Speaks on Unofficial Links with Taiwan's Democratic Progressive Party", Reuters, 9 August 1994.

16. *Lianhe Zaobao*, 30 September 1997, p. 17.

17. "Former Parliamentary Leader Urges Beijing to Move towards Peace Talks", *Sing Tao Jih Pao*, 6 May 1996, p. A2, from Reuters, 7 May 1996.

18. *Lianhe Zaobao*, 13 September 1997, p. 26. Emphasis added.

19. In the election, the D.P.P. grabbed 12 out of the 23 seats available, leaving 8 to the K.M.T. and 3 to the non-partisan independent candidates.

20. Willy Wo-Lap Lam, "Beijing Warns D.P.P. over Splittist Line", *SCMP*, 6 December 1997. Emphasis added.

21. Lee San Chouy, "Taiwan Opposition Party Backs Talks with China", *ST*, 26 September 1997.

22. Ibid.

23. Joanne Lee-Young, "Beijing Happy to Speak If Opposition Takes Reins", *SCMP*, 21 February 1998.

24. From my interviews with Chinese strategists in both Beijing and Shanghai in June 1998.

25. See Lee Teng-hui's remarks in *ST*, 3 July 1995, p. 18.

26. There are many such reports. For example, see *Lianhe Zaobao*, 8 October 1998, p. 23, and 25 September 1998, p. 21.

27. Central News Agency, "Report Released on U.S. Reaction to Threat of War with Mainland", 2 April 1996, from Reuters, 4 April 1996.

28. "Japan Cautious of Rapping Chinese Missile Tests", Jiji Press (Tokyo), from Reuters, 8 March 1996.

29. Paul Jacob, "Show Restraint or Setback Will Be Immense", *ST*, 14 March 1996.

30. Julian Baum and Susan V. Lawrence, "Breaking the Ice", *Far East Economic Review*, 15 October 1998.

31. See Lee Teng-hui's speech in "Taiwan Wants Non-Political Sino Talks", *ST*, 21 October 1998.
32. Mary Kwang, "Jiang, Taiwan's Koo Have Frank, Amicable Dialogue", *ST*, 19 October 1998.
33. Ibid.
34. See remarks by Chinese Foreign Ministry spokesman Tang Guoqiang in Mary Kwang, "China Rejects Reunification Conditions", *ST*, 21 October 1998.
35. "Taipei Envoy Firm on Sovereignty", *SCMP*, 19 October 1998.
36. Ching Cheong, "War Awaits If Taiwan Rejects Talks, China Hints", *ST*, 22 October 1998.
37. Ching Cheong, "Taiwan Convince China of Its Existence", *ST*, 23 October 1998.

10

The Splash of the "Two States" Theory

After several rounds of negotiation between Li Yafei, deputy secretary of A.R.A.T.S. and his S.E.F. counterpart, Jan Jih-horng, Wang Daohan announced in late June 1999 that he would pay a return visit to Taiwan in the coming October. China hoped that there would be no restriction on the topics for discussion. To prepare for Wang's visit, Beijing planned to hold a forum in late August on mainland China–Taiwan ties and would invite senior Taiwanese statesmen responsible for handling contacts with the mainland. The two sides agreed to a visit by Taiwanese legal experts to China in July and a visit by a Chinese agricultural delegation to Taiwan in August. Jan suggested building detention centres in Xiamen for mainland Chinese who were caught illegally entering Taiwan. Li said that China was willing to co-operate, but would not be able to take full responsibility for the problem.[1] China hoped that a hotline would be set up between the two sides after Wang's visit. The hotline would be of a "higher status" than routine communications between A.R.A.T.S. and S.E.F. China's wish list for the Wang-Koo talks also included closer co-operation on economic issues, such as on agriculture, and listing political matters.[2]

Taiwan Makes a Big Splash

To the surprise of many, in an interview with the German radio station Deutche Welle on 9 July 1999, Lee Teng-hui for the first time openly defined the relations between mainland China and Taiwan as "between two countries (*guojia*), at least a special relation between two countries". With this definition he dumped Taiwan's previous position of "two equal political entities", although according to him, this was actually equal to "two countries". He also noted that there was no need for Taiwan to declare independence again since it (R.O.C.) had been an independent country since 1912.[3]

Taiwan's Foreign Minister Hu Chih-chiang, S.E.F. Chairman Koo Chen-fu, M.A.C. Chairman Su Chi, and other high officials immediately confirmed this as the government position. Koo changed his previous position (i.e. that he had held in his meeting with Wang Daohan in October 1998) and publicly called cross-strait ties country-to-country (*guojia*) relations. M.A.C. was thus instructed to replace any reference to "two equal political entities" with the new notion of "two countries (*guojia*)" in subsequent government documents, and to drop completely the reference to "one country".[4] On 12 July, M.A.C. Chairman Su Chi claimed that from then on Taiwan would drop references to the idea of "one China".[5] Later, M.A.C., under pressure, came out with an English version of Lee's theory of "two countries". It was translated into "two states of one nation", avoiding using the sensitive word "countries" (*guojia* in Chinese can be translated into either country, state or nation).[6] On 22 July, it changed the term to "special state-to-state relations."[7]

The Presidential Office and a central K.M.T. meeting disclosed that the "two states" concept was the product of a year-long study by the "Select Group on Strengthening the Sovereignty Status of the Republic of China", which was headed by the secretary-general of the Presidential Office, Huang Kun-huei.[8] Therefore, the "two states" theory was not a personal slip of the tongue, but a set government policy. Taiwan said this was a fundamental policy change and would be followed by a series of changes in policy and law, such as the State Security Law, Regulations Governing Cross-Strait Relations and the Nationality Law. Lee was expected to raise other corresponding new political, economic and social policies before leaving office.[9]

He was also expected to push ahead with constitutional amendments to give the notion a firm legal foundation. This was expected to take place together with a major overhaul of the constitutional and legal framework, covering all aspects of laws ranging from the definitions of state and institutions to territories and people. Under the present Constitution, Taiwan is referred to as the "freedom area of China" while the mainland is described as the "Republic of China territories other than Taiwan". Amendments were needed to confine the R.O.C. territories to Taiwan proper, Penghu, Kinmen, Matsu and other islands. All government decrees, notices, memoranda and propaganda materials, including websites, would be revised to reflect the new status. Government ministries were told to draw up a full list of documents that needed amendments.[10]

On 14 July, following a meeting of the standing members of the K.M.T. Central Committee, Taiwan announced the launch of a major diplomatic offensive to sell its "two states" policy to the international community. The initiative included dispatching the chairman of the Council for Economic Planning and Development Chiang Pin-kung to attend the A.P.E.C. meeting in New Zealand in September, where he would explain the "new principle" to the world leaders at the gathering. It would ask its allies in the United Nations to help explain its "two states" concept whenever they addressed the international assembly. In addition, it would ask them to co-sponsor a motion that would allow Taiwan to join the U.N. on the new basis. Previously, its bid to re-enter the world body was made by asking for a repeal of the U.N. Resolution No. 2758 of 1971, which gave the seat to the P.R.C. In a change of strategy Taipei would now ask for permission to join the U.N. as a new and separate state, using the German model to support its motion. It would also instruct all its foreign representative offices to explain to their host governments the applicability of the German model, which was embodied in the "Grundlagenuertrag", or Fundamental Treaty of 1972, between the two Germanies.[11]

Chinese and International Pressure

Taiwan's new initiative, as expected, provoked China's fury. Wang Daohan warned that the "two states" policy had removed the basis for further dialogue between A.R.A.T.S. and S.E.F. He demanded an explanation from Taiwan. Otherwise, he hinted, he might be compelled to cancel his October visit to Taiwan. China demanded a retraction of the "two states" statement and a return to the "one China" position. It claimed that Lee had taken an "extremely dangerous step" towards splitting China and warned him against playing with fire. It reaffirmed that it had never renounced the use of force to prevent Taiwan's independence and warned Taiwan not to underestimate its determination and capability to uphold the nation's sovereignty, dignity and territorial integrity. It warned that Lee had taken "the people of Taiwan, as well as his foreign patrons, hostage down his road of destruction and into his suicidal, separatist adventures".[12]

Newspapers, mostly in Hong Kong, quoted unspecified Chinese sources, saying that China was considering a military response. The P.L.A. exercises, though small-sized and far away from Taiwan, were reported to be warnings. Chinese newspapers carried many editorials and articles, denouncing Lee's "two states" theory. Chinese military specialists and scholars, in their personal capacities, issued stern warnings, also mainly through media in Hong Kong. For example, Hong Kong's *Wen Wei Po* quoted a senior researcher at P.L.A.'s Academy of Military Science, Yan Zhao, as saying that military conflict in the Taiwan Strait could erupt at any moment. He also said Beijing would not stop using force even if the United States intervened.[13]

Pressure also came from the international community. The United States, Japan, the EU, Russia and many other countries reaffirmed their "one China" policy.

Taiwan Explains

First, Lee blamed the media for "misquoting" him. The President's Office explained that what Lee said was "special state-to-state relations" and not a "two states" theory. On 26 and 27 July, Lee said: "As a matter of fact, I did not mention 'two states theory' in the interview with the German radio ... I realise my idea would be better understood if the queries the German reporter raised could be read carefully." He said that the "two states theory" was coined by the media.[14]

It was a play of words. The crux here was not who coined the term "two states theory". Actually, Lee did not use the term itself in the interview. However, the description of the "two states" theory given by the international media was not wrong. He had not been "misquoted" since Koo Chen-fu, Su Chi and other Taiwan high officials also changed their tune following Lee's interview.

Then, Lee insisted that this state-to-state relationship was a special one. The term "special" referred to the special emotional ties between the people of Taiwan and China ("[They] have special feelings towards each other").[15] However, he did not clarify what he meant by "special" . In other words, this special emotion could also mean hatred or what was popularly expressed in Taiwan as *"bei qing"* [the complex of being victimized (by the mainlanders)]. This would imply hatred and revenge instead of love. Koo's clarification on 30 July and M.A.C.'s statement on 1 August did not succeed in making it better.[16]

Such ambiguity and self-contradiction could also be found in Lee's explanation that he had no plan to declare independence. In the interview on 9 July, he said, as quoted above, that there was *no need* for Taiwan to declare independence again since it (the R.O.C.) had been an independent country since 1912. That being said, Lee's "concession" that he had no plan to declare independence did not mean anything. At the same time, M.A.C. insisted: "The two sides of the Taiwan Strait have been divided into two states and China's sovereignty and territory have been cut apart."[17] This was a refutation of the Chinese insistence that a country's administration could be cut apart but not its sovereignty.

China and Taiwan also differed in their usage of the term "independence". When Lee said that he would not declare Taiwan's independence, in essence he meant that he would not declare a Republic of Taiwan. However, to China, the term "independence" meant a split from China, whether in the name of the Republic of Taiwan or the Republic of China. To declare that the R.O.C. and the P.R.C. were two separate and independent sovereign states was to split China and therefore declare Taiwan's independence, especially as the D.P.P. had declared Taiwan's independence as the R.O.C. instead of the R.O.T.

Lee assured Washington that Taiwan's mainland policy remained "intact". Yet in the same interview of 9 July Lee had said: "Since we made our constitutional reforms in 1991, we have redefined cross-strait relations as state-to-state". In other words, if cross-strait contact since 1991 was already what Lee described as "state-to-state", then Taiwan's mainland policy was indeed "intact". However, China and many other countries had been told that cross-strait dealings should be conducted on this state-to-state basis only after July 1999.

Lee said that he made the "two states" claim so that Taiwan would be treated as China's equal in future talks on reunification.[18] In the past, Taiwan insisted on "two equal *political* entities". Now, this equality had changed to equality in terms of sovereignty, not even in the sense of two central governments representing one state, but of two separate states. It called this a necessary step to prepare Taiwan for talks on unification and offered to agree to China's demand of holding some form of political dialogue, if China accepted Taiwan's new status.[19] Presidential deputy secretary-general Lin Pi-chao said:

> We have made preparations to push for political dialogue and drafted several proposals based on Taiwan's new status as declared by President Lee Teng-hui. We are willing to adopt a more positive attitude at the negotiation table if their reaction is practical and rational. We definitely would not want to see a backward step in cross-strait relations, and we hope Wang Daohan will visit Taiwan as scheduled."[20]

Taiwan knew only too well that Beijing would never accept the "two states" theory in exchange for political dialogue, for that dialogue would be about having one state, not two.

Taiwan made another "concession" by claiming to return the 1992 consensus between A.R.A.T.S. and S.E.F. The consensus, it said, was that there was "*yi ge zhong guo, ge zi biao shu*" [one China but free interpretations] and both sides agreed to disagree. Accordingly, Taiwan now interpreted "one China" as being a future state. At present there were two states.[21] Taiwan also cited Jiang Zemin's eight-point proposal which had said that both sides could come together to talk about anything. Taiwan claimed that this meant it could talk in this way.

Beijing was annoyed. It accused Taiwan of distorting the facts and denied that it ever agreed to disagree on "one China". It had agreed not to discuss the political content of "one China" in talks on pragmatic matters.[22] It also accused Taiwan of distorting Jiang's words. When Jiang had said that both sides could discuss anything, it was within the framework of "one China", which was clearly stated at the very beginning of Jiang's eight-point proposal.

With these "explanations,"[23] Taiwan's claim that it had not abandoned the "one China" policy and sought eventual unification with China did not appease China. As U.S. Secretary of State Madeleine Albright said in late July, these explanations "thus far don't quite do it."[24] Taiwan resisted this pressure. Lee insisted that Taiwan and China deal with each other on a "state-to-state" basis. Though the theory had not been included in the state constitution, it had, by the end of August, been enshrined, by way of a K.M.T. resolution, in the party charter. Thus, for the first time, it became a formal document. At the same time, as another "concession", the K.M.T. reaffirmed Lee's assurance that

Taiwan had no plan to draft it into the constitution. However, in early September, Taiwan's National Assembly voted to extend its four-year term by another 25 months. The reason given by its speaker Su Nan-cheng on 6 September was that it planned to "suspend" or "temporarily freeze" the present constitution and would instead draft a "basic law" to "reflect its current constitutional reality". According to him, the extension was necessary "to provide sufficient time and space for a major constitutional revision".[25] In other words, Taiwan could keep its word by not revising the constitution to encompass the "two states" theory. However, it was going to "suspend" or "freeze" the constitution (it had never promised not to do so) and draft a new basic law to "reflect its current constitutional reality", i.e. the "special state-to-state relations" with China.

The Motivation

Lee's motivation for choosing this time to bring up the "two states" theory has been subject to various interpretations. In my view, Lee wanted to lay a firmer groundwork for what he had in mind for future Taiwan before his presidential term expired. This reflected his lack of confidence in the next president. Lee explained in August 1999: "I will no longer be the president at this time next year. ... But I realise my redefinition of statehood might allow my successor to handle the issue more easily."[26] He wanted to mould his successor. After the "two states" position had been formally accepted by the K.M.T., into the party charter, as it was in late August, and by the government, it would be difficult for the new president to challenge it. It would undermine those presidential candidates, especially Soong Chu-yu, who did not agree with Lee's mainland policy.

However, this also hurt the K.M.T.'s presidential candidate, Lien Chan. The D.P.P. had lost votes in the previous presidential election because the electorate were worried about cross-strait stability once the D.P.P. was in power. This was one of the K.M.T.'s trump cards. It claimed that it was the only party capable of handling the stability across the Strait and used this card to scare the votes away from the D.P.P. Now, Lee's controversial remarks and China's expected angry reaction would deprive the K.M.T. of much credibility.

There was speculation[27] that Lee used the contradiction between Soong Chu-yu and Lien Chan to break the widely-supported Lien-Soong partnership for the presidential election in 2000 and weaken Soong. After this, he undercut Lien Chan by depriving him of such a trump card. And who benefited from this? None other than the D.P.P. which had claimed Lee's "two states" theory was a gift to its presidential candidate Chen Shui-bian. The latter, during a visit to the United States in April 1999, had described China–Taiwan relations as special international country-to-country relations.

Back in October 1996, Wang Daohan told me: "Lee Teng-hui does not trust Soong Chu-yu and Lien Chan because of their mainland background". Later, Lee did indeed dump Soong. As for Lien Chan, even if he were to win the presidential election in March 2000, he would then have already been cut into the shape by Lee on his mainland policy. Without Lee's support, he could not win the presidential election. With Lee around as the K.M.T. chairman, and the "two states" theory being formally incorporated into the K.M.T. party charter, he would not have much room to move about. As Taiwan's *China Times Express* put it, "He [Lee] does not trust the political line of his successor, so he's simply taking it upon himself to force the situation to a point of no return."[28]

Second, while his controversial remarks prompted a flurry of angry protests and threats from Beijing, Lee continued to mock the P.L.A. In a meeting at the Presidential Office on 10 August 1999, he said the controversy would benefit Taipei in the end. "The more controversy, the better. Only in this way will everyone pay attention to the key of the Republic of China's existence. When the whole world is aware of the Republic of China's difficult situation, it will be easier to do things."[29] This encapsulated Lee's strategy for Taiwan: constant international "splashes" which attract constant international attention, and more international sympathy.

This international sympathy, at the present, helps Taiwan's security. Time is not on Taiwan's side if its status continues unresolved for another 20 or 30 years when the balance across the Strait will likely tilt against Taiwan. This reality once again brings Lee's motivation into question: Lee may have been exploiting American sympathy and worsening China–U.S. relations to cement U.S. military commitment to a no-return end.

Lee must have known that the Chinese had become very irritable and emotional after the U.S. bombing of the Chinese embassy in Belgrade on 8 May. The United States was also alarmed by the nation-wide anti-American student demonstrations in China after the bombing and China's rising challenge. A U.S. policy of containment could possibly be in the pipeline. Why did Lee choose *this time* to raise this long-prepared and highly provocative "two states" theory? It could be that he hoped to incite Beijing into going further than just carrying out military exercises as it did in 1996, as this would mean the United States would have to get involved, especially as no American statesmen could afford to tolerate China's military response against a democratic Taiwan around the time of the U.S. presidential election. Should a military clash occur between China and the United States, China–U.S. relations could worsen irreconcilably. Like Kosovo and South Korea, Taiwan could be assured of clear and firm U.S. military commitment. Its status as an independent sovereign state would be secured in much the same way as South Korea's. Even if the United States does not position its troops in Taiwan like it did in South Korea or has a firm military commitment as in the Kosovo case, U.S.–China relations would be too rigid for China to play around. If China took military action, Lee could make this a hot issue in the March 2000 presidential election, as he did in 1996, to overshadow pressing social issues. He could even declare a state of emergency or war in Taiwan to postpone the coming election. Then he would remain in office as president for a few more years. If China's response was not strong, he could take more steps, before leaving office, towards the institutionalizing of the "two states" theory, both at home and abroad (i.e. more international awareness and acceptance).

China's Dilemma

It was my impression during my talk with Wang Daohan in mid-June 1999, only three weeks before Lee's "two states" theory announcement, that China still had hope in Taiwan. Wang Daohan listed three scenarios for his October visit to Taiwan, namely, (1) a big sensation like *Huanzhu Gege*;[30] (2) being humiliated and coming back with a bleeding nose; (3) somewhere in between. He said the first one was very difficult, but he would direct his efforts towards getting the third one. My impression from interviews with him and many other Chinese Taiwan specialists was that China still seemed to believe that many Taiwanese did not have an accurate picture of China's Taiwan policy because of Lee's influence. Once they got the picture, the situation would improve. For this purpose, it was better for Wang to visit Taiwan to tell the people there in person and in detail what China's Taiwan policy was so as to correct their misunderstanding.

The wide support in Taiwan of Lee's "two states" theory may have made Beijing think twice about this and the rationale behind its "peaceful reunification" strategy. Is there still any basis for the strategy that emphasized the "two trusts", namely "the trust in the Taiwan government and trust in the people of Taiwan (of their intention for reunification)". This strategy, in effect since 1979, can only be said to have been a failure with such a result.

Trust the K.M.T.?

China gave up hope on Lee Teng-hui after his U.S. visit in June 1995. It had not completely, however, given up on the K.M.T. This was shown by its reception of Koo Chen-fu in China in October 1998 and Wang Daohan's planned visit to Taiwan in October 1999. Beijing was aware that Koo would not bring many concessions when he visited in October. The trip was mainly to reduce the pressure from both the United States and home to resume cross-strait contacts, and to show the people in Taiwan that the K.M.T. was better than the D.P.P. at handling cross-strait relations for the coming legislative, mayoral and city council elections in December 1998.

Why did China agree to Koo's visit when there were no prospects of substantial concessions? One factor was its concern about the forthcoming legislative, mayoral and city council elections in December 1998. Some Chinese analysts believed that the K.M.T. could lose its majority in parliament to the D.P.P. No matter how China distrusted Lee, it still preferred the K.M.T. to be in power. Agreeing to Koo's visit was a way of helping the K.M.T. in the coming elections by giving them credit for being able to improve cross-strait relations. This motivation was revealed by Yu Keli, deputy director of China's Institute of Taiwan Studies in Beijing, an elite think-tank for Beijing's Taiwan policy-making. When commenting on Ma Yin-jeou's victory over Chen Shui-bian as Taipei mayor, he said that Ma's victory had something to do with China's tacit support in agreeing to Koo's China visit.[31]

China also hoped that the K.M.T. victory this time would also diminish the prospect of the D.P.P.'s victory in the 2000 presidential election. Since China had no trust in Lee whatsoever, it placed high hopes on the presidential election and was prepared to engage in more serious talks with the new president, so long as he was not a hard-line advocator of Taiwan's independence. Therefore, by entertaining Koo's visit, China tried to maintain some "reasonable" ties with the K.M.T., before Lee left office in 2000. It hoped that through these ties it would be able to influence the younger generation of K.M.T. leaders after Lee Teng-hui, such as Soong Chu-yu, Lien Chan and Ma Yin-jeou. These younger leaders had some policy differences with Lee despite their claimed support of Lee. Soong was in open conflict with Lee over the issue of freezing the Taiwan Provincial Government and Taiwan's mainland policy. Unlike Lee, Soong, Lien and Ma had not made any remarks about reunification that would be considered too provocative by China and helpful to those advocating Taiwan's independence. China was interested in Lien Chan's proposal in late 1995 (although it was not implemented) for setting up a special zone for direct trade and shipping with China besides the government's plan for the offshore transhipment centre. He called for efforts to boost exchanges with China for a win-win situation. He had laid down the principles of the "three no's", i.e. "no Taiwan independence, no immediate unification and no confrontation", and the "three wants", i.e. "want peace, want exchanges and want a win-win situation". He also once pushed for the re-opening of dialogue between Beijing and Taipei, saying that talks *could include any issue* and should be held without any pre-conditions.[32]

For the sake of their own political interest, these younger leaders generally did not encourage *benshengren* (the natives of Taiwan) to marginalize *waishengren* (the mainlanders). China of course wanted to see more *waishengren* and those who had strong feelings towards China remaining in power. It had once had a preference for a coalition between Lien, Soong, Ma, and those K.M.T. leaders who had been marginalized by Lee on the reunification issue.[33]

To meet the D.P.P. challenge, this K.M.T. younger generation had wanted to "play the China card" and seek some kind of tactical political co-operation from China. It was often a great political advantage to demonstrate to the voters the capability for cross-strait stability. This was where Beijing could exert its influence.

This expectation had been plunged into doubt with the wide support within the K.M.T. of Lee's "two states" theory. In the past, Lee had, on occasion, made controversial remarks, which the K.M.T. government had been quick to dilute by describing them either as "being misquoted" by the press or "a slip of the tongue" or a personal opinion. This time it was different. The "two states" theory had not only been prepared for a long time within the K.M.T. but was also given support by many K.M.T. leaders including those of the younger generation. It was endorsed in the K.M.T. party charter. This prompted Beijing to seriously doubt one primary element of the basis of its "peaceful reunification strategy", i.e. whether the K.M.T. in future should be trusted for reunification. This doubt and frustration was revealed when, for example, Chinese Vice-Premier Qian Qichen used the expression "Taiwan separatist forces with Lee Teng-hui at the core".[34] In the past China had only targeted Lee without mentioning other political figures at all. This time it also made veiled verbal attacks on Koo Chen-fu, Su Chi and other Taiwan officials (though without mentioning their names) and warned them that following Lee further would come to no good end.

Trust the People in Taiwan?

The other "trust" in the basis of China's "peaceful reunification" strategy, i.e. the trust of the people in Taiwan, was also plunged into doubt by the high percentage of support given by people in Taiwan to Lee's "two states" remarks. For example, in an opinion poll conducted by T.V.B.S. on 11 July 1999, more than 56 per cent of respondents sided with Lee, while only 22 per cent disapproved of his remarks. Thirty eight per cent said they realized Lee's words would lead to tension, while 45 per cent foresaw no strains with China. Some 43 per cent believed Taiwan's ties with China had moved in the right direction during Lee's tenure, while 25 per cent disapproved of his policy.[35] In another poll taken by *The United Daily* on 11 July 1999, 71 per cent said Taiwan was a sovereign country, 13 per cent disagreed and the rest had no opinion. Forty-nine per cent agreed with Lee that relations with China were "state-to-state" matters.[36] A poll commissioned by the K.M.T. showed over 60 per cent backing the categorization of Taiwan–China relations as "special state-to-state" ties rather than as "political entities".[37] Though many Taiwanese thought that it was neither feasible nor absolutely necessary and preferred to maintain the status quo for the moment given the political reality, they were pleased that their president had finally spoken out on what they saw as a political reality, i.e. Taiwan was nothing less than a sovereign state.

Beijing felt that it could not be more tolerant towards Taiwan. Feeling wronged, many Chinese asked me the following questions during interviews: Would the United States be as tolerant as to agree to practising the "one country two systems" formula in its own soil by allowing the co-existence of a communist government? How many central governments in the past two thousand years of Chinese history have made so many concessions as China has done so far? If it were the C.C.P. who had lost the Civil War and retreated to Taiwan, would the K.M.T government in Beijing (or Nanjing) be willing to treat the C.C.P. regime as another independent sovereign state or another central government of China? They felt that the concession and trade benefits given to the people in Taiwan did not really work. They complained that when China was soft in its approach, Taiwan did not take it as a favour, nor returned with favour. They mistook it as a signal that Beijing was now weak, it could not do anything about Taiwan and was in need of Taiwan. Then it would demand more and often the impossible (see the evolution of Taiwan's demands in the past ten years as discussed above). They complained: "We don't know when and where it will end its endless demands." They highlighted what Lee Teng-hui once said in a private talk with other Taiwanese officials: "You [Beijing] want reunification? Then, you must first of all recognize the fact of [Taiwan] being independent. ... Once the C.C.P. is thus trapped, then it will have no more control over what happens next".[38] Many Chinese I interviewed were concerned that Taiwan would not return with favour any further concessions. Whenever China's response was strong, even though it was directed against Lee alone, the Taiwanese would support Lee all the more, as was the case when China denounced Lee's "two states" theory. In response, more people in Taiwan identified themselves as "Taiwanese" instead of "Chinese". A public opinion poll, conducted after Lee's "two states" theory had been publicized, found a record high 44.8 per cent of respondents considered themselves Taiwanese rather than Chinese, up 7.9 percentage points from the last such poll conducted in April. In the poll, 39.9 per cent of the respondents said they considered themselves both Taiwanese and Chinese, down 5.5 percentage points from the April survey. Only 13.1 per cent said they considered themselves solely Chinese.[39]

What Will China Do?

Thus, the situation left China with only two choices. One was to accept Lee's position. This was simply out of the question, at least for the present. This left China with no other choice but to do something to stop this trend in Taiwan.

But how? It now could not "trust" the K.M.T. government (nor the D.P.P.) and giving more "sweeteners" to Taiwanese businessmen would not work magic on the Taiwanese people. Taiwan had accumulated more than US$90 billion profit from cross-strait trade over 1979–99.[40] Yet this was not about to make the Taiwanese, as a whole, change their position on statehood to suit Beijing's taste. Given this, it would be logical to assume that Beijing would fundamentally revise its previous "peaceful reunification" strategy, in essence if not in name. At the very least it would revise the "two trusts" as the basis. "Sweeteners" would not work without convincing military back-up. Therefore military modernization, especially high technology, would be placed high on the agenda with greater urgency.

A Phased Response

China took a phased response to see whether Taiwan would back off under pressure. It indicated that it would normalize relations with Taiwan if it retracted the "two states" statement. Taiwan has so far taken a defiant stance. Instead of rescinding the "two states" theory, it had adopted it into the K.M.T. party charter and indicated that it would suspend the constitution and draft a "basic law" to "reflect its current constitutional reality". It also took a crucial step by making an official decision, at this sensitive moment, to join the U.S.-led T.M.D., if invited.[41]

China was preparing itself for the worst. The decisive action it took against Falun Gong from July 1999 showed that it was more than merely dealing with a cult. It was also testing its capability for grass-root control. Without its own house in order, it could not take military action, if required, against Taiwan. At the same time, it mobilized the nation by bombarding the public with articles, editorials, TV interviews, seminars, lectures, conferences by scholars and well-known figures of various circles condemning Lee's "two states" theory. This was, in effect, psychological and political preparation of the people for possible military action.

Meanwhile, it was also preparing the international ground. At China's request, many countries had reaffirmed their "one China" policy. Of course, the biggest concern was the United States, for which China took both soft and hard tactics. It depicted Taiwan as the troublemaker for normal China–U.S. relations at the expense of the U.S. strategic interest. It asked the Clinton Administration to press Taiwan to retract its "two states" theory. It also asked the United States to stop giving misleading signals by encouraging further provocation from Taiwan through, for example, arms sales and the T.M.D. development. Jiang Zemin wrote Clinton a letter in this spirit in August. Through public press and diplomatic channels, China repeatedly warned the United States not to intervene on Taiwan's behalf.

On 2 August 1999, China test-launched a new *Dongfeng*-31 intercontinental ballistic missile and tested *Dongfeng*-41. *Jane's Defence Weekly* estimated that the *Dongfeng*-31 had an 8,000-km range, and was capable of carrying a 700-kg nuclear warhead.[42] It could cover part of the U.S. mainland. It came with an improved Global Positioning System that made it more accurate. It was solid fuelled and therefore highly mobile. It did not use a silo but was vehicle-mounted, vehicle-erected and vehicle-launched. *Dongfeng*-41 was estimated to have a 13,000-km range, capable of covering the whole U.S. mainland. Equipping China's submarines with such missiles would greatly enhance its strategic deterrence as this would mean that these submarines could launch *Dongfeng*-41s to hit any part of the world from China's own territorial waters.[43]

China kept up its pressure on Taiwan, warning that it was fully prepared to launch an attack on the island if necessary, regardless of the cost.[44] It said: "The Chinese Government has always been devoted to a peaceful resolution of the Taiwan issue, but if the Taiwan authorities think the mainland can only launch a propaganda or psychological war [as Taiwan described], they are mistaken. If the Taiwan authorities think they can depend on the shelter of external forces, they are mistaken."[45] "The mainland has made various preparations to use force against Taiwan. Military mobilization, military deployment, combat-readiness training and logistics have all been completed."[46]

It should be noted that China's military threats were mostly reported by newspapers in Hong Kong and other countries. China itself avoided using its top leaders to make these threats, using instead scholars, specialists and newspaper commentators. Military exercises were conducted but, according to the United States and Taiwan, these were just routine. The airforces on both sides of the Strait also engaged in military activities, but there was nothing abnormal to suggest that a large-scale military operation was underway.

By taking this posture, China was trying to send a stern warning to Taiwan as well as the United States, but at the same time it did not want to give Lee an excuse to postpone the presidential election. It was watching for the turnout of the coming presidential election in March 2000. By then, the celebrations for the fiftieth anniversary of the P.R.C. would be over and the hand-over of Macao to Chinese sovereignty on 20 December 1999 would be completed. It would also by then have levelled the ground at home with political and military preparations for a possible large-scale military operation should there be such a need.

This was China's phased response. From this, there are two likely scenarios.

Economic Competition

The first scenario is that, should Taiwan take no further provocative action that would leave China with no choice, the current tension will not lead to Chinese using actual force on Taiwan. China will use political and diplomatic means to cushion the impact of Lee's "two states" theory. So long as there is no international acceptance of the "two states" theory, China can afford to put up with it, even if Lee does not retract the "two states" theory. This would be in line with its overall modernization agenda, which China does not want to be undermined and hijacked by the Taiwan issue. China does not expect any dramatic breakthrough on the Taiwan issue in the near future but only hopes to constrain Taiwan's pushes towards further independence.

However, even though a war can be avoided at present, China will likely reassess the feasibility of its "peaceful reunification" strategy. Even if it does not drop it in name, out of concern for the international repercussions, it will likely change some of its essentials following the collapse of the "two trusts". One logical question is whether handing out huge economic sweeteners *at this time*, if not later, will help towards reunification without military backing. Many of those sweeteners were given at the expense of China's own national and private industries. The US$90 billion trade profit earned by Taiwanese businessmen over the past 20 years has not made them more sympathetic to China or more supportive of reunification. Many Taiwanese businessmen talked about reunification only when in China.

Taiwan's ability for sustained confrontation with China is supported by its strong military and political resources, which in turn come from its social resources, i.e. its social cohesion and stability. This social stability is fundamentally decided by its economic success. Lee Teng-hui himself also said in August 1999 that whether Taiwan can stand up against China in future will fundamentally depend on its own economic development.[47]

In the early 1970s, after the first world oil crisis, Taiwan adopted a correct economic development strategy, i.e. it developed its electronic industry, while China was deep in the domestic turmoil of the Cultural Revolution. This correct development strategy benefited Taiwan with strong economic resources and social stability, which it has skilfully used in its political bargaining with China for nearly 30 years.

China's Cultural Revolution is now over, and it is trying hard to catch up. If it competes with, instead of supplementing Taiwan's development, it may exhaust and eventually overtake Taiwan, or at least make it very difficult for Taiwan to continue to enjoy such a huge gap between itself and China as it used to. Taiwan's industry will feel the pressure and will have to keep spending massively to upgrade in order to stay ahead. And Taiwan's industry is at the very stage that needs massive investment to upgrade itself in terms of industrial structure. It has a lot of money. However, this pool of money is being drained by, for example, its increasingly huge arms purchases (in 1997, it spent US$4.049 billion, making it the top importers of weapons in the world);[48] its costly economic diplomacy; the increasing politicization of its economic development.[49]

China can, if it wants to, cut off some of Taiwan's revenue resources. For example, a significant part of the huge deficit, on China's part, in cross-strait trade is the result of Taiwanese businessmen importing semi-raw materials or even raw materials from Taiwan, instead of locally. China can adopt certain policies to encourage its own industries to produce these materials of acceptable quality to cut down on imports from Taiwan. This policy will help its own industries. At the same time, the profit of the Taiwanese businessmen in mainland (but not those industries in Taiwan that produce those materials) will not be adversely affected because of the lower cost of transportation and lower price of the materials. This economic competition will benefit China's economic development tremendously because many of China's industries will have a clear competitor (i.e. Taiwan). Taiwan's industries are a good target for many, although not all, of China's industries. This is not only because they are more advanced but also because most of them are heading in the right direction (they know the international market better) which Chinese industries should follow. In other words, carefully observing the development of Taiwan's industries and their market strategy will provide valuable and fast information about the international market to many of China's industries that so far are not very familiar with it. Even if China cannot catch up with Taiwan in the short run, it will benefit tremendously from this "close-tailing" before it eventually overtakes Taiwan. Taiwan, with a shrinking pool of economic resources and more competition, will find it more and more difficult to compete.

China will also likely make efforts to ensure that Taiwan does not become a regional economic centre, financial centre, transportation centre, or even high science and technology centre. The depletion of Taiwan's economic resources will take its toll, in the long run, on Taiwan's political confrontation with China.

With this awareness, Taiwan has cancelled its plan to become a regional economic centre (as discussed in the previous chapter, without China's co-operation, it is impossible for Taiwan to become such a centre). Instead, it wants to become a regional centre of science and technology. This will not be easy either. Not only China is now intensifying its effort to become a major power of high technology, but Hong Kong has recently also mapped out its plan to be a regional technology centre. Taiwan's basic science research cannot match that of the United States or even China. Its application science and technology cannot match that of Japan and the United States as well. What is more, with over 93 per cent of its industries being medium and small-sized, and with its economic resources depleting against an increasingly competitive China and world market, Taiwan will find technological upgrading very difficult. Taiwan's businessmen will likely continue to make money, for most of them are small in size and therefore flexible. But its industries as a whole will not easily step higher on the ladder of high technology, either globally or regionally. Moreover, despite a slumping external market, China, with its huge domestic market, can continue its economic growth if it can successfully stimulate its domestic demand. Taiwan cannot. The strategic significance of these points will tell in the long run, depending on whether China can skilfully play these factors to its own advantage.

However, the game is not simply between Taiwan and China. Out of their own strategic interests, some countries may give Taiwan better access to their markets and high technology in order to stimulate Taiwan's economy and sabotage China's strategy. Taiwan will make a good use of this advantage. In early September 1999, Koo Chen-fu was invited to Japan to discuss building a closer partnership of high technology between Japan and Taiwan.[50] On the other hand, China's ambition to become a world-class economic power through modernization may not be smooth sailing. The unco-operative Taiwan is not likely to remain idle. For example, it may make use of China's setbacks to push its "pragmatic diplomacy" further in the world. Taiwan will continue to consume a lot of China's political, diplomatic and economic resources which could otherwise be used for China's faster rise. This may make some Chinese leaders think that an earlier and once-and-for-all solution for Taiwan, though costly in the short term, will still be much more cost-effective than letting it drag on for a long time. Should China become more powerful economically and militarily, Taiwan might still not agree to reunification. Economic prowess may not guarantee an automatic reunification. For example, facing the powerful United States, some of its small neighbours like Cuba from 1950s, Panama under General Manuel Noriega in the late 1980s and Grenada in the early 1980s, refused to back off under U.S. pressure. And the United States had to use force, e.g. against Grenada in 1983 and Panama in 1989.

Military Modernization

Following Lee's announcement of the "two states" theory, Beijing began to seriously contemplate the eventual use of force against Taiwan. The immediate use of force was unlikely because Beijing preferred to wait until Lee stepped down as president. However, no matter who the president is in Taiwan, a highly accelerated Chinese military modernization is inevitable, for which Taiwan has accidentally played an impetus role by default. It has provided the P.L.A. with a clear target for its determined modernization. With a clear focus and target, an army will more easily catch up. For example, in the 1950s and 1960s, though China was very poor with a very backward economic and scientific infrastructure, it nevertheless took many by surprise by turning out its own nuclear weapons, satellites and long-range missiles. The clear focus and strong determination played a crucial role. Taiwan is now playing this catapult role, though unintentionally, in the P.L.A.'s determination towards accelerated modernization.

From Beijing's perspective, the cross-strait tussle in essence has always been a China–U.S. issue though called the "Taiwan issue" in public. If China has the capability to deter the United States from intervention, the "Taiwan issue" will be easily solved. The accelerated P.L.A. modernization, therefore, is also targeted at the United States' intervention. Shortly after Lee's announcement of the "two states" theory, the C.C.P. Politburo held an enlarged meeting in Beidaihe in early August, where the "998 National Security System Project" was proposed. Its main points include (1) to develop new strategic and tactical weapons; (2) to develop ship (submarine)-launched missiles and cruise missiles; (3) to equip the army, earlier than originally planned, with electronic weapons, laser guns and other directed-energy weapons; (4) to terminate consultation with the United States on proliferation of weapons; (5) to partially revise the non-first-use nuclear policy; and (6) to revise the out-dated position of non-alliance and non-grouping.[51]

These proposals seem targeted at the potential U.S. deployment of the T.M.D. and National Missiles Defence (N.M.D.) systems and emergencies on the Taiwan issue. Much depends on Beijing's reading of the developments on these issues to decide how far it will go in carrying out these proposals.

There have been some new P.L.A. developments in this direction: To deter the United States from intervention in Taiwan, the P.L.A. is further developing its intercontinental ballistic missile *Dongfeng*-31 and *Dongfeng*-41 missiles to be equipped with the low-power propulsion technology, a new technological breakthrough that can alter the path of offensive missiles.[52] In other words, the Chinese missiles can dance along from designated points at different angles, thus making them almost impossible for the potential U.S. T.M.D. and N.M.D. systems to intercept. It is also building its first Type-094 missile-carrying nuclear submarine, whose missiles, with a range of 11,906km, can be launched from within the Chinese waters but are still able to strike at any place in the United States.[53]

As a further obstacle to U.S. aircraft carrier intervention, the P.L.A. is fielding a new Passive Coherent Location (PCL) system — a revolutionary new anti-aircraft early-warning defence system that can detect US stealth aircraft, including the F-117 bomber and even the futuristic F-22 fighter.[54]

To boost its military pressure over Taiwan, it is further developing land-attack cruise missiles (LACM) for medium-to-long-range missions. Its official aerospace publications recently indicated two such land-attack missiles: *Chang Feng* and *Chang Feng-JIA*. Similar to U.S. *Tomahawk* LACM, the Chinese versions employ technologies such as GPS/Inertial mid-course guidance and most critically, terrain contour matching to increase its accuracy. The P.L.A. will field these cruise missiles with more advanced *Hong Niao* LACM.[55]

Its air force has its own airborne warning and control system (AWACS),[56] and may soon acquire a few Russian AWACS. Its AWACS, coupled with its Su-27SK and its recent acquisition of Su-30MKK and Su-27UBK advanced jet fighters will greatly improve its air control.

The purchase and deployment of more diesel-electric submarines such as the Russian-designed *Kilo*-class 636-series, and destroyers such as the *Sovremenny-*

class, and possibly longer-range *Yakhont* missiles will greatly improve China's naval capability.

China has also acquired the co-production license of the Russian *Zvezda* Kh-31P missile. The missile is specifically designed to counter the U.S.-made *Patriot* and *Aegis* systems. It is reportedly developing FT-2000/2500 missiles based on Russia's S-300PMU missiles capable of homing in on radiation emitted by E-2s. It has also acquired Russian-designed anti-AWACS missiles, dubbed KS-172/AAM-L, capable of being launched from a jet fighter. Subsequently, Taiwan's E-2Ts, future P-3s, land-based and (future) sea-based missiles will be subject to the P.L.A.'s anti-radiation threats.[57] These weapons can critically enhance the P.L.A.'s edge over Taiwan, rapidly establishing air and naval superiority, and disrupting U.S. intervention.

The accelerated P.L.A. modernization will not exhaust China in the same manner the Soviet Union was crippled in its arms race with the United States in the Cold War, because its cost is manageable and, therefore, affordable. One reason is that its pace is likely to be, just as it has been, under Beijing's careful control and well-calculated, based on the assessment of how much its economy can afford. Second, unlike the Soviet Union, China is not expanding across its national borders and has undertaken no costly security obligations to protect any other countries.

Third, the theory that diverting resources from the economy to a military build-up had caused the Soviet collapse is misleading. Actually, military spending could, if well-planned, bring about faster economic modernization by high technology breakthroughs that could be quickly converted for civilian use. The Soviet Union did not collapse from military spending — apart from political and other reasons, its collapse was due to the *excessiveness* and *distorted pattern* of its military spending. It had failed to develop a mechanism that could quickly and efficiently convert breakthroughs in its military technologies for civilian use to strongly promote its overall industrial development. It also made the mistake of slipping to the American-favoured rules of the game, i.c. to comprehensively upgrade and excessively produce all weapons and weapons systems along the lines of what the Americans were developing when its economy could ill afford it.

Given this lesson, if China plays the game according to its own rules, i.e., developing a few well-chosen, lower-cost but very effective weapons technologies (instead of following the United States to produce many glaringly expensive weapons), it will not be exhausted like the Soviet Union. There is no substantial difference between the potential of paralysing a country ten times and that of thousands of times. The United States, as the global leader, may need the latter capability. As for China, the former is enough, — for the purpose of deterrence but not for world leadership. This could be the philosophy underlining the principles for the P.L.A. weapon procurement and production, i.e., "*Shao Shengchan, Duo Yanzhi*" [less weapon production, more military R&D], "*Xiao*

Piliang, Gao Shuiping" [produce only a small quantity of weapons but seek higher technological level], and *"Shao Chubei Wuqi, Duo Chubei Jishu"* [maintain fewer weapons but more weapon technologies].

Therefore, China may feel that instead of "economic security", there should be "a security economy", i.e., to use security needs to promote a faster economy. For example, the P.L.A.'s modernization at this stage emphasizes electronic information technology and precision heavy machinery. Breakthroughs and resources (including talents and education) spent in these two areas will not only break the bottleneck of China's military modernization but its economic development as well. The significance for its rapid and sustained rise is immense. In this sense, with Taiwan as the target, China could have a much faster military as well as economic modernization so long as it keeps in mind the key point, i.e., to deter rather than go to war.

One side advantage is that Taiwan (as well as the U.S. T.M.D. and N.M.D. pushes) as the claimed target of a "forced" military modernization response will make it inconvenient for other countries to call out "China threat". Once China has enhanced its military leverage against Taiwan, its deterrence against other big powers would also be enhanced and so would be its position in the region and the world. At the same time, the Taiwan issue, if skilfully handled, will arouse strong patriotic feelings (instead of a national split) that China could make use of for its internal cohesion.

Also, with the Taiwan political challenge, Beijing will sooner or later have to improve its governance (including democracy, human rights, and anti-corruption) for legitimacy rule and policy-making efficiency — this is another side advantage, enhancing its soft power as well. Competition makes man tough and a country as well. In other words, theoretically, China could turn the Taiwan issue from a liability into credit. In reality, it depends on Beijing's wisdom, skill and determination. Should this come true, Taiwan would be a blessing in disguise for China.

Notes

1. Tara Suilen Duffy, "Taiwan, China Seek to Restart Talks", AP, 28 June 1999.
2. Willy Wo-Lap Lam, "Post-Talks Hope for Cross-Strait Hotline", *SCMP*, 15 February 1999.
3. "Taiwan Redefines China Relations", AP, 10 July 1999; *Lianhe Zaobao*, 11 July 1999, p. 2; *Chung Kuo Shih Pao*, 11 July 1999.
4. David Briscoe, "U.S. Calls for China–Taiwan Dialogue", AP, 12 July 1999; *Lianhe Zaobao*, 11 July 1999, pp. 2 & 11.
5. Ibid.
6. *Chung Kuo Shih Pao*, 13 July 1999. "*Guojia*" in Chinese can be translated into either "countries" or "states".
7. Michael Laris, "Taipei Softens Wording but Reiterates It's Coequal", *IHT*, 22 July 1999.

8. "Taiwan Moves to Sell 'Two States' Policy World-Wide", *ST*, 15 July 1999; *Lianhe Zaobao*, 14 July 1999, p. 16.
9. *"Ziwo Biaobang, Yugai Mizhang"* [A Wild Bragger and A Poor Liar], *Renmin Ribao*, 6 August 1999, p. 4.
10. Ching Cheong, "Teng-Hui Pushing Changes to Constitution", *ST*, 14 July 1999.
11. "Taiwan Moves to Sell 'Two States' Policy World-wide", *ST*, 15 July 1999.
12. Ivan Tang, "Beijing Anger at Congressman", *SCMP*, 14 August 1999.
13. "Taipei Denies Mainland Jets Crossed Line", *SCMP*, 14 August 1999.
14. Ching Cheong, "Press Coined '2 states' Idea, Says Teng-Hui", *ST*, 28 July 1999.
15. Annie Huang, "Taiwan President Warns China", AP, 28 July 1999. Also "China Rejects Taiwan President", AP, 29 July 1999.
16. See Koo's statement of 30 July 1999, *Chung Kuo Shih Pao*, 30 July 1999. It generally reiterated what Lee Teng-hui had said. Regarding the "special state-to-state relationship" he said: "First, the shared cultural and ethnic origins have cultivated a very unique affection between the two states. Second, the intensifying cross-strait exchanges in civil, commercial as well as other sectors are unparalleled when compared with other divided countries past and present. Third, and most importantly, both sides should have the common will to pursue a unified China in the future by engaging in negotiations on the basis of parity." Also see "Unification with China Still the Goal", *ST*, 31 July 1999.
17. See M.A.C.'s statement of 1 August 1999, *Chung Kuo Shih Pao*, 1 August 1999.
18. Annie Huang, "Taiwan President Warns China", AP, 28 July 1999.
19. Annie Huang, "Taiwan President Stands by Statehood", AP, 20 July 1999.
20. Jason Blatt, "Taipei Dialogue Offer Aims to Cool Tensions", *SCMP*, 14 July 1999.
21. Also see Koo's statement of 30 July 1999, *Chung Kuo Shih Pao*, 30 July 1999. Koo said: "We believe one China is in the future, but at the moment the sides are coexisting as equals." Annie Huang, "Taiwan Reaffirms Statehood Claim", AP, 30 July 1999.
22. For a detailed discussion of the different interpretations of the 1992 consensus, see Chapter 5.
23. The two major official statements from Taiwan to explain Lee's "two states" theory are Koo Chen-fu's written explanation of 30 July 1999 and the M.A.C.'s statement of 1 August 1999. See Notes 16 and 17.
24. Tom Raum, "Albright: U.S.–China Tensions Easing", AP, 25 July 1999.
25. Ching Cheong, "Taipei Plans to Suspend Charter", *ST*, 7 September 1999.
26. Jason Blatt, "Taipei 'to Face Beijing Force'", *SCMP*, 11 August 1999.
27. See Yan Xuetong, *"Yijian Duodiao de 'Lianguolun' Jiqi Weixian"*[The Danger of the Multi-Purpose "Two states" Theory], *Lianhe Zaobao*, 19 July 1999, p. 14.
28. *China Times Express*, quoted in "Two Likely Reasons for Controversial Declaration", *ST*, 13 July 1999.
29. Jason Blatt, "Taipei 'to face Beijing force'", *SCMP*, 11 August 1999
30. *Huanzhu Gege* [My Fair Princess] is a Chinese TV series that had caused a big sensation throughout Taiwan in 1998.
31. CCTV (overseas), News Program, 7 December 1998.
32. "Two Takes on Cross-Strait Ties", *ST*, 20 February 1998.
33. For example, see Yan Xuetong, *"Lian'an Zhengzhi Tanpan de Zhenjie yu Qianjing* [Crux and Prospect for Cross-Strait Political Negotiations], *Lianhe Zaobao*, 30 March 1998, p. 13.
34. "Committed to Peace", *ST*, 20 August 1999.

35. "President Backed in Poll", *SCMP*, 14 July 1999.

36. "Taiwanese Back Their President", *SCMP*, 14 July 1999.

37. *ST*, 15 July 1999.

38. Zheng, *Gudao Chanmeng* [Lingering Dreams over the Isolated Island], p. 616.

39. This poll was commissioned by the Mainland Affairs Council and conducted by the China Credit Information Service. See "Highest Percentage Ever Consider Themselves Taiwanese", Central News Agency, 3 September 1999.

40. Xinhua, "*Jianchi 'Lianguolun' Jiushi Beipan Taiwan Renmin*" [The "Two states Theory" is Betrayal of People of Taiwan], *Renmin Ribao*, 3 August 1999, p. 4.

41. "I Am Just Telling the Truth, Says Lee", *SCMP*, 20 August 1999.

42. "Beijing Gives Details of Missile Test", *ST*, 13 August 1999.

43. *Hong Kong Business Daily* reported the Chinese test of *Dongfeng*-41 on 2 August 1999, quoted in *Lianhe Zaobao*, 4 September 1999, p. 2.

44. "I Am Just Telling the Truth, Says Lee", *SCMP*, 20 August 1999.

45. Ibid.

46. "Committed to Peace", *ST*, 20 August 1999.

47. *Lianhe Zaobao*, 23 August 1999, p. 23.

48. See Table 2.

Table 2   Military Spending and Weapons Import

	Military Spending as Percentage of GDP 1996/97	Weapon Imports (million U.S. dollars) 1997	World Ranking of Weapon Imports 1997
Taiwan	3.7	4049	1*
China	1.9**	1816	3
Egypt	3.1***	808	9
India	2.5	1085	6
Malaysia	2.4	1346	4
Russia	3.7	n.a.	n.a.
Saudi Arabia	13.2	2370	2
South Korea	3.2	1077	7
Turkey	4.3	1276	5
U.S.	3.6	656	12

*Taiwan's purchase of arms continued to grow in the 1990s, rising from No. 9 in 1993 to No. 6 in 1995 and No. 3 in 1996.

**China's official figure is 1.1 per cent. The figure in the table is based on the *SIPRI Yearbook 1999*.

***1995 figure.

Sources: Stockholm International Peace Research Institute, *SIPRI Yearbook 1998* (London: Oxford University Press, 1998), pp. 229–233 & 300–301.

49. Tien Chang-lin, former president of University of California, Berkeley, pointed out that Taiwan was paying too much attention to politics at the expense of overall economic development. This increasing politicization, if not held back, would eventually hurt Taiwan's economy. See Tien's remarks in *Lianhe Zaobao*, 17 August 1999, p. 22.
50. CTN TV, News Program, 6 September 1999.
51. *Lianhe Zaobao*, 14 June 2000, p. 23. Directed-energy weapons may include laser guns, micro-wave beams, particle beams, high energy radio frequency [HERF], accoustic cannons, plasma guns, high energy ultrasonic weapons, and subsonic wave weapons.
52. "Spacecraft Launch 'a Victory for PLA'", *SCMP*, 23 November 1999. Also see *China Business Times*, 22 November 1999.
53. *The Washington Times*, quoted in Greg Torode, "New Nuclear Sub Can Target 'Any US City'", *SCMP*, 7 December 1999.
54. Current U.S. anti-aircraft defences are cued by radar that detects and tracks incoming aircraft. But the radar is vulnerable because its signals can be jammed or missiles can be launched to ride back down the radar beam to destroy the transmitter. But China's new Passive Coherent Location (PCL) system tracks the signals of civilian radio and television broadcasts and picks up aircraft by analysing the minute turbulence their flights cause in the commercial wavelengths. Because the PCL does not transmit, its receivers cannot be detected and jammed or destroyed. Its strategic implication is significant because it can defeat current U.S. air force tactics against enemy defences. This has alarmed the United States defence community to the cost of defending Taiwan as it will make U.S. air power suddenly vulnerable. See *Newsweek* (U.S. Edition), 6 December 1999, quoted in "Anti-Plane System Causes Concern in U.S.", *SCMP*, 30 November 1999.
55. Holmes S. Liao, "What Taiwan's Military Needs for Its Survival", *Taipei Times*, 19 April 2000.
56. A photo of one P.L.A. AWACS was published in *Lien Ho Pao*, 29 November 1993, p. 1.
57. Liao, op. cit.

Index